The BOWTIE has been the trademark for Chevrolet since its early days. The Chevrolet BOWTIE was inspired by a hotel wallpaper sample that W.C. Durant brought back from France in 1908.

BOWTIES
of the
FIFTIES

By
James H. Moloney

My Chevrolet Dedications

My first dedication in this book goes to my Aunt Gertrude Krebser who started this whole car thing with me, bringing me a tootsietoy car from Lake Arrowhead, California when I was just 18 months old.
Born: September 18, 1899 - Died: September 29, 1972

The second dedication in this book goes to my good friend Frank Waterhouse who unfortunately died in a fiery crash April 20th 1957.
Born: June 27, 1929 - Died: April 20, 1957

The third dedication in this book goes to the best boss anyone could ever have had. Fred Donnelly, my boss at the Chevrolet zone office in Los Angeles, California. Fred is now retired and lives in Walnut Creek, California.

I wish to thank General Motors for their assistance in helping me compile the "BOWTIES of the FIFTIES."

Thanks to all my Chevrolet friends who helped in any way toward making this endeavor happen.

Published by
Amos Press, Inc.
911 Vandemark Road
Sidney, Ohio 45365

Cars & Parts Magazine is a division of Amos Press, Inc.

Printed and bound in the United States of America

ISBN 1-880524-42-2

CONTENTS

8

INTRODUCTION

I have always held Chevrolet as my favorite car. Some model years I like better than others, but no matter. They all rate number one with me. In a way, my fondness for these cars may seem strange as, in 1957, I was involved in a very serious automobile accident that took the life of a very good friend of mine, and nearly took my own.

The accident was caused by a Chevrolet with less than 300 miles, that had brakes which were faulty. The car caught on fire, and laid me up in the hospital for the next couple of years.

I guess you'd say, I'm either nuts, or dedicated to the marque. Having owned more than 30 Chevrolets throughout my life, kind of sums it up that I like them. Probably my all-time favorite model is the 1958 Impala. I've owned four of them at one time and currently own two, one of which has been with me since I purchased it new. That Silver Blue Coupe is a "keeper." It has 62,000 original miles and still looks and runs as it did the day I took delivery of it.

This book, dealing with the Chevrolets of the 1950s will show you some of my very favorite models. I hope you'll enjoy browsing through it once and, maybe, even give it a second look, sometime later.

- Jim Moloney

Showing only minor trim changes from the new body style that was introduced in 1949 is the 1950 DeLuxe Styleline Sport Sedan. Note the small "V" chevrons under the parking light directional signal unit and the gold emblem made the main distinctions for the front-end appearance over the 1949 cars. This model, referred to as 2103 for factory comparisons, was the most popular model in the Chevrolet line for 1950. It delivered for $1,529, weighing 3150 pounds. The production run amounted to 316,412 units delivered.

Chevrolet for 1950

The 1950 Chevrolet models were, basically, the same offering as the first post-war body styles of 1949. Only minor trim changes were added to the crisp new body style. The company offered a more pleasing grille with small chevrons added under the parking lights to help distinguish it from the 1949 cars. From the rear, a new deck lid handle was the most noticeable trim change over the previous year. Larger bumper guards enhanced both the front and rear of the vehicles.

One new model was added to the 1950 line and it was the sharp new body style called "Bel Air." This model was technically referred to as Model 2154. It was, basically, a convertible with a non-detachable solid roof. The car was an instant success with a production of over 76,000 manufactured. The vehicles sold for $1,741.

Mechanically, another first for one of the Big Three was Chevrolet being the one to offer an automatic transmission! They referred to it as "Powerglide." The

11

In the Special Series, there were two coupes available. From the exterior they were identical. Only when looking in the inside would you see the difference. One was classed as a Sport Coupe which was the more popular having a rear seat. It carried a price of $1,408 and weighed 3050 pounds. The other example was this version known as the Styleline Business Coupe. It was called Model 1504, weighing 3025 pounds. The cost of this model was $1,329, and it had a run of 20,984 units. As a side note, this example was my brother-in-law's (Charles Chodzkos) first brand-new car, purchased February 10, 1950 in Pasadena, California, with payments of $51.00 a month for three years. He owned it for two years before going to work for a trucking firm in Los Angeles. The trucking firm gave him a brand new Chevrolet every two years until his retirement last year when he bought a new car for the first time since 1950. This time, for retirement, he purchased a new Buick Roadmaster. I guess the term, "You've come a long way, Baby," easily applies to my brother-in-law.

unit was of the torque converter type, with low and drive positions, and reverse. This new transmission brought about the revision of the 235.5 cubic-inch truck engine for the passenger car. Hydraulic valve lifters and larger intake valves were put to use, and the engine now used a 3 9/16-inch bore and a 3 15/16-inch stroke. It developed 105 horsepower at 3600 RPM. This transmission was only available in the DeLuxe Series. The regular 216.5 cubic-inch engine continued to be used in all regular models developing 90 horsepower at 3300 RPM.

The wheelbase on the 1950 cars continued to be the same as on 1949 cars — 115 inches. The overall length increased to 197.5 inches in all models except for the station wagon, which carried an overall length of one inch more.

The Special series was known as Series HJ and DeLuxe cars were referred

Looking similar to the above-described Styleline Sport Coupe, is its cousin, the DeLuxe Sport Coupe. This example was far more popular with a production run of 81,536 units delivered. It was called Model 2124. These coupes sold for $1,498 and tipped the scale at 3090 pounds. The fender skirts were standard equipment on all DeLuxe models, but considered extra cost on the Styleline cars. The most distinguishing marks between DeLuxe cars and the Styleline models was the stainless side trim running from the tip of the front fenders to the trailing edge of the front doors, and the stainless scuff pad affixed to the rear quarter panel on 2-door models. The interior of DeLuxe cars showed fancier appointments from door armrests to a higher quality gray broadcloth upholstery.

to as HK models. Chevrolet continued to hold on to the number one sales slot for 1950 with a calendar year run of 1,520,577 units delivered. The model year sales amounted to 1,371,535 vehicles produced.

The 1950 cars saw quite an array of factory approved accessories from a glove compartment lamp in the Special Series for $1.00, to a Custom DeLuxe Push Button Radio and Antenna for $74.50. The factory-approved equipment really added some luxury to an already good looking car.

Prices for the 1950 cars ranged from $1,329 for a three-passenger Special Styleline Business Coupe to the Model 2119 eight-passenger DeLuxe Station Wagon that delivered for $1,994. This was now the second year for the all steel Station Wagon which was a big plus for Chevrolet, as far as sales were concerned. A total of 166,995 Wagons were produced. The buyer had his choice of three colors for the Wagon model: Oxford Maroon, Rodeo Beige and Crystal Green. As far as regular models were concerned, the two-tone varieties were only available in the Styleline Series. A total of seven single colors could be ordered for Sedans, 2-Door Sedans and Coupes. Moonlight Cream was only available for the Convertible models, as well as the Bel Air Hardtop, Moonlight Cream with Falcon Gray top was more popular than the solid cream color. Additional choices were Falcon Gray top with Grecian Gray bottom; Black top with Mist Green bottom; Grecian Gray top with Windsor Blue bottom, and solid Black, making a variety of five color choices for Bel Air owners.

Sedan Delivery models, known as 1508 vehicles, are sometimes referred to in the truck category. I prefer to think of them as passenger car models, due to the front end being that of a passenger car. The Model 1508 vehicles for 1950 saw a production run of 23,045 units produced.

The latest in design is what Chevrolet referred to as its new 1950 Bel Air Hardtop Coupe. This example was called Model 2154. The smart fresh new styling was an instant success as it was in the entire GM line. A dealer, in my hometown of Pasadena, California, said one day he couldn't get enough of them. The model sold for $1,741 and weighed 3225 pounds. A total of 76,662 went to customers during the year.

Another view of the 1950 Bel Air Hardtop Coupe. This example came with a nice variety of factory appointments such as the front and rear fender guards costing $29.50 for the set of four; stainless steel 15-inch wheel discs set of four for $19.95; pushbutton radio with fender-mounted antenna for $74.50, and whitewall tires with prices varying on the manufacturer. I'd say this was done in the popular color combination of Mist Green and Black top.

Not as popular a body style as the DeLuxe Styleline was this Special Fleetline DeLuxe Model 2153 with a production run of 124,187 units delivered. This example sold for $1,529 and weighed 3145 pounds. It was also available as a Special Fleetline 4-door Sedan. That example, minus the skirts and other fancy trim, sold for $1,450, weighing 3115 pounds. It was known as Model 1553.

Always a favorite, especially with the young, was the 1950 DeLuxe Styleline Convertible, Model 2134. The model only came in the DeLuxe line and was available in all regular factory colors with Moonlight Cream being one color only available to it and the Bel Air Hardtop Coupe. This example weighed 3380 pounds and delivering for $1,847, making it second to the most expensive Chevrolet for 1950. A total of 32,810 sales were made possible, mainly due to this attractive body style.

A view as seen many times for Chevrolet advertisements and in sales brochures from the early days of the good old Cast Iron Wonder right up to the 1950s. This particular engine was probably destine for a 1950 mode. I wonder if by chance it's still in operation?

This was a very popular accessory seen not only on Chevrolets for the 1950 era, but on all makes of cars. This visor gave owners many comfortable hours of driving and, when the car was parked in the sun, assisted in keeping the interior cooler. For wintertime driving in areas where snow and ice were prevalent, the visor helped in eliminating it on the windshield. The list price for this accessory was $19.95.

A front close up view of a 1950 Chevrolet grille area showing off the front bumper guard accessory unit. The unit included the rear guards also. The complete package sold for $29.50, list. The extra cost accessory hood ornament could be ordered for $5.85 list price.

The rear view of a 1950 Chevrolet Fleetline Deluxe 2-Door Sedan with the factory bumper guard accessory. Also the factory back up lights could be purchased for $9.00 on non-Powerglide cars. Those equipped with the automatic transmission cost an additional 75 cents.

The Styleline DeLuxe Station Wagon came in Oxford Maroon, Crystal Green and Rodeo Beige. The eight-passenger Wagon employed an all steel body with the wood appliquè making it appear to be finished in wood. The wagon saw 166,995 produced, weighing 3,460 pounds and selling for $1,994, making it the most expensive vehicle in the Chevrolet lineup for 1950.

A variety of factory-approved accessories are shown below for the 1950 cars, along with the price list effective January 1, 1950.

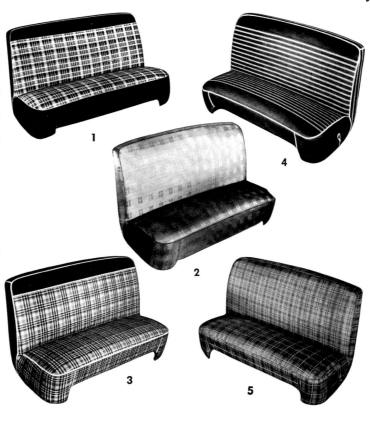

1 DeLuxe Saran Plastic

For the first time in Chevrolet history, plastic Seat Covers are being offered to car owners. The most outstanding features of this new saran plastic material are its fade-proof colors and longer wear. These Covers, made of a combination plastic, leatherette, and rayon materials, give a distinctive appearance to the interior of the Chevrolet.

2 DeLuxe Nylon-Rayon

This ultra-smart set of Seat Covers is the finest in the Chevrolet line. The subtle duotone shades of maroon and taupe fabric lend a distinctive air of richness and beauty. By using both the nylon and rayon threads, the Seat Cover designers have been able to combine greater durability with more luxurious patterns.

3 DeLuxe Fiber Plaid

Unexcelled for style and service, these Covers have a beautiful multi-color plaid trimmed in the finest red leatherette which adds the final su-

perlative touch of beauty to the Chevrolet interior. The fabric material has been finished with clear lacquer to enhance the color tone and brilliance of this attractive pattern.

4 DeLuxe Fiber Green Stripe

This new all-fiber Seat Cover has been styled to harmonize beautifully with the green and gray automobiles which make up a larger percentage of our passenger car production. The most outstanding feature of these Covers is the bolster-type construction which eliminates the objectionable seam usually found across the seat back of most Covers.

5 DeLuxe Rayon

The new Rayon Seat Cover, styled in rich chocolate brown with bright orange and green stripe, supplies a beautiful contrast to the interior upholstery and gives a distinguished look of individualized tailoring. This heavy denier material is designed to offer long lasting service.

1 Mirror—Glare-Proof Inside

A proven favorite among Chevrolet customers, this duo-purpose Mirror gives true daylight reflection and no glare vision for night driving. A flick of the finger adjusts this Mirror to either day or night driving.

2 DeLuxe Steering Wheel

This newly designed Wheel is ultra-modern, combining a handsome golden center-medallion, bright chrome, and plastic, colored to harmonize with the fittings of the 1950 Chevrolet. The rubber-cushioned horn-blowing ring responds to the lightest touch.

3 Auxiliary Lamps

These new 1950 Lamps, easily installed on the front splash pan, provide greater protection by casting a powerful beam of light to help improve drivers' visibility during inclement weather. By using the time-tested and approved sealed beam unit, these Lamps are engineered for longer service.

4 Mirror—Vanity Visor

A handy make-up Mirror for the ladies. This Mirror is easily clipped on to the right hand visor. It has

provisions for recording service data, too, having specially designed frosted areas.

5 Back-Up Lights

Chevrolet has designed a new Dual Back-Up Lamp Unit for 1950. These Lamps are a flush-body type mounting, and automatically provide diffused white light over the entire rear area when the car is in reverse.

6 Safetylight

The door-mounted Safetylight offers the Chevrolet owner additional driving safety and convenience, for its beam can be concentrated in any direction. It is an indispensable aid for doctors and salesmen too as it makes spotting of road markers and house numbers easier.

7 Outside Rear-View Mirror

This Mirror is designed and engineered to be mounted on either the left or right side of the automobile by simply adjusting the "clamp-on" bracket, and is made of the finest chrome plated, rust resistant metal. When mounted on the right side of the car, the Mirror may be adjusted so the driver can see either approaching cars or the curb for easier parking.

1 Locking Gas Cap

This highly polished stainless steel gas Cap has been designed to safeguard the gasoline supply and the cap itself. The Cap is so engineered that the key cannot be removed until the Cap is locked.

2 Front Fender Shield

Here is a matched pair of highly polished stainless steel Shields which are designed to add a note of distinction to the Chevrolet. The stainless steel material assures these Shields longer lasting beauty and utility.

3 Wheel Trim Rings

Here's another way to give your car a mark of distinction. These Trim Rings are made of highly polished stainless steel, and designed to wedge firmly into the wheel ring. They make the wheels look smaller, the tires more impressive.

4 Direction Signal

Chevrolet has developed for the 1950 Model, an all-new Direction Signal. This Signal, attractively designed to match the interior of the automobile, features an automatic turn-off control.

5 Outside Visor

By installing a new Chevrolet outside Visor, driving fatigue is lessened

for it reduces sun glare and helps to keep rain, snow, and sleet from the windshield. This Visor is of all-metal construction trimmed with high appealing stainless steel.

6 Hood Ornament

The Hood Ornament for the 1950 Chevrolet has been styled to add a personalized touch to your car. It features the graceful lines of a winged bird; thereby symbolizing the smoothness of the new Chevrolet.

7 Front Fender Guards

These new 1950 Guards have been designed to follow the lines of the Chevrolet automobile. They fit securely around the ends of the bumper and thus help to protect that part of the car against serious damage. Made of heavy gauge, highly polished, chrome plated steel, these Guards are engineered to retain their beauty.

8 Rear Fender Guards

To protect the rear Fenders against danger of over-ride, Chevrolet has styled a beautiful new set of Rear Fender Guards. These Guards are the wrap-around type which help to protect the side of the Fenders as well as the rear. Constructed of heavy gauged steel, they are chrome plated to withstand rust and corrosion.

1 Heater & Defroster Unit — Air-Flow

Chevrolet feels that this is the last word in automotive heating equipment. This Heater is thermostatically controlled to desired temperatures. By utilizing outside air for heating, passengers are insured a complete change of air periodically.

2 Tissue Dispenser

Mounted conveniently and securely on the cowl trim pad, this Dispenser places tissues available for many uses. The container is designed to hold one small box of tissues and is equipped with a tension spring which always pushes the tissues to the front.

3 Auxiliary Speaker

Installation of the new Chevrolet engineered Auxiliary speaker, developed for the occupants of the rear seat, now insures complete radio enjoyment for all passengers. This is a 5 x 7 elliptical speaker with four-way switch control.

4 Clocks

For the 1950 Models, Chevrolet again offers handsomely designed Electric and Spring-Wind Clocks to harmonize with the instrument panel and interior of the automobiles. With extra thick crystal and prominent face markings, the readability of these Clocks has been increased.

5 Custom DeLuxe Manual Tuning

This Radio offers a superb performance at a lower price. It is a two unit set and lists such other fine features as a full-tone six inch speaker, continuous variable tone control, and dial illumination which may be controlled by the instrument panel light dimmer switch.

6 Heater & Defroster Unit — Dash Recirculating

One of the best and most economical Heaters designed to keep comfortable temperatures circulating throughout the car, while the defroster helps to prevent windshield clouding.

7 Windshield Washer

The instant action Windshield Washer is fast becoming the proven favorite among Chevrolet customers. By simply pressing a button in the Windshield Wiper control, the washer action goes into operation immediately. This is an excellent item for helping to keep the windshield clean under all conditions.

8 Custom DeLuxe Push Button

This attractive six-tube set (including rectifier) is the finest Radio ever offered by Chevrolet. The set consists of two units; the radio frequency, and audio frequency, which are designed to be an integral part of the instrument panel. There are five vertical push buttons for station preference.

Chevrolet Accessories for 1950

Dealer's Confidential

PRICE LIST

Effective January 1, 1950

ALL PRICES SUBJECT TO CHANGE WITHOUT NOTICE

NEW CAR AND TRUCK ACCESSORIES

Description	Part. No.	Unit	Net Price	List Net
Antenna - Cowl - Truck	986069	1	$4.05	$6.75
Antenna - Fender - Pass	986257	1	3.57	5.95
Block Unit - Wiring Junction	986395	1	.90	1.50
Bracket - Truck Mirror	986381	1	1.05	1.75
Cap - Gas Tank, Locking	986326	1	1.35	2.25
Carrier - Umbrella	985929	1	1.35	2.25
Clock - Electric - Pass	986271	1	11.10	18.50
Clock - Electric - Pass	986384	1	11.10	18.50
Clock - Hand Wind - Pass	986261	1	5.70	9.50
Clock - Hand Wind - Pass	986385	1	5.70	9.50
Condenser - Radiator - Overflow - Truck	985528	1	1.77	2.95
Condenser - Radiator - Overflow - Pass	986282	1	2.10	3.50
Cover - Accelerator Pedal (6 Covers)	986325	6	3.60	6.00
Cover - Radiator - Truck	986127	1	2.85	4.75
Cover - Seat - Plaid - Styleline - 2 Door	986331	Set	13.50	27.50
Cover - Seat - Plaid - Styleline - 4 Door	986332	Set	13.50	27.50
Cover - Seat - Plaid - Fleetline - 2 Door	986333	Set	13.50	27.50
Cover - Seat - Plaid - Fleetline - 4 Door	986334	Set	13.50	27.50
Cover - Seat - Plaid - Spt. Coupe	986335	Set	13.50	27.50
Cover - Seat - Plaid - Bus. Cpe & Front Seat	986380	Set	5.70	14.50
Cover - Seat - Gray Stripe - Styleline - 2 Door	986336	Set	13.50	27.50
Cover - Seat - Gray Stripe - Styleline - 4 Door	986337	Set	13.50	27.50
Cover - Seat - Gray Stripe -Fleetline - 2 Door	986338	Set	13.50	27.50
Cover - Seat - Gray Stripe - Fleetline - 4 Door	986339	Set	13.50	27.50
Cover - Seat - Gray Stripe - Spt. Coupe	986340	Set	13.50	27.50
Cover - Seat - Green Stripe - Styleline - 2 Door	986374	Set	13.50	27.50
Cover - Seat - Green Stripe - Styleline - 4 Door	986375	Set	13.50	27.50
Cover - Seat - Green Stripe - Fleetline - 2 Door	986376	Set	13.50	27.50
Cover - Seat - Green Stripe - Fleetline - 4 Door	986377	Set	13.50	27.50
Cover - Seat - Green Stripe - Spt. Coupe	986378	Set	13.50	27.50
Cover - Seat - Green Stripe - 2 Door	986421	Set	16.50	27.50
Cover - Seat - Green Stripe - 4 Door	986422	Set	16.50	27.50
Cover - Seat - Plaid - 2 Door	986423	Set	16.50	27.50
Cover - Seat - Plaid - 4 Door	986424	Set	16.50	27.50
Cover - Seat - Plastic - 2 Door	986425	Set	27.60	46.00
Cover - Seat - Plastic - 4 Door	986426	Set	27.60	46.00
Cover - Seat - Rayon - Styleline - 2 Door	986341	Set	14.85	29.75
Cover - Seat - Rayon - Styleline - 4 Door	983642	Set	14.85	29.75
Cover - Seat - Rayon - Fleetline - 2 Door	986343	Set	14.85	29.75

Description	Part No.	Unit	Net Price	List Net
Cover - Seat - Rayon - Fleetline - 4 Door	986344	Set	14.85	29.75
Cover - Seat - Rayon - Spt. Coupe	986345	Set	14.85	29.75
Cover - Seat - Rayon - Bus. & Front Seat	986379	Set	6.30	15.50
Cover - Seat - Nylon Rayon - Styleline - 2 Door	986346	Set	26.10	48.50
Cover - Seat - Nylon Rayon - Styleline - 4 Door	986347	Set	26.10	48.50
Cover - Seat - Nylon Rayon - Fleetline - 2 Door	986348	Set	26.10	48.50
Cover - Seat - Nylon Rayon - Fleetline - 4 Door	986349	Set	26.10	48.50
Cover - Seat - Nylon Rayon - Spt. Coupe	986350	Set	26.10	48.50
Cover - Seat - Truck Cab - 1949	986289	Set	8.10	13.50
Cover - Seat - Truck Cab - 1950	986405	Set	8.10	13.50
Cover - Steering Wheel (6 Covers)	986356	6	5.40	9.00
Cushion - Air - Green (6 Cushions)	986435	6	14.22	23.70
Cushion - Air - Red (6 Cushions)	986436	6	14.22	23.70
Disc - Stainless Steel - 15" Wheel - Set	986352	4	11.97	19.95
Disc - Stainless Steel - 15" Wheel - Single	986358	1	3.00	5.00
Disc - Stainless Steel - Do-Nut Type - Set	986417	4	8.85	14.75
Disc - Stainless Steel - Do-nut Type - Single	986416	1	2.40	4.00
Dispenser - Tissue	986353	1	1.40	2.35
Extension - Pipe Exhaust	986382	1	1.50	2.50
Filter - Unit - Gasoline (12 Filters)	986399	12	14.04	23.40
Frame - License Plate	986371	Pair	1.77	2.95
Garment Bag and Hanger Unit, Ladies (3)	986437	3	6.72	10.35
Garment Bag and Hanger Unit, Men's (3)	986438	3	6.72	10.35
Glareshade - Windshield - Styleline	986354	Pair	5.97	9.95
Glareshade - Windshield - Fleetline	986355	Pair	5.97	9.95
Guards - Bumper - Truck	986113	Pair	3.90	6.50
Guard - Grille - Light Truck	986152	1	12.90	21.50
Guard - Grille - Heavy Truck	986153	1	12.90	21.50
Guard Unit - Front and Rear	986260	Set	19.50	32.50
Guard Unit - Front and Rear Fender	986413	Set	17.70	29.50
Heater and Defroster - Air Flow	986401	1	36.45	59.75
Heater and Defroster - Dash Recirculating	986400	1	21.65	35.50
Heater and Defroster - Air Flow - Truck	986104	1	37.00	58.00
Heater and Defroster - Dash - Truck	986248	1	21.65	35.50
Horns - Matched - Truck	986099	Pair	8.37	13.95
Jack - Mechanical	986177	1	3.57	5.95
Kool Kushion	986357	1	2.85	4.75
Lamp - Aux. - Dual - Pass	986234	Pair	9.45	15.75
Lamp - Back-Up - (except Powerglide)	986239	1	4.65	7.75

Description	Part. No.	Unit	Net Price	List Net
Lamp - Back-Up - (W/O Powerglide)	986408	Pair	5.40	9.00
Lamp - Back-Up - (With Powerglide)	986409	Pair	5.85	9.75
Lamp - Glove Compartment	986262	1	.60	1.00
Lamp - Load Compartment - Truck	986310	1	3.00	5.00
Lamp - Luggage Compartment	986238	1	.90	1.50
Lamp - Underhood	986250	1	.90	1.50
Lamp - R.H. Tail - Truck	986299	1	4.05	6.75
Lamp Unit - Service - Magnetic	986174	6	10.44	17.40
Lighter - Cigarette - Illuminated	986403	1	1.65	2.75
Mirror - Inside Rear-View - Pass.	985994	1	2.37	3.95
Mirror - Outside Rear-View - Pass.	986305	1	1.80	3.00
Mirror - R.V. Extension - Truck	986129	1	2.10	3.50
Mirror - Rain Deflector	986178	1	1.35	2.25
Mirror - Vanity Visor	985268	1	.90	1.50
Ornament - Hood - Pass.	986254	1	2.51	5.85
Ornament - Head - Pass.	986410	1	3.51	5.85
Ornament - Hood - Commercial	986161	1	4.20	7.00
Ornament - Hood - Truck	986162	1	4.20	7.00
Panel - Rear Fender	986290	Pair	9.40	14.50
Plate - Running Board Safety Tread	986328	Pair	4.50	7.50
Pocket - Cowl Trim Pad	986315	1	1.70	2.85
Radio Unit - Truck and Cowl Antenna	986185	1	47.68	74.50
Radio Unit-Custom-Deluxe - Push Button and Antenna	986390	1	44.25	73.75
Radio Unit - Custom Deluxe - Manual Training and Antenna	986391	1	35.85	59.75
Receiver - Ash - Pass.	986394	1	1.77	2.95
Reflector - Red Reflex	985223	1	.90	1.50
Rest - Arm Door - Pass. - 1949	986320	Pair	6.00	10.00
Rest - Arm Door - Pass. - 1950	986392	Pair	4.65	7.75
Rest - Arm - Door - Truck	986154	1	2.10	3.50
Rest - Arm - Door - Suburban	986167	1	2.10	3.50
Ring - Trim - 15" Wheel - Set	986258	5	5.97	9.95
Ring - Trim - 15" Wheel - Single	986259	1	1.50	2.50
Safetylight and Bracket Unit - Truck	986173	1	11.00	18.35
Safetylight and Bracket Unit - Pass.	986302	1	11.70	19.50
Safetylight and Bracket Unit - Pass.	986308	1	11.00	18.35
Safetylight and Bracket Unit - R.H. Pass	986327	1	11.70	19.50
Shaver - Electric	986418	1	14.97	24.95
Shield - Front Fender	986330	Pair	3.00	5.00
Sidewall Unit - White - 15" Wheel - Set	986269	4	5.97	9.95
Sidewall Unit - White - 15" Wheel - Single	986297	1	1.50	2.50
Signal - Direction - Automatic	986402	1	9.30	15.50
Signal - Direction - Truck	986179	1	15.60	24.50
Signal - Parking Brake	986323	1	1.08	1.80
Speaker - Rear Seat - Radio	986351	1	5.85	9.75
Track Unit - Tire	986108	Pair	2.10	3.50
Tool Kit - w/Bag	986362	1	1.65	2.50
Ventshade Unit - Styleline - 2 Door	986272	Set	7.50	12.50
Ventshade Unit - Styleline - 4 Door	986274	Set	7.50	12.50
Ventshade Unit - Fleetline - 2 Door	986275	Set	7.50	12.50
Ventshade Unit - Fleetline - 4 Door	986276	Set	7.50	12.50
Ventshade Unit - Coupe	986273	Set	3.90	6.50
Visor - Outside Car - Pass	986433	1	11.97	19.95
Visor - Outside Car - Pass.	986324	1	11.97	19.95
Visor - R.H. Sun - Pass. - 1949	986322	1	2.55	4.25
Visor - R.H. Sun - Pass. - 1950	986393	1	2.55	4.25
Visor - R.H. Sun - Truck	986155	1	1.80	3.00
Washer - Windshield - Truck	986041	1	3.75	6.25
Washer - Windshield - Pass.	986404	1	4.17	6.95
Wheel - Steering - Pass.	986306	1	7.65	17.75
Wheel - Steering - Pass.	986383	1	10.65	17.75

SERVICE ACCESSORIES

Description	Part No.	Unit	Net Price	List Net
Anti-Freeze - W/S Washer (12 - 6 oz. bottles)	986180	12	4.32	7.20
Caroma Evaporator Unit	983715	12	2.16	3.60
Cleaner Unit - White Sidewall (12 - 13 oz.)	986283	12	3.60	6.00
Cleaner - White Sidewall (gallon)	986284	1	1.50	2.50
Cleaner Unit - Sponge (12)	986225	12	3.12	5.88
Cleaner - Fabric (gallon)	986285	1	1.95	3.25
Cleaner Unit - Pre-Wax - Liquid (12 - 16-oz.)	986071	12	3.24	6.00
Cleaner Unit - Pre-Wax - Paste (12 - 11 oz.)	986073	12	3.24	6.00
Cleaner Unit - Fabric (12 - 16 oz.)	986076	12	3.96	6.60
Cleaner Unit - Glass (12 cans)	986193	12	3.24	5.40
Cleaner - Upholstery, 1/2 Gal.	985260	1	1.75	NL
Cleanser - Cooling System (12 cans)	986052	12	6.72	12.00
Cloth Unit - Polishing (12 cloths)	986077	12	3.60	6.00
Compound - Hand Rubbing, 5 Gal.	985559	1	5.70	NL
Compound - Hand Rubbing, 1 Gal.	985560	1	1.50	NL
Compound - Machine Rub., 1 Gal.	986092	1	1.50	NL
Compound - Machine Rub., 5 Gal.	986093	1	5.70	NL
Compound - Unit - Valve Grinding (36 - 4 oz)	986078	36	5.04	9.00
Door Ease - Stick Lubricant	985093	12	.68	1.20
Finish - Black Rubber - Gal.	985229	1	1.40	NL
Flush Unit - Radiator (12 - 16-oz.)	986079	12	3.12	5.88
Injector - Static Eliminator Powder	986033	1	.75	1.25
Oil Unit - Dripless Pene. (36 - 4 oz.)	986082	36	4.68	9.00
Oil Unit - General Use (36 - 4 oz.)	986054	36	4.68	9.00
Paste Unit - Gasket (12 - 16 oz.)	986083	12	13.80	22.77
Polish Unit - Chromium (12 - 8-oz.)	986084	12	2.52	4.20
Polish Unit - Triple Action (12)	986085	12	5.40	9.00
Polish - Triple Action - Gal.	985888	1	1.89	3.15
Porcelainize - Liquid (24 - 8-oz.)	986175	24	60.00	105.60
Porcelainize - Wash Cream (24 - 8-oz.)	986176	24	8.64	14.40
Porcelainize - Cleaner (gallon)	986363	1	4.75	NL
Powder Unit - Static Eliminator (12)	986087	12	2.88	4.80
Preventive Unit - Rust (24 - 4-oz.)	986086	24	3.60	6.00
Remover - Tar and Road Oil (12 cans)	986226	12	3.60	6.00
Ru-Glyde - G.M. (12 - 8 oz)	986046	12	3.60	6.00
Ru-Glyde - G.M. - Gallon	986047	1	2.15	3.60
Scraper Unit - Windshield (24 scrapers)	986194	24	5.72	9.36
Sealzit Unit - Glass Sealer (12 bottles)	986199	12	6.12	10.20
Sponge Unit (12 Florida)	986089	12	13.00	NL
Sponge Unit (6 Rock Island)	986090	6	19.00	NL
Sponge Unit (6R.1 Sheepswool)	986091	6	13.00	NL
Spot Remover Unit (12 - 8-oz.)	986075	12	3.60	6.00
Stop Leak Unit - Radiator (12 - 10-oz.)	986088	12	3.12	5.88
Undercoating (54 gallons)	986359	1	49.50	NL
Wax Unit - Auto - Paste (12 - 7-oz.)	986074	12	5.40	9.00
Wax Unit - Auto - Liquid (12 - 16-oz.)	986072	12	5.40	9.00

For 1950 Chevrolets interiors were more inviting, more attractive, and more luxurious than ever before. Shown here is an interior view of a Styleline DeLuxe 4-Door Sedan.

This is the 1950 Chevrolet Fleetline DeLuxe 2-Door Sedan, Model 2152 that weighed 3,115 pounds and delivered in base form for $1,482. A total of 189,509 of this body style were produced. I personally favored this fastback styling to the humpback model, but sales were indicating the other version was receiving more of an applause.

This example belonged to my sister, Mary Chodzko, of La Habra, California. It was the Model 2102 DeLuxe Styleline Town Sedan which was now ranked as Chevrolet's second most popular model with sales amounting to 248,567 units. The car weighed 3100 pounds and cost exactly the same as the fastback, version $1,482.

This 1950 Chevrolet Special 4-Door Sedan, as seen here, is a total original with only 6,000 true miles recorded as of 1990. It is for sure a bare bones car. The model weighed 3120 pounds and found 55,644 customers for the season. New, it sold for $1,450. The main thing it has going for it is the mileage.

CHEVROLET

Chevrolet's enduring quality is your reward for <u>thoughtful</u> buying

Size up the Styling

Road-test the Ride

Put it through its Paces

...and try Chevrolet's finer Time-Proved

POWERglide

Automatic Transmission *

The Styleline De Luxe 4-Door Sedan
(Continuation of standard equipment and trim illustrated is dependent on availability of material.)

Pound for pound, feature for feature, Chevrolet sizes up as America's *largest* and *finest* low-priced car!

It's *longest* and *heaviest* in its field, and you'll know that for a fact by the solid way it takes to the road, and the sweeping lines of its Body by Fisher.

It's *far ahead in fine-car features,* and every one adds greatly to *lasting* value! Unitized Knee-Action ride for *more lasting* smoothness— Valve-in-Head engine for *more lasting* economy— Center-Point Steering for *more lasting* handling ease—

Jumbo-Drum brakes for *more lasting* safety.

More size, more quality, *more car,* in the lowest-priced line of the low-price field. That's your reward for choosing—Chevrolet! Chevrolet Division of General Motors, Detroit 2, Michigan

Combination of Powerglide automatic transmission and 105-h.p. engine optional on De Luxe models at extra cost.

MORE PEOPLE BUY CHEVROLETS THAN ANY OTHER CAR!

One of my "pride and joys" is this 1951 Bel Air Hardtop Coupe. This example is shown when I purchased it in 1972 as a truly "Plain Jane" vehicle. New, it delivered for $2,286.28.

Chevrolet for 1951

The Chevy lineup for 1951 was basically the same car it had been from the year before. Small changes to the grille area and extended rear quarter panels, making the car appear both larger and wider, were the most noticeable differences from the previous year. Personally, of the four-year run for this body style, the 1951s were my favorite. I have a 1951 Bel Air Hardtop Coupe which I've owned for over 20 years. It was a real "Plain Jane" when I purchased it, but being fortunate enough to locate all the original accessories for the car has turned it into a real winner today. In this chapter, the car is shown here in its before and after photo. This unit is totally original, which has also added to its value. As a side note, one thing this car has in common with a 1950 Oldsmobile that I own is that my parents purchased the Olds new on December 12, 1950 and the Chevrolet was delivered to its first owner in Walnut Creek, California, on that very same day. This was the first 1951 Chevrolet car sold in Walnut Creek. The delivered price was $2,286.28 and included an Air Flow Heater, Directional Signals, Outside Rear View Mirror, Exhaust Extension and Tool Kit. These accessories, when installed, amounted to $97.25, according to the bill of sale that came with the car. How things have changed!

The 1951 cars were designated as Series JJ in the Special line, and JK for the DeLuxe models. Mechanically, all went along the same as in the previous year except that Bendix brakes were used in place of Huck brakes. The 1951 cars came with carburetors produced by Carter, Stromberg and Rochester which was a case of take what you get. The supply was limited and, with the Korean Conflict in full swing, the factory was agreeable to take what was available. Some suppliers were also unable to complete their fulfillments to the factory, as was the situation in the entire industry. As an example, very few cars came with white wall tires, as the ingredients for these were needed for the Korean affair. Chromium also saw its needs in other areas than bright work on the new cars.

Color choices for 1951 cars amounted to nine single tones:

Onyx Black
Thistle Gray
Aztec Tan
Burgundy Metallic
Trophy Blue
Shadow Gray
Fathom Green
Aspen Green
Moonlight Cream

Moonlight Cream was available only on the Convertible and the Bel Air Hardtop Coupe. Two-tone combinations were limited to Thistle Gray with Shadow Gray, Trophy Blue with Shadow Gray and Fathom Green with Aspen Green. The Bel Air Hardtop was more often seen in Moonlight Cream with Onyx Black top. My Bel Air came with the more rare version of solid Moonlight Cream, which I preferred.

Chevrolet continued to hold the number one sales position for another year, with calendar sales amounting to 1,118,096 units sold. The model year production consisted of 1,250,803 vehicles delivered. The DeLuxe line was the more popular of the two series selling 1,044,896 cars.

Here is the same car after being spruced up quite a bit in a matter of just a few weeks. Made quite a difference, wouldn't you agree? This unit delivered in the full single-tone color, rather than with the black top which most cars were equipped with. The color trade name was Moonlight Cream. We call her "Buttercup".

A typical factory production photo shows the more common version of Model 2154 Bel Air Hardtop Coupe with the black roof and Moonlight Cream body. It always amazes me how these cars get in these snow scenes without a bit of mud and slush on the body, nor even a tire track in the snow as the car drove out to be photographed. Guess I'm just being picky.

Looks like another one of my favorite hardtop models for 1951. The only additional equipment which this unit employs, appears to be the Powerglide transmission from the view of the gear selector placed in the park position, and the two tone paint combination. Hardtop models were equipped with two-tone gray striped nylon cord and genuine leather bolsters. Full floor carpeting came as standard equipment.

Chevrolet's 1951 Convertible, Model 2134, saw a production of 20,172 units. The base price for this sharp looking vehicle was $2,030. The whitewalls were an additional cost item. On convertible models, the outside left-mount side mirror was standard equipment. For the convertible models in 1951, they came with a choice of four different two-tone interiors complimenting the exterior colors. Only the convertible employed the use of 7.10 x 15-inch tires. All other models continued with 670 x 15-inch tires. The clear view plastic rear window was very popular with owners, chiefly due to its extended width. However, after it was only a few years old it became discolored, owners favored the older glass arrangement used on convertibles of an earlier era. The strong and durable top, went up and down automatically.

Again, Chevrolet's most popular car came as Model 2103, the DeLuxe Styleline 4-Door Sedan. It delivered for $1,680 in base form and weighed in at 3125 pounds. Most noticeable differences between this model and the Special 4-Door Sedan were the use of stainless stone guards on the rear door, and the fender stainless trim continuing from front fender into the front door. The Special 4-Door, referred to as Model 1503, delivered for $1,594. For an additional $86.00, the buyer received far more car by purchasing the DeLuxe Styleline.

Prices ranged from $1,460 for the three-passenger Special Styleline Business Coupe, weighing 3040 pounds, to the Station Wagon, Model 2119, which tipped the scale at 3470 pounds and sold for $2,191.

The 1951 Chevrolet three-passenger Business Coupe Model 1504 delivered for $1,460 and weighed 3040 pounds. A total of 17,020 units were produced during the year. The model came with a large compartment behind the rear seat which was beneficial to the traveling salesman. The rear compartment consisted of a rubber floor mat. The rear windows were stationary. This example sports a few frills to give it more appeal. The items consist of the sun visor which cost an additional $17.50; wheel trim rings for $10.95, and white sidewall tires. Appearing exactly the same, externally, was the Special Styleline Sport Coupe which had a production run of 18,982 units sold. Its delivered price was $1,545, and it tipped the scale at 3060 pounds. The Sport Coupe was Model 1524.

A 1951 Chevrolet Special Model 1553 Fleetline 4-Door Sedan had a run of 3364 vehicles sold for its final year of production. This unit delivered for $1,594. The fender skirts were optional equipment on the Special series but were standard equipment on all DeLuxe models. Note how the fender skirts improve the looks of the rear quarter panel. As on the Coupe Model, the rear vent windows were stationary.

Classed in the Special series was the Model 1508, better known as the Sedan Delivery. This model was classed and catalogued in the passenger car production. The company only saw a run of 20,817 units sold. The delivery unit delivered for $1,648. Basically, it used the same body shell as did the Pontiac of this era.

The most expensive Chevrolet for 1951 came as this Model 2119, better known as the *Styleline DeLuxe Station Wagon. The vehicle weighed 3470 pounds and delivered for $2,191. A total of 23,586 were produced for the model run. Note the rear door scuff plate is the same configuration as on the 1950 models, rather than that used on all other DeLuxe models. Interior-wise, the seats were done in tan imitation leather with tan rubber floor mats. The headliner consisted of a combination simulated wood and leather with roof bows having a woodgrain finish. The seating allowed for eight passengers with the rear and intermediate seats being interchangeable and allowing for additional cargo.*

This is a rear interior view of the 1951 Chevrolet Station Wagon. The front seat came with a full-width foam rubber cushion, while both the intermediate and rear seat were supported by rugged resilient coil springs.

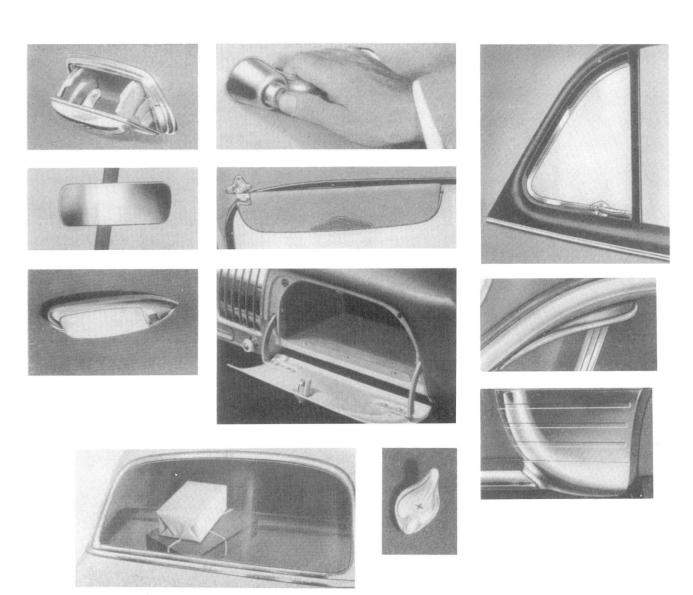

Features of the 1951 Chevrolet

Convenience in every detail was seen on the 1951 models as well as in all years of Chevrolet. Here are some views of small details that went into every Chevrolet: conveniently placed ash tray in the rear of the front seat of DeLuxe model cars; the finger tip ease of the push button door handles; easily adjusted rear view mirror; the dome light which automatically came on when front doors opened in DeLuxe models; the spring-friction sun visor could be adjusted without thumb screw setting and, except in Bel Air and Convertible models, it could easily pivot from front to side. DeLuxe cars came with two sun visors. The glove compartment was conveniently placed in the instrument panel offering ample capacity for maps and various paraphernalia. A locking button came in all models. The no-draft vent panels permitted instant ventilation in all kinds of weather also being locked tightly by a locking button mounted on the ventipane. The drip shield openings directed the flow of water away from the window. Gravel shields on the rear fenders (stainless on DeLuxe models and rubber on Special cars) saved the paint from much abuse especially in highway driving. Other small details included coat hooks above the rear quarter windows and a package shelf behind the rear seat which added additional carrying space for shopping tours and other occasions.

A three quarter rear view of the 1951 DeLuxe Styleline Sedan offered many of the more advanced styling features of larger G.M. cars of that era. The panoramic rear view window giving additional vision for both passengers and driver.

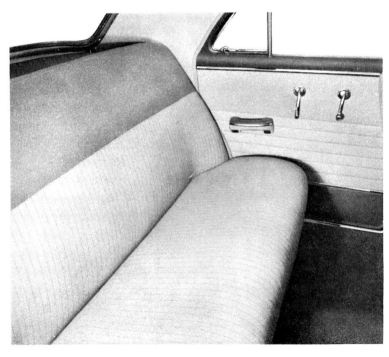

The rich deep upholstery and tasteful trim design with tailored striped light grey broadcloth set off by dark gray broadcloth on the seat backs were part of the package offered for all DeLuxe models in the 4-Door, 2-Door and Club Coupe models for 1951 Chevrolets.

A
C
C
E
S
S
O
R
I
E
S

AIR FLOW

HEATER AND DEFROSTER UNIT

Provides the maximum efficiency in heat distribution and temperature control. This Heater is thermostatically controlled to desired temperatures to insure the passengers of maximum driving comfort.

SPEAKER—REAR SEAT

A completely new Rear-Seat Radio Speaker. Full size 5" x 7" elliptical type Speaker, powered for dependable performance. Incorporated with this Speaker is a four-way switch.

MIRROR—OUTSIDE REAR-VIEW

This Mirror is sturdily mounted to keep vibration at a minimum, assuring you of sharp, clear images. Made of the finest chrome-plated, rust-resistant metal—Is engineered to be mounted on either the right or left side of the automobile.

ELECTRIC VANITY VISOR MIRROR

The Chevrolet Electric Vanity Visor Mirror has been attractively designed in appealing gray to harmonize with the interior of the car. The Mirror is framed in durable tenite, and it embodies full electrical safety features.

WINDSHIELD WASHER

This De Luxe Equipment is an excellent item for helping to keep the windshield clean under all conditions. Simply press a button on the windshield wiper control and the washer goes into action immediately, shooting a double spray of water on your windshield for six seconds.

CLOCK

For the 1951 Models, Chevrolet offers completely new designed Electric and Spring Wind Clocks that harmonize with the instrument panel and interior of the automobile. Complete with ultra-modern housing to enhance the beauty of the car.

HEATER AND DEFROSTER UNIT
DASH RECIRCULATING AIR-FLOW

The newly designed Recirculating Air-Flow Heater is one of the best and most economical Heaters designed to maintain even temperatures throughout the car.

RADIO—CUSTOM DE LUXE MANUAL TUNING

This Radio offers a superb performance at a lower price. It is a single Unit set and lists a new 5" x 7" Alnico permanent Magna-type Speaker. Variable tone control and dial illumination which can be controlled by the instrument panel light dimmer switch.

RADIO—CUSTOM DE LUXE PUSH-BUTTON

The 1951 Custom De Luxe Chevrolet Radio features a single unit with five station selector buttons. This highly sensitive Radio has six tubes (including rectifier) combined with a 6" x 9" Alnico permanent Magna-type Speaker.

AUXILIARY LAMPS

These new 1951 brightly chromed Lamps have 32 candlepower sealed-beam bulbs, and are easily installed on the front splash pan. Chevrolet Auxiliary Lamps project a wide low beam that reduces reflection and helps give better vision whatever the weather.

MIRROR—GLARE-PROOF INSIDE

The new 10" Glare-Proof Mirror is another FIRST in Chevrolet De Luxe Equipment. Designed to give full view at the rear, this duo-purpose Mirror gives full daylight reflection plus a no-glare vision at night. A flick of the finger adjusts the Mirror to either day or night driving.

BACK-UP LIGHTS

A new dual Back-Up Lamp Unit for 1951. These Lamps are a flush-body type mounting. Chevrolet Back-Up Lamps throw out two powerful beams of 32 candlepower each, to let you see what's behind you. They provide a bright warning to approaching cars and to pedestrians. The Lights flash on whenever the motor is running and shift lever is in reverse.

TISSUE DISPENSER

Mounted conveniently and securely under the glove compartment, this new De Luxe Tissue Dispenser is designed to take one full box of tissues. Made of a high luster plastic, this Dispenser will add to the beauty of the automobile.

DIRECTION SIGNAL

Chevrolet 1951 Direction Signal features an automatic turn-off control, and is attractively designed to match the interior of the automobile. The styling of this distinctive Direction Signal gives a neat built-in look of beauty.

WHEEL TRIM RINGS

These Trim Rings are made of highly polished stainless steel, and add a brilliant touch of sparkle to the wheels of the automobile. Do not rust or lose their luster even after long service.

FRONT AND REAR FENDER GUARDS

The new 1951 Fender Guards have been especially designed for Chevrolet. Made of heavy gauge, highly polished, chrome-plated steel, these Guards fit securely around the ends of the bumpers and thus help to protect that part of the car against serious damage.

TRUNK GUARD

The horizontal lines and the blended radii of heavy steel chrome-plated Trunk Guard enhances the rear appearance of the 1951 Chevrolet. This Guard was primarily designed to protect the trunk and rear license plate; also, relieving the plainness between the trunk and the bumper guards. Massively good looking, this Guard is bolted to the bumper guards. It also helps to prevent annoying overriding when parking.

LOCKING GAS CAP

This Cap has been designed to safeguard the gasoline supply and the Cap itself. This highly polished stainless steel Gas Cap is so engineered that the key cannot be removed until the Cap is locked.

HOOD ORNAMENT

The new Hood Ornament for the 1951 Chevrolet has been designed to add elegance to the automobile. It features the graceful lines of a gazelle, symbolizing smoothness and grace of the new Chevrolet.

SAFETYLIGHT

The heavily chromed and highly polished Chevrolet Safetylight is available with right or left-hand bracket. A unique feature on the 1951 Safetylight is a rear view mirror which turns with the light and can be adjusted to suit the driver's convenience.

Shown here are a variety of brilliant new genuine Chevrolet approved accessories for 1951. Further in this section is the list of accessories that customers could order along with the price of each.

The 1951 Chevrolet DeLuxe Fleetline 2-Door Sedan Model 2152 was always a favorite of mine. Next to my Bel Air Hardtop Coupe, this was my Number 1 model with its fastback styling. This unit weighed 3125 pounds and cost $1,629. Chevrolet delivered 131,910 of this model. It was not as popular with the customers as the 2-Door Sedan with a bustle back trunk. In fact, the fast back styling was only available in the 2-Door line for one more season.

Not nearly as sharp looking as its DeLuxe sister is this Special Fleetline 2-Door Sedan which wasn't around too long in 1951. Both it and the Special Fleetline 4-door Sedan were phased out during the 1951 model year. This example was known technically as Model 1552. It weighed 3090 pounds and sold for $1,541. Chevrolet found 6,441 customers for this "Plain Jane" model.

Distinction and beauty in every detail pretty much sums it all up in the views of 1951 styling from the panoramic windshield to the hood ornament designed to resemble a jet fighter plane.

An interior view of my 1951 Bel Air Coupe sporting the rare and highly sought after ornamental steering wheel. The part number for this accessory was 986545 and, when ordered new, cost the buyer $18.75. I'd hate to think what a N.O.S steering wheel would cost today.

A right side view showing a fuller interior shot of the dashboard with factory radio, Part Number 986517, when installed, cost $74.85. Note also the facial tissue dispenser, still with its 1951 tissue, costing $3.25. The part number for this accessory was 986546.

Factory antenna for the 1951 Coupe was interchangeable with 1949-1952 cars. It listed for $5.25 with a part number 986257. Also sharing the limelight for factory equipment was the combination spotlight and mirror, part number 986407. Installed, this accessory listed for $19.95.

A rear view of the 1951 hardtop coupe decked out in all its finery.

A close up view of the three-piece wrap-around rear window treatment. This styling was also shown on Pontiac and Oldsmobiles for this time span.

To add a little splash to the front fender treatment on these cars was this stainless shield that cost an additional $5.75 per pair. The part number was 986535.

The full package of rearview accessories consisted of gas door protecting guard, rear fender molding unit (which, on early models, came as standard equipment) back-up lamps, tailpipe extension, trunk guard, and rear fender guards.

A three-quarter front view of my 1951 Bel Air Hardtop Coupe with all its factory-approved accessories. The car now shows slightly over 70,000 without a major overhaul, as yet.

The debut of the name "Impala" appeared on the 1951 cars. If the owner wished to order the special Gazelle ornament, it sold for $7.80 additional. Its part number was 986528.

1951 Chevrolet Bel Air Sport Coupe

Chevrolet Accessories For 1951

Retail Salesman's

PRICE LIST

Effective Nov. 15, 1950

ALL PRICES SUBJECT TO CHANGE WITHOUT NOTICE

1951 ACCESSORIES

PASSENGER CAR

Description	Part No.	Unit	List Price
Antenna - Fender	986257	1	5.95
Block - Wiring Junction	986442	1	1.60
Cap - Gas Tank, Locking	986326	1	1.60
Clock - Electric	986526	1	2.25
Clock - Spring Wind	986525	1	9.95
Condenser - Radiator Overflow	986282	1	3.95
Cover - Accelerator Pedal 1/6	986325	1	1.25
Cover - Seat - Plastic - All Models		Set	37.50
Cover - Seat - Fiber - All Models (except Convertible)		Set	23.50
Cover - Seat - Rayon - All Models (except Convertible)		Set	27.50
Cover - Steering Wheel 1/6	986356	1	1.50
Disc - Stainless Steel - 15" Wheel - Set	986352	4	14.75
Disc - Stainless Steel - Do-Nut Type - Set	986417	4	15.75
Dispenser - Tissue	986546	1	3.25
Extension - Exhaust Pipe	986382	1	2.95
Filter Unit - Gasoline 1/12	986620	1	1.95
Frame - License Plate	986371	Pair	2.95
Garment Bag and Hanger Unit - Ladies 1/3	986437	1	3.95
Garment Bag and Hanger Unit - Men 1/3	986438	1	3.95
Glareshade - Windshield - Styleline	986354	Pair	9.95
Glareshade - Windshield - Fleetline	986355	Pair	9.95
Glareshade - Windshield - Bel Air & Convertible	986539	Pair	9.95
Guard Unit - Front and Rear Fender	986496	Set	32.50
Guard - Gas Tank Filler Fender 1/6	986552	1	1.50
Guard - Trunk	986538	1	8.95
Heater and Defroster - Air-Flow	986492	1	59.90
Heater and Defroster - Recirculating Air-Flow	986513	1	35.90
Hook Unit - Garment 1/12	986537	1	1.25
Lamp - Auxiliary Dual (Fog)	986523	Pair	15.75
Lamp - Back-Up (Conventional Trans.)	986408	Pair	8.90
Lamp - Back-Up (Power Glide)	986409	Pair	8.90
Lamp - Glove Compartment	986489	1	1.25
Lamp - Luggage Compartment	986238	1	1.50

Description	Part No.	Unit	List Price
Lamp - Underhood	986250	1	1.50
Lamp Unit - Service Magnetic 1/6	986174	1	2.90
Lighter - Cigarette - Illuminated	986488	1	2.75
Mirror - Door Top L.H. - R.V.	986533	1	3.00
Mirror - 10" Glare-proof Inside R.V.	986530	1	3.95
Mirror - Outside Rear-View	986305	1	3.00
Mirror - Vanity Visor	985268	1	1.50
Mirror - Vanity Visor - Bel Air and Convertible	986605	1	1.50
Mirror - Electric Vanity Visor	986439	1	4.50
Ornament - Hood	986528	1	7.80
Panel - Rear Fender	986519	Pair	14.50
Radio Unit - Push-Button and Antenna	986517	1	74.85
Radio Unit - Manual Tuning and Antenna	986518	1	61.50
Receiver - Ash	986487	1	1.35
Rest - Arm Door	986553	Pair	7.95
Ring - Trim 15" Wheel - Set	986258	5	10.95
Safetylight and Mirror - L.H./Brkt.	986407	1	19.95
Shaver - Electric 6V - 110V	986418	1	24.95
Shield - Front Fender	986535	Pair	5.75
Sidewall Unit - White 15" Wheel - Set	986269	4	9.95
Signal - Direction - Self-Cancelling	986514	1	15.50
Signal - Parking Brake	986529	1	1.80
Speaker - Rear Seat Radio	986532	1	9.75
Spotlight - Portable	986555	1	7.95
Tool Kit - With Bag	986362	1	2.75
Ventshade Unit - All Models (except Coupe)		Set	12.50
Ventshade Unit - Coupe	986273	Set	6.50
Visor - Outside Metal	986433	1	17.50
Visor - R.H. Sun	986544	1	4.50
Viewer - Traffic Light	986550	1	2.50
Washer - Windshield	986404	1	6.95
Wheel - Steering - Ornamental	986545	1	18.75

TRUCK

Description	Part No.	Unit	List Price	Description	Part No.	Unit	List Price
Antenna - Cowl	986069	1	6.75	Lamp - Underhood	986250	1	1.50
Bracket - Mirror R.H.	986441	1	1.85	Lamp Unit - Service Magnetic	.1/6 986174	1	2.90
Condenser - Radiator Overflow	985528	1	2.95	Lighter - Cigarette - Illuminated	986403	1	2.75
Cover - Radiator	986127	1	4.75	Mirror - R.V. Extendable	986440	1	3.95
Cover - Seat - Fiber	986405	Set	13.50	Ornament - Hood - Commercial	986161	1	7.00
Filter Adapter - Gasoline	1/6 986621	1	.50	Ornament - Hood - Truck	986162	1	7.00
Frame - License Plate	986371	Pair	2.95	Plate - Running Board Safety Tread	986328	Pair	7.50
Glareshade - Windshield	986604	Pair	10.95	Radio unit - Push-Button and Antenna	986444	1	69.50
Guard Unit - Bumper	986113	Pair	6.50	Reflector - Red Reflex	985223	1	1.50
Guard - Radiator Grille - Commercial	986486	1	23.50	Rest - Arm Door	986154	1	3.50
Guard - Radiator Grille - Truck	986536	1	23.50	Safety and Bracket Unit	986173	1	18.50
Heater and Defroster - Air-Flow	986104	1	59.00	Shaver - Electric 6V - 110V	986418	1	24.95
Heater and Defroster - Dash Recirculating	986248	1	35.90	Signal - Direction Lamp Unit	986551	1	24.50
Horns - Matched	986397	Pair	12.50	Spotlight - Portable	986555	1	7.95
Lamp - Auxiliary Dual (Fog)	986524	Pair	14.50	Tool Kit - With Bag	986362	1	2.75
Lamp - Glove Compartment	986489	1	1.25	Visor - R.H. Sun	986155	1	3.25
Lamp - Load Compartment	986310	1	5.00	Washer - Windshield	986041	1	6.25
Lamp - R.H. Tail	986299	1	7.00	Washer - Windshield - Foot-operated	986527	1	6.25

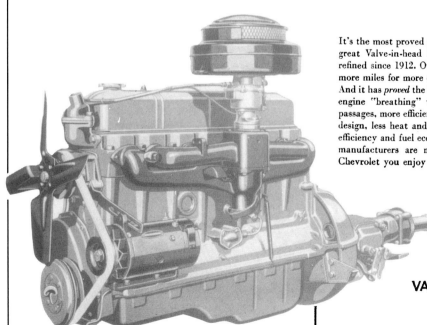

A long drive in this smart Sport Coupe leaves you rested, relaxed and ready for fun.

Smooth as a fine tennis court—that's Powerglide automatic transmission with extra-powerful Valve-in-Head engine and Automatic Choke. Optional on De Luxe models at extra cost.

Colorful as the most scenic golf course. Chevrolet offers a choice of 26 solid colors and two-tone color combinations with color-matched interiors in De Luxe models.

Room for two foursomes in this handsome Chevrolet Station Wagon with all-steel Body by Fisher. Four doors for easier entrance and exit.

Continuation of standard equipment and trim illustrated is dependent on availability of material.

Pleasure? . . . Full measure!
Price? . . . Pleasant surprise!

If you think that high quality in a motor car goes hand in hand with high cost, your Chevrolet dealer has a very pleasant surprise for you.

You'll be surprised at the style and quality of Chevrolet's Body by Fisher . . . the *only* Body by Fisher in the low-price field.

You'll be surprised at the smoothness of new Centerpoise Power . . . with Chevrolet's famous valve-in-head engine centered, poised and cushioned in rubber by new high-side mountings.

You'll be surprised at the comfort of Chevrolet's improved Knee-Action ride . . . at the easy way this car handles and its solid feel on the road.

In *every* respect, this fine, big Chevrolet offers you a full measure of motoring pleasure. And yet—most pleasant surprise of all—it's the lowest-priced line in its field! See your Chevrolet dealer soon and satisfy yourself that there's no reason for paying more. Chevrolet Division of General Motors, Detroit 2, Michigan.

MORE PEOPLE BUY CHEVROLETS THAN ANY OTHER CAR!

The Only Fine Cars PRICED SO LOW!

Looking virtually the same as the 1951 Chevrolet Station Wagon is this Model 2119 eight-passenger wagon. The most noticeable change this year came with the five teeth on the middle bar of the grille. Sales were way down this year, mainly because Ford came out with their new wagon offering an entirely new body style. Chevy wagon sales amounted to only 12,750 units. The vehicle weighed 3475 pounds and sold for $2,297, making it still the company's most expensive vehicle. The wagon was only available in four solid colors: Emerald Green, Sahara Beige, Saddle Brown, and Regal Maroon, as mentioned in the text.

Chevrolet for 1952

This was the final year for this attractive four-year body style. I know it really isn't true but, over the years, it seems as though nearly everyone I've spoken with, at one time or another, has owned a Chevrolet with the 1949-1952 body design. In our own family, we've had three of these automobiles, ranging from a 1950 Styleline Business Coupe, to the 1951 Bel Air Hardtop Coupe mentioned in the previous chapter. Being in the final year of this body design, little was done to change the nice lines of the vehicle. The usual grille change only amounted to placing five teeth in the center bar which did alter its front end appearance. The most noticeable change was seen in the DeLuxe line where an additional bit of side trim was employed on the rear quarter panel. Also, the DeLuxe nomenclature was removed from the front fender to the rear quarter panel, directly above the stainless gravel deflector. As for the past three years, fender skirts were standard equipment on DeLuxe models and available on Special cars for an additional $16.75. Few purchased them as most people, buying the lower-priced cars, were not interested in the luxury appointments.

A larger selection of colors was now becoming available on Chevrolets as the new approach, to try to appeal to women with wilder color combinations, was just around the corner. A customer now had a choice of 10 solid colors in regular closed cars, and 5 two-tone combinations. The Bel Air was available in 4 solid colors and 11 two-tone choices. Convertible models could be ordered in 10 solid colors with 5 varieties of fabric tops from black, green, blue, gray and tan. The Station Wagon was available in 4 colors:

Emerald Green
Sahara Beige
Saddle Brown
Regal Maroon

The Station Wagon interior continued to be of the sturdy leather fabric which retained its good looks in spite of hard usage and heavy loads.

One new item that became popular at this time, which really hasn't been mentioned by many authors of various automotive books, was the use of tinted glass. Chevrolet was the first in its field to offer this special safety plate glass on all their 1952 cars, at an additional cost. They referred to it as E-Z Eye Glass.

A sharp looking 1952 Bel Air Hardtop Coupe, Model 2154, that delivered for $2,006. This vehicle weighed 3215 pounds, selling 74,634 units for the year. This example was done in one of Chevrolet's new color choices called Beach White and Bittersweet, a color choice only available on the Hardtop Coupe. It also proved to be very popular with purchasers.

At first, it wasn't received very well as it was shaded too deeply and, for night driving, many people complained because vision was impaired.

The 1952 Chevrolet Club Coupe in the DeLuxe Styleline was technically referred to as the Sport Coupe Model 2124. Production reached 36,954 vehicles sold for the model run. The Sport Coupe weighed 3100 pounds and delivered for $1,726. Note the 1952 cars are shown with black wall tires in all their promotional advertising. This was actually the case with all manufacturers due to the Korean Conflict. The zinc used in the whitewalls found a better use at this time. The color combination from this color photo shows the coupe done in Admiral Blue over Twilight Blue.

Still Chevrolet's best seller was this DeLuxe Styleline 4-Door Sedan, Model 2103. The 4-Door saw a production run of 319,736. It weighed 3145 pounds and delivered for $1,761. The DeLuxe Sedan came with color coordinated chevron pattern cloth with plain broadcloth inserts. The buyer had his choice of green, blue or gray upholstery to coordinate with the vehicle's exterior color. E-Z Eye Glass was first available on these 1952 models.

The number of body styles offered were fewer than the previous year. The 4-Door Fleetline and Special Fleetlines were not introduced for the 1952 model run. Only the Fleetline DeLuxe 2-Door Sedan remained in the Fleetline lineup. A total of 11 models were left for the year. The Specials were called Model KJs while the DeLuxe line was known as Series KK. The DeLuxe Styleline 4-Door Sedan, Model 2103, again was the most popular car from Chevrolet for the year. A run of 319,736 units were sold at a base price of $1,761. The Company continued to hold the first sales slot for the year, with calendar sales amounting to 877,947 units delivered and model year sales consisted of 827,317 vehicle purchases.

This vehicle was my brother-in-law's first company-owned vehicle. It's the Special Styleline 2-Door Sedan, Model 1502. It weighed 3085 pounds and delivered for $1,614. The car performed well, as a Chevy should. In the two years he drove it, he racked up 45,000 trouble-free miles. The only appearance problem developed when it was barely eight months old. Typical of all cars at that time was the lack of the proper ingredients in the chrome, a problem attributed to the Korean Conflict. All the chrome wore thin and pealed off the grille. This unit came in a bland green color known as Spring Green.

The last year to appear is this DeLuxe Fleetline Fastback 2-Door Sedan, Model 2152. The production run amounted to 37,164. The car weighed 3110 pounds and sold for $1,707. This particular body style was not available as a two-tone paint combination like the DeLuxe Styleline 2-Door Sedan.

Shown here are some of the fashionable Chevrolet approved accessories for 1952.

The lowest production model in the DeLuxe lineup was Model 2134 which happened to be the Convertible. The vehicle weighed 3380 pounds and delivered for $2,128. A total of only 11,975 were manufactured, making them fairly rare to obtain today. The convertibles were upholstered in genuine leather with a choice of five colors to harmonize with the exterior.

The overall lowest production unit from Chevrolet in 1952 was the Special Styleline Sport Coupe which drew only 8906 buyers. The car weighed 3050 pounds and delivered for $1,620. Looking exactly the same from the exterior was the Styleline three-passenger Business Coupe which saw a production run of 10,359 units, weighed 3045 pounds, and selling for $1,530. Looking inside and seeing a rear compartment minus a seat was the only telltale difference.

This 1952 Special Sedan Delivery sold for $1,648 and weighed 3100 pounds. Again, it was called Model 1508, with a production run of 9,175 units sold. The vehicle had a 1000-pound weight capacity. The car used the same body shell as that of the station wagon. This unit is all decked out with whitewalls wheel trim rings and even sports factory fender skirts which certainly adds to its appearance. The vehicle is a service vehicle for Time Lines, a Texas Corporation, as the 1952 Texas license plates indicate it is home based.

Being the most popular model in the 2-Door line of vehicles for 1952 was the DeLuxe Styleline 2-Door Sedan, Model 2102. This unit weighed 3110 pounds and carried a tab of $1,707. A total of 215,417 saw the light of day. Note the side trim difference on this DeLuxe model from the 1951 cars. The nameplate DeLuxe appeared on the rear quarter panel above the gravel shield, rather than on the front fender as in 1951 models.

A nicely equipped 1952 DeLuxe Styleline 4-Door Sedan shown from the three-quarter, left-rear view. I photographed this vehicle in the late '60s when it barely had 19,000 miles on the odometer.

A front three-quarter view of the DeLuxe Styleline Sedan. The unusual thing on this vehicle was that you could tell the chrome still had the lacquer coating on the finish from new. I took this photo of the car when it was 17 years old. It sported a factory sun visor, spotlight, and 1953 Bel Air wheel covers. A very clean original automobile. I wonder where it is today?

A brand new 1952 Bel Air Hardtop Coupe taken in the summer of 1952 at Lake Arrowhead, California. The color combination was Beach White and Bittersweet. Nicely equipped wouldn't you say?

EXTERIOR COLORS

Single colors

Color Description	Color Name — Body, Sheet Metal, and Wheels	Wheel Stripes	All Sedans, Sport and Business Coupes	Bel Air	Convertible	Station Wagon
Black	Onyx Black	Argent Silver	✔	✔	✔	
Dark Gray	Dusk Gray *	Argent Silver	✔			
Light Gray	Birch Gray	Onyx Black	✔		✔	
Dark Blue	Admiral Blue *	Argent Silver	✔		✔	
Light Blue	Twilight Blue	Onyx Black	✔	✔	✔	
Dark Green	Emerald Green *	Argent Silver	✔	✔	✔	✔
Light Green	Spring Green	Onyx Black	✔		✔	
Beige	Sahara Beige	Onyx Black	✔		✔	✔
Brown	Saddle Brown *	Argent Silver			✔	✔
Maroon	Regal Maroon *	Argent Silver	✔			✔
Red	Cherry	Argent Silver			✔	
Cream	Honeydew	Onyx Black		✔	✔	

Two-tone combinations

Color Description	Color Name — Upper Body	Lower Body, Sheet Metal, and Wheels	Wheel Stripes	Styleline Sedans, Sport and Business Coupes	Bel Air
Dark Gray over Light Gray	Dusk Gray *	Birch Gray	Onyx Black	✔	
Dark Blue over Light Blue	Admiral Blue *	Twilight Blue	Onyx Black	✔	
Dark Green over Light Green	Emerald Green *	Spring Green	Onyx Black	✔	
Light Green over Dark Green	Spring Green	Emerald Green *	Argent Silver		✔
Black over Maroon	Onyx Black	Regal Maroon *	Argent Silver	✔	✔
Black over Light Gray	Onyx Black	Birch Gray	Onyx Black		✔
Black over Cream	Onyx Black	Honeydew	Onyx Black		✔
Light Gray over Dark Blue	Birch Gray	Admiral Blue *	Argent Silver		✔
Light Gray over Light Blue	Birch Gray	Twilight Blue	Onyx Black		✔
Light Gray over Light Green	Birch Gray	Spring Green	Onyx Black		✔
Brown over Beige	Saddle Brown *	Sahara Beige	Onyx Black		✔
Beige over Brown	Sahara Beige	Saddle Brown *	Argent Silver		✔
Beige over Maroon	Sahara Beige	Regal Maroon *	Argent Silver		✔
Off-white over Coral	Beach White	Bittersweet **	Bittersweet		✔

* – Metallic Color.
** – Beach White Wheels.

Chevrolet Accessories For 1952

DEALER LIST AND NET PRICE SCHEDULE

Effective April 1, 1952

ALL PRICES SUBJECT TO CHANGE WITHOUT NOTICE

The "List Prices" shown in this schedule are suggested prices for sales to consumers.

1952 ACCESSORIES

Description	Part No.	Unit	Net Price	List Price
Antenna - Fender - Pass.	986652	1	3.96	6.60
Antenna - Cowl - Com'l. and Truck	986069	1	4.49	7.48
Block - Wiring Junction	986442	1	.99	1.65
Bracket - Mirror - R.H. Com'l. and Truck	986441	1	1.10	1.83
Cap Battery Filler (12)	986781	12	10.00	16.68
Cap - Gas Tank, Locking	986689	1	1.56	2.60
Clock - Electric	986677	1	12.60	21.00
Clock - Spring Wind	986678	1	6.65	11.08
Condenser - Radiator Overflow - Pass	986282	1	2.31	3.85
Cover - Accelerator Pedal (6)	986325	6	4.20	7.00
Cover - Seat - Plastic - 2-Door, 4-Door, Bel Air		Set	24.23	40.38
Cover - Seat - Fiber - 2-Door, 4-Door, Bel Air		Set	15.45	25.74
Cover - Seat - Rayon - 2-Door, 4-Door, Bel Air		Set	16.35	27.25
Cover - Seat - Fiber - Com'l. and Truck	986644	Set	8.87	14.79
Disc - Stainless Steel - Do-Nut Type -Set	986417	4	9.56	15.93
Disc - Stainless Steel - Do-Nut Type Single	986416	1	2.59	4.32
Dispenser - Tissue	986546	1	2.02	3.37
Extension - Exhaust	986382	1	1.87	3.12
Filter Cooling System Unit	986705	1	6.57	10.95
Filter & Element Cooling System 6 Filters, 2 Elements	986760	6	52.74	87.90
Filter & Element Cooling System 24 Filters, 8 Elements	986761	24	210.96	351.60
Filter - Gasoline Pass (Autochoke)	986640	12	15.84	26.40
Filter - Gasoline (12) - Pass	986620	12	14.99	24.98
Filter Adapter - Gasoline (6) - Truck	986621	6	1.92	3.20
Frame - License Plate - (Pair)	986708	Pair	1.96	3.27
Garment Bag and Hangers - Ladies (3)	986437	3	7.11	11.85
Garment Bag and Hangers - Men (3)	986438	3	7.11	11.85
Glareshade - Windshield - Styleline	986354	Pair	6.20	10.33
Glareshade - Windshield - Fleetline	986355	Pair	6.20	10.33
Glareshade - Windshield - Bel Air and Conv't.	986539	Pair	6.20	10.33
Glareshade - Windshield - Com'l. and Truck	986604	Pair	6.60	11.00
Guard Unit - Front and Rear Fender	986496	Set	20.17	33.61
Guard - Bumper - Commercial	986113	Pair	4.34	7.23
Guard - Radiator Grille - Commercial	986486	1	14.16	23.60
Guard - Radiator Grille - Truck	986536	1	15.48	25.80
Guard - Gas Tank Filler Fender (6)	986552	6	5.83	9.72
Guard - Bumper (Truck)	986538	1	6.75	11.25

Description	Part No.	Unit	Net Price	List Price
Heater and Defroster - Air-Flow	986492	1	42.54	69.73
Heater and Defroster - Recirculating Air-Flow	986513	1	25.29	41.46
Heater and Defroster - Air-Flow - Com'l. & Trk.	986104	1	43.01	67.41
Heater and Defroster - Dash Recirculating -Trk.	986248	1	25.26	39.59
Hook Unit - Garment (12)	986537	12	9.00	15.00
Horns - Matched - Com'l. and Truck (Pair)	986397	Pair	7.99	13.32
Kit - Seat Cover Installation	986432	1	3.30	NL
Lamp - Auxiliary Dual (Fog) - Pass	986686	Pair	10.09	16.82
	986697	Pair	10.09	16.82
Lamp - Auxiliary Dual (Fog) Comm'l. & Truck	986524	Pair	9.29	15.48
Lamp - Back-Up - Conventional Trans. (Pair)	986408	Pair	5.70	9.50
Lamp - Back-Up - Power Glide (Pair)	986409	Pair	5.70	9.50
Lamp - Glove Compartment	986489	1	.70	1.17
Lamp - Luggage Compartment	986238	1	.93	1.56
Lamp - R.H. Tail - Comm'l. and Truck	986299	1	4.48	7.47
Lamp - Underhood	986250	1	.93	1.56
Lighter - Cigarette - Illuminated - Pass.	986488	1	1.72	2.87
Mat Unit - Rubber Floor (Blue) (6)	986765	6	6.30	10.50
Mat Unit - Rubber Floor (Red) (6)	986766	6	6.30	10.50
Mat Unit - Rubber Floor (Green) (6)	986767	6	6.30	10.50
Mat Unit - Rubber Floor (Black) (6)	986768	6	6.30	10.50
Mirror - 8 1/2" Glare-proof Inside R.V.	986632	1	2.37	3.95
Mirror - Outside Rear-View - Body Mounting	986762	1	2.08	3.47
Mirror - Outside Rear-View - Rain Deflector	986692	1	1.80	3.00
Mirror - Outside R.V.	986305	1	1.88	3.13
Mirror - R.V. Extendable - Comm'l. and Truck	986440	1	2.19	3.65
Mirror - Vanity Visor	985268	1	.93	1.56
Mirror - Vanity Visor - Bel Air and Conv't.	986605	1	.94	1.57
Mirror - Electric Vanity Visor	986439	1	2.80	4.67
Moulding Unit - Rear Fender	986702		4.83	8.05
Panel - Rear Fender (Pair)	986519	Pair	10.05	16.75
Radio Unit - Push Button and Antenna	986517	1	48.35	80.58
Radio Unit - Manual Tuning and Antenna	986518	1	39.32	65.53
Radio Unit - Push Button and Antenna - Com'l. and Truck	986444	1	45.55	75.91
Receiver - Ash	986676	1	.84	1.40
Reflector - Red Reflex	985223	1	.95	1.58
Rest - Arm Door (Pair) - Pass.	986682	Pair	5.26	8.77
Rest - Arm Door - Truck	986154	1	2.34	3.90

Description	Part No.	Unit	Net Price	List Price
Ring - Trim - 15" Wheel - Set	986258	5	6.45	10.75
Ring - Trim - 15" Wheel - Single	986259	1	1.62	2.70
Safetylight and Mirror - L.H./Bracket - Pass	986407	1	13.17	21.95
Safetylight and Bracket - Com'l. and Truck	986173	1	11.43	19.05
Shaver - Electric - 6V-110V	986418	1	14.97	24.95
Shield - Front Fender (Pair)	986535	Pair	3.71	6.18
Sidewall Unit - White - 15" Wheel Set	986269	4	6.60	11.00
Sidewall Unit - White - 15" Wheel - Single	986297	1	1.66	2.77
Signal Direction - Self-Cancelling	986679	1	9.93	16.55
Signal - Direction Unit - Com'l. Truck	986636	1	19.06	31.76
Signal - Direction Lamp Unit - Com'l and Truck	986551	1	15.66	26.10
Signal - Parking Brake	986529	1	1.33	2.21
Speaker - Rear Seat Radio	986532	1	6.39	10.65
Spotlight - Portable	986555	1	4.96	8.27
Tool Kit - With Bag	986362	1	1.85	2.80
Undercoating - 54 Gal. Drum	986359	1	49.50	NL
Undercoating - 54 Gal. Drum	986637	1	49.50	NL
Undercoating - 80 Drum Carload	986548	1	3283.20	NL
Undercoating - 80 Drum Carload	986638	1	3283.20	NL
Ventshade - Styleline 2-Door	986272	Set	7.94	13.23
Ventshade - Styleline 4-Door	986274	Set	7.94	13.23
Ventshade - Fleetline 4-Door	986276	Set	7.94	I3.23
Ventshade - Coupe	986273	Set	4.13	6.88
Ventshade - Truck	986623	Set	4.13	6.88
Visor - Outside Metal	986433	1	10.90	18.17
Visor - R.H. Sun - Pass.	986544	1	2.91	4.85
Visor - R.H. Sun - Truck	986155	1	2.01	3.35
Viewer - Traffic Light	986550	1	1.59	2.65
Washer - Windshield - Pass.	986404	1	4.35	7.25
Washer - Windshield - Foot Operated Com'l. and Truck	986527	1	4.06	6.77
Wheel - Steering - Ornamental	986545	1	11.46	19.10

SERVICE ACCESSORIES

Description	Part No.	Net Price	List Price
Anti-Freeze - 100% Methanol (24-1qt. Cans)	986700	9.00	6.30
Anti-Freeze - 100% Methanol (6-1 Gal. Cans)	986701	9.00	5.88
Anti-Freeze - 100% Methanol (54-Gal. Drum)	986369	81.00	48.60
Anti-Freeze - Ethylene-Glycol (24-1Qt. Cans)	986698	24.00	16.08
Anti-Freeze - Ethylene-Glycol (6-1 Gal. Cans)	986699	22.50	15.06
Anti-Freeze - "Zerex" - (24-1Qt. Cans)	986645	24.00	16.08
Anti-Freeze - "Zerex" - (6-1 Gal. Cans)	986646	22.50	15.06
Anti-Freeze - "Zerone" - (24-1Qt. Cans)	986647	9.00	6.30
Anti-Freeze - "Zerone" - (6-1Gal. Cans)	986648	9.00	5.88
Anti-Freeze - "Zerone" - (54 Gal. Drum)	986649	81.00	48.60
Anti-Freeze - W/S Washer (12-6oz. Bottles)	986180	7.20	4.32
Caroma Evaporator - Unit (12 Vials)	983715	3.60	2.16
Cleaner Unit Fabric (12-16 oz. Cans)	986076	6.60	3.96
Cleaner - Fabric (1 Gal.)	986285	3.25	1.95
Cleaner - Sponge (12)	986225	5.88	3.12
Cleaner - White Sidewall, Tire (1 Gal.)	986284	2.50	1.50
Cleaner Unit Glass (12-10 oz. Cans)	986193	5.40	3.24
Cleaner Upolstery (1/2 Gallon)	985260	NL	1.75
Cleaner - Cooling System (12 Cans)	986052	12.00	6.72
Cloth Unit - Polishing (12 Cloths)	986077	6.00	3.60
Compound - Hand Rubbing (1 Gal.)	985560	NL	1.50
Compound - Machine Rubbing (1 Gal.)	986092	NL	1.50
Compound - Valve Grinding (36-4oz. Cans)	986078	9.00	5.04
Element - Cooling System Replacement	986706	1.85	1.11
Finish - Black Rubber (1 Gal.)	985229	NL	1.40
Flush Unit - Radiator (12-16oz. Cans)	986079	5.88	3.12
Injector - Static Eliminator Powder	986033	1.25	.75
Lock-Ease (12-4oz. Cans)	986434	4.20	2.80
Lubricant - Stick door-ease (12 Sticks)	985093	1.20	.68
Oil Unit - Dripless, penetrating (36-4 oz. Cans)	986082	9.00	4.68
Oil Unit - General Use (36-4 oz. Cans)	986054	9.00	4.68
Perfect Seal - Gasket Paste (Single)	985872	1.75	1.05
Polish Unit - Chromium (12-8 oz. Cans)	986084	4.20	2.52
Polish Unit - Triple Action (12-16 oz. Cans)	986085	9.00	5.40
Polish - Triple Action (1 Gal.)	985888	3.15	1.89
Porcelainize Liquid (24-8 oz. Bottles)	986175	105.60	60.00
Porcelainize Wash Cream (24-8 oz. Bottles)	986176	14.40	8.64
Porcelainize Cleaner (1 Gal.)	986363	NL	4.75
Powder Unit Static Eliminator (12 envelopes)	986087	4.80	2.88
Preventive Unit - Rust (24-4 oz. Cans)	986086	6.00	3.60
Ru Glyde (1 Gallon)	986047	3.60	2.15
Sealer Unit - GM Chrome Protective	986680	15.00	9.00
Sealzit Unit - Glass Sealer (12-2 oz. Bottles)	986199	10.20	6.12
Spot Remover Unit (12-8 oz Cans)	986075	6.00	3.60
Stop Leak Unit Radiator (12-10 oz. Cans)	986088	5.88	3.12
Wax Unit Auto, liquid (12-16 oz. Cans)	986072	9.00	5.40

Without a doubt, one of the finest cars I've ever owned was this Bel Air 2-Door Sedan, Model 2403. Possibly, the fact that it was my first brand new car, made it the best. Chevrolet produced 144,401 of this model for the year's run. The base price was $1,820, minus the factory accessories with which this car came equipped, as shown here.

Chevrolet for 1953

The 1953 Chevrolet will always be considered as one of my favorite cars from my favorite manufacturer. Even without knowing what the new car was to look like, I had my heart set on owning a 1953 Chevy. In those days, debut day seemed always to be on a Friday, early in January. Shortly after Christmas, I'd see these new models arriving on these long transport trucks into Pasadena, California (where I then resided). Each car was completely covered with its own tarpaulin where nothing could be seen. One day, when the covers were removed from a blue and ivory Bel Air Sedan, I was there to take some pictures of it. No way was I allowed to shoot it. I guess they thought I was from the local newspaper, the Pasadena Star News, hoping to get a first-hand story about the new models. I was told not to take pictures and just be on my way. Well, to make a long story short, I was attending USC at the time and, every afternoon for the week that the GM Motorama was being held at the Shrine Auditorium, I would traipse up Figueroa Street from school, to the auditorium just to look at all the GM products that were on display. For some reason, I always wandered over to the Chevy display to look at the Bel Air Hardtop Sport Coupe done again in Horizon Blue and India Ivory. The tab was in the $2800-range and I just didn't know how I could swing it. A friend of mine, whom I'd known since grade school and who was also going to SC, had just taken delivery of the exact model. When I saw it, I wanted it even more. As things worked out, I also liked the Sahara Beige or Woodland Green-Campus Cream (two-tone), as well as the blue and ivory model, and July 3, 1953 turned out to be one of the happiest days of my life. That was the day I got my first brand new car. It wasn't the hardtop, but close enough to make me very proud. It was a Bel Air 2-Door Sedan, Model 2402. The color choice was Campus Cream bottom with a Woodland Green top. The car was well-equipped with a lot of stuff I really didn't want but, to get rid of a "lemon" '47 Olds that I had, I needed to take all the accessories on this car so they could make a profit. That night my dad and I went to the C.S. Mead Chevrolet Dealership in Pasadena to sign papers for a $54.00 a month commitment for the next three years. Now, the last part of this long epistle. I really loved everything about this car, as it was totally trouble free. However, the day after Thanksgiving, I received a brown envelope in the mail telling me Uncle Sam would like my assistance for the next two years. I was sick! What will I do with my new car? A payment of $54.00 and I was bringing in $74.00 a month.Guess you can see, I lived it up for the next two years!

Liking 1953's so well, I later owned two more. This example came into the family as somewhat of a derelict, which I felt sorry for. After some new chrome, removing the seat covers and finding near perfect seat upholstery, replacing the tires with whitewalls, and a few other bits of new accessories, it stayed in the family with my sister being its main caretaker for the next five years. The day after she turned it in on a 1968 Chevelle, it was involved in an accident with the front end sustaining much damage. The car's new owner had even used a hammer to nail the license plate into the hood. I don't lose my cool too often but, when I saw it, I gave him a piece of my mind! Guess that just tells us, we can't have total control of them forever.

Now, getting back to the 1953 cars, themselves. For the first time, they came in three distinct series. The low-priced models were called the 150 Specials, ranging in price from $1,524 for a two-passenger Business Coupe that weighed 3140 pounds, to the 4-Door Handyman Wagon which tipped the scale at 3420 pounds, delivered for $2,010, and had sales amounting to 22,408 vehicles.

The middle line of cars was referred to as the "210 Model" available in seven styles ranging in price from $1,707 for the 4-Door Sedan which weighed 3215 pounds and received a very good sales run of 247,455 units sold, to the most expensive vehicle in the 210 lineup, Model 2134, denoting it to be a Convertible. Incidentally, it was the poorest seller for the year producing only 5,617 units. It was phased out of production at the end of the model year and was not to return during the next three years of the 210 production. The best selling Chevy for 1953 was the 210, 4-Door Sedan, seeing a run of 332,497 cars being delivered. This vehicle weighed 3250 pounds and carried a price tag of $1,761.

From the success of the Bel Air nameplate which was introduced in 1950, Chevrolet felt it was a good sign to introduce it as a complete series and so came the Bel Air name appearing on four models ranging from the Model 2402 Bel Air 2-Door Sedan weighing 3230 pounds and selling for $1,820. A total of 144,401 units were delivered in 1953. The lowest production in the Bel Air line went to the Model 2434, being a Convertible. It sold for $2,175 with delivery to 24,047 customers. To me, the best looking model came as the Bel Air Hardtop Coupe weighing 3310 pounds, selling for $2,051, and finding 99,028 registrants. The best seller in the Chevrolet lineup for Bel Airs was the 4-Door Sedan Model 2403. It saw a production run of 247,284 units that delivered for $1,874. This Sedan weighed in at 3275 pounds.

Chevrolet was now getting "big time," offering optional equipment such as power steering, autronic eye, and special wire wheel covers. Items that had never even been thought of until this year.

Here is the 1953 Bel Air Sedan after a mini restoration. I've been told this car is still running around Santa Barbara but, once again, in as horrible condition as it was when I retrieved it from going to the crusher back in 1963.

A factory photo of a Model 2403 Bel Air Sedan. This 1953 vehicle was one of the most popular cars Chevrolet produced for this model run. They delivered 247,284 units for the year. The Sedan weighed 3275 pounds and carried a price tag of $1,874.

Chevrolet's color choices abounded for 1953. As mentioned earlier, color and women were now being acknowledged by General Motors and Chevrolet did its part with a nice array to choose from (colors, not women). Single tones available in the entire line amounted to:

Black
Saddle Brown
Horizon Blue
Regatta Blue
Sahara Beige
Dusk Gray
Surf Green
Woodland Green
Madeira Maroon
Driftwood Gray

Two-tone choices were:

Top	Bottom
India Ivory	Black
Saddle Brown	Sahara Beige
Sahara Beige	Saddle Brown
India Ivory	Horizon Blue
India Ivory	Regatta Blue
Regatta Blue	Horizon Blue
Dusk Gray top	Driftwood Gray
Woodland Green	Surf Green
Woodland Green	Campus Cream
Campus Cream	Woodland Green

The color choice of Sungold was available only in the Bel Air line. It also came as a two-tone, which was more popular with a Sungold bottom and India Ivory top. Campus Cream and Target Red, as single colors, were only available on Convertibles. Target Red roof with India Ivory bottom were seen only on Bel Air and 210 4-Door Sedans, which were used in the beginning only as Chevrolet demonstrators. So, if you happen to own a red and white Bel Air or 210 4-Door Sedan, you have a rare demonstrator.

All the Bel Air models came with a contrasting color sweep rear quarter panel which added a little splash to the cars' appearance. Full wheel covers and fender skirts were standard equipment on the Bel Air line for the two-year run of this model.

The basic engine for the 1953 cars was referred to as the Blue Flame Six developing 108 horsepower with the standard transmission, and a 235.5 cubic-inch displacement. If the customer preferred the Powerglide model, it could be ordered in either the 210 or Bel Air line for an additional $178. These vehicles came with a 115-horsepower engine with a 7.5:1 compression ratio. The Powerglide models only came with full pressure lubrication which would become standard on non-automatic transmissioned cars the following year. The Powerglide 1953 cars came with aluminum pistons and self-adjusting hydraulic valve lifters.

What a difference whitewalls can make in a car's appearance. The Korean conflict still wasn't over for the early model releases, but the government apparently found enough supplies to allow whitewall production to be reissued. This example came in Sun Gold and India Ivory; a color combination available only in the Bel Air line.

My third 1953 Bel Air. This time it's the twin I mentioned in the text for 1953 cars. That's right, a true copy of the model that I saw at the 1953 Motorama in Los Angeles. It is an India Ivory and Horizon Blue, Model 2454 Bel Air Hardtop Coupe or, as it was better referred to, the Bel Air Sport Coupe. This vehicle, in base form, sold for $2,051 and weighed in at 3310 pounds. As you can see, this vehicle came pretty much loaded; even included was power steering!

All 1953 cars rode on a 115-inch wheelbase using 6:70 x 15-inch tires in all models except for the Convertibles which required 7:10 x 15-inch rubber.

Even though this book is basically about Chevrolet passenger cars, two models at the opposite end of the spectrum, that I feel deserve mentioning, are the Sedan Delivery, and the Corvette.

The Sedan Delivery, described earlier in the first chapter, was a part of Chevrolet history, from the late 1920s through to the 1960 model run.

Not as dolled up as mine, is a basic 1953 Bel Air Sport Coupe. The deluxe wheel covers and fender skirts were classed as standard equipment for all Bel Air cars that year. A total of 99,028 of this model were delivered for the year.

A basic 1953 Bel Air 2-Door Sedan. The lowest priced model for 1953 happened to be this example. All the Bel Air models offered richness in exterior and interior appointments, giving the series a distinction never previously achieved in the Chevrolet market. The 2-Door and 4-Door Sedans in the Bel Air line came with a ladder pattern cloth and broadcloth in harmonizing colors of gray, blue, green and tan to compliment the exterior choices.

The most expensive model for 1953 came as this Model 2434 Bel Air Convertible. It sold for $2,175 in base form. The Convertible used a fabric-baked plastic material, which was fade resistant and easy to keep clean. A choice of six colors were available: blue, green, tan, black, yellow, and red with a white bolster to contrast in the seating arrangement. Note that all Bel Air models came with carpeted flooring, also a first for the low-priced cars.

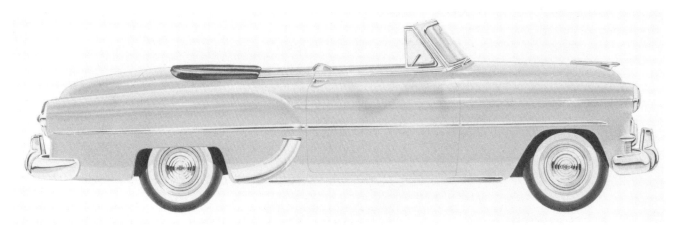

The lowest production model in the 210 line for 1953 came as this Model 2134 Convertible Coupe. The vehicle was only $82 less than the Bel Air Convertible and saw only 5,617 purchasers. The model was discontinued early in the season. Its price tag was $2,093. Those who chose it had a choice of red, blue, green or tan for vinyl seating materials. The floor material was matching rubber with the interior color choice.

The Corvette was an instant success, at least for people to admire in dealer show rooms. The sharp little sport car saw a production of only 300 vehicles for the year. All were done in Polo White with a red interior. The seats were bucket style made of a vinyl material. The side curtains were not of the type one would expect when you paid over $3500. These were only snap-on side curtains in place of the expected wind-up windows. All 1953 Corvettes came with the

Again, Chevrolet's most popular and best seller for the year was this 210 4-Door Sedan. A total of 332,497 were produced. It weighed 3250 pounds and carried a price of $1,761. Less decorative trim was employed on the 210 models, as can be seen here: small hub caps, no skirts and fewer deluxe appointments such as the rear quarter contrasting color swatch, as seen on the Bel Air models.

The first photo I took of my 1953 Bel Air 2-Door Sedan leaving the C.S. Mead Chevrolet Agency on July 3, 1953.

An early photo of the above-mentioned Chevy. Probably it was all of one-week old, as the car didn't even have its new license plate on it at this time. Note for we pack rats: I still have the license plates which I used on my blue Sport Coupe.

Almost as rare a car as the 210 Convertible is this 210 Sport Coupe which shared the basic body as the Bel Air Sport Coupe. The big difference between the two vehicles is that only 14,045 vehicles drew customers and it was discontinued at the end of the model run. The car delivered for $1,967 and weighed in at 3295 pounds.

automatic transmission which didn't appeal too much to the true sports car enthusiast. Engine-wise, the vehicles came with the 6-cylinder engine of 235 CID developing 150 horsepower at 4200 RPM. The compression ratio was raised to 8.0:1. Triple side-draft carburetors were employed for the 300 vehicles manufactured from the July 1, 1953 production date in Flint, Michigan, until its relocation to St. Louis, Missouri on January 1, 1954.

This is a rear view of the Bel Air Sport Coupe wearing a Stylecraft "falsy" continental kit. These proved fairly well, especially with those not wishing to pay the full tab for the real thing. This accessory was not a factory accessory. I note, from the license plate frame on the original photo, the car was sold by H. H. Rhodes Chevrolet of Beverly Hills, California. This was a leading dealership in Los Angeles County, at that time.

This example was the best seller in the "150" series. It was known as a 2-Door Sedan in the Special Series, and its technical title was Model 1502. Weighing 3180 pounds, it delivered for $1,613. A total of 79,416 vehicles were produced for 1953.

For the 1953 model year production of regular cars it amounted to 1,356,413 units delivered. The calendar year sales consisted of 1,477,287 vehicle sales putting Chevrolet again in the number one sales slot!

This is the 1953 Special Business Coupe Model 1504 that sold for $1,524 and weighed 3140 pounds. The vehicle from the outside was identical to the Special Series "150" Club Coupe Model 1524 that delivered for $1,620 and tipped the scale at 3150 pounds. Interior is where the difference occurred. The Business Coupe carried a large rubber platform in the rear compartment, in place of a rear seat. Both models were discontinued at the end of the model year.

A variety of 1953 models on the display floor of a Chevrolet dealership. In the foreground sits a Bel Air Sport Coupe with a nice variety of bumper and grille guard equipment and the accessory hood bird ornament. Directly behind it is a top-down Bel Air Convertible and behind these two sits a "210" 4-Door Sedan and the low-priced "150" 2-Door Sedan.

Basically classed in the "150" Series is this Model 1508 Sedan Delivery. This vehicle was chiefly classed as a model within the station wagon line with blanked-out side windows. A total of 15,523 units were produced which was one of the best production figures ever for this body style. The vehicle weighed 3160 pounds and sold for $1,648.

Popular as a station wagon was this "210" Handyman Model 2109. Like the "210" Townsman, this example came minus the wood trim. The Handyman sold for $2,123 while the Townsman Model 2119 delivered for $2,273 to 7,988 customers. For 1954, this Townsman came only in the Bel Air line as a nine-passenger vehicle.

In its first year, and not received too well, is this sharp looking Corvette Sports car, Model 2934. The low production figure of only 300 cars delivered was not the fault of the car as it was just getting into production. As stated in the text, it was an instant success, but this was chiefly for people viewing it at auto shows, motoramas, and in dealer showrooms. As the example leaves the assembly line, it is equipped with Bel Air wheel covers which were not the right equipment for the vehicle.

Shown here is the Polo White Corvette wearing the correct wheel discs, but it's still missing the final side body trim. Early examples were only to have the small nameplate on the front fender but, before any left the factory, the 102-inch wheelbased car saw complete side trim on all 300 examples. Its base price was just a little over $3,500.

Chevrolet

CORVETTE

sensational styling
extra-low center of gravity
outstanding performance
amazing acceleration

Since its introduction in January 1953 as an experimental "dream car," the revolutionary Chevrolet Corvette—equipped with Chevrolet's famous Powerglide Automatic Transmission—has been thoroughly proved by thousands of miles of strenuous testing, and now is being produced in limited numbers. Sensational in styling and performance, it sets the standard for a coming field— THE AMERICAN SPORTS CAR. Designed exclusively for sports-loving, fun-loving people, it combines the graceful silhouette, light weight, sparkling action, and free-as-a-breeze companionship of the true sports car with the comforts, conveniences, and riding qualities that are expected in an automobile today. It's real fun to drive a Chevrolet Corvette.

Chevrolet Accessories for 1953

DEALER LIST AND NET PRICE SCHEDULE

Effective April 1, 1953

ALL PRICES SUBJECT TO CHANGE WITHOUT NOTICE

**The "List Prices" shown in this schedule are
suggested prices for sales to consumers.**

1953 CHEVROLET ACCESSORIES PRICE SCHEDULE

Description	Part No.	Unit	List Price	Net Price
Adapter - Gas Filter (6)	986621	6	3.20	1.92
(Single Unit Price)			(.53)	(.32)
Antenna - Fender Type - Pass.	986627	1	6.35	3.81
Antenna - Cowl Type -				
Comm. & Truck	986069	1	7.48	4.49
Autronic Eye	986804	1	49.50	37.12
Blade - W/S Wiper Self De-Icing	986882	1	2.50	1.50
Block - Junction	986630	1	1.75	1.05
Bracket - Rear-View Mirror -				
R.H. & L.H.	986441	1	1.63	.98
Bracket - Inside Rear-View Mirror	986875	1	1.30	.78
Cap - Locking Gas Tank	986691	1	2.90	1.74
Cap - Sav-A-Battery (12)	986781	12	16.68	10.00
(Single Unit Price)			(1.39)	(.83)
Clock - Spring Wind	986633	1	10.25	6.15
Clock - Electric	986634	1	19.70	11.82
Condenser - Radiator Overflow	986643	1	3.85	2.31
Cover - Seat - Plastic - 2 Dr. & 4 Dr.		Set	39.75	23.85
Cover - Seat - Nylon - 2 Dr. & 4 Dr.		Set	49.75	29.85
Cover - Seat - Fiber - 2 Dr. & 4 Dr.		Set	26.75	16.05
Cover - Seat - Plastic - Convertible		Set	39.75	23.85
Cover - Seat - Nylon - Sport Coupe		Set	49.75	29.85
Cover - Seat - Fiber -				
Comm. & Truck	986798	Set	14.60	8.76
Cover - Accelerator Pedal (6)	986325	6	7.00	4.20
(Single Unit Price)			(1.17)	(.70)
Cover - Wheel - Stainless Steel 15"				
(Set of 4)	986656	4	19.75	12.84
Dispenser - Tissue	986672	1	3.50	2.10
Element - Cooling System Filter (6)	986706	6	11.10	6.66
(Single Unit Price)			(1.85)	(1.11)
Extension - Exhaust	986382	1	3.12	1.87
Extension - Exhaust	986885	1	3.25	1.95
Filter - Cooling System	986705	1	10.95	6.57
Filter & Element - Cooling System				
6 Filters, 12 Elements, 1 cut away				
Display Filter	986760	6	87.90	52.74
Filter & Element - Cooling System				
24 Filters, 48 Elements, 4 cut away				
Display Filters	986761	24	351.60	210.96
Filter - Gasoline (Automatic Choke) (12)	986640	12	26.40	15.84
(Single Unit Price)			(2.20)	(1.32)
Flap Mud - (2 Pair Per Carton)	986783	2	27.50	16.50
(Single Wheel Trucks & Trailers)				
(Single Unit Price (Pair))			(13.75)	(8.25)
Flap Mud - (2 Pair Per Carton)	986784	2	39.00	23.40
(Dual Wheel Trucks & Trailers)				
(Single Unit Price (Pair))			(19.50)	(11.70)
Frame - License (Pair)	986708	Pair	3.27	1.96
Glareshade - Windshield	986683	1	8.50	5.10
All Except Convertible & Sport Coupe				
Glareshade - Windshield	986685	1	8.50	5.10
Convertible & Sport Coupe				
Glareshade - Windshield -				
Comm. & Truck	986604	Pair	11.00	6.60
Guard Unit - Front & Rear Fender	986780	Set	39.00	23.40
Guard - Grille Safety Bumper - Pass.	986803	1	13.50	8.10
Guard - Grille Safety Bumper - Truck	986536	1	25.80	15.48
Guard - Grille Safety Bumper - Comm.	986486	1	23.60	14.16
Guard - Gasoline Tank Filler Door (6)	986789	6	9.72	5.83
(Single Unit Price)			(1.62)	(.97)
Heater & Defroster - Air-Flow - Pass.	986629	1	76.50	46.67
Heater & Defroster - Recirculating,				
Air-Flow Type - Pass.	986628	1	40.50	24.71
Heater & Defroster - Recirculating -				
Comm. & Truck	986248	1	38.41	23.43
Heater & Defroster - Air-Flow - Truck	986709	1	68.25	43.54
Hook Unit - Garment (12) (D)	986537	12	15.00	5.00
(Single Unit Price)			(1.25)	(.75)
Horn Unit - Comm. & Truck	986799	1	6.25	3.75
Kit - Tool	986362	1	2.80	1.85
Kit - Seat Cover - Installation	986432	1	NL	3.30
Lamp - Tail R.H. Universal Mounting	986299	1	7.27	4.36
Lamp - Luggage Compartment	986625	1	1.85	1.11

Description	Part No.	Unit	List Price	Net Price
Lamp - Underhood	986642	1	1.73	1.04
Lamp - Glove Compartment (1500 Series Pass., Comm. & Truck)	986693	1	1.23	.74
Lamp - Courtesy (Pair)	986806	Pair	2.75	1.65
Lamp - Back-Up Conventional Trans. (Pair)	986663	Pair	5.55	3.33
Lamp - Back-Up Power Glide Trans. (Pair)	986664	Pair	5.95	3.57
Lamp - Dual Fog - Comm. & Truck (Pair) (D)	986524	Pair	15.48	5.00
Lighter - Cigarette	986631	1	2.95	1.77
Mat Unit - Floor - Rubber - Blue (6)	986765	6	10.50	6.30
Mat Unit - Floor - Rubber - Red (6)	986766	6	10.50	6.30
Mat Unit - Floor - Rubber - Green (6)	986767	6	10.50	6.30
Mat Unit - Floor - Rubber - Black (6)	986768	6	10.50	6.30
(Single Unit Price of All Mats)			(1.75)	(1.05)
Mirror - R.V. Outside W/Extendable Arm. Comm. & Truck	986440	1	3.65	2.19
Mirror - Outside R.V. Clamp on Type.	986641	1	3.13	1.88
Mirror - Inside R.V. - Glareproof	986651	1	3.95	2.37
Mirror - Outside R.V. - Rain Deflector R.H. & L.H.	986692	1	3.00	1.80
Mirror - Outside R.V. - Body Mounting R.H. & L.H.	986762	1	3.47	2.08
Mirror - Outside R.V. - Inside Remote Control	986805	1	8.15	4.89
Mirror - Vanity Visor	986605	1	1.57	.94
Ornament - Hood - Pass.	986785	1	7.50	4.50
Panel - Rear Fender - Prime (Pair)	986619	Pair	16.00	9.60
Radio & Antenna - Push Button Comm. & Truck	986444	1	75.91	45.55
Radio & Antenna - Push Button - Pass.	986670	1	80.25	48.15
Radio & Antenna - Manual - Pass.	986671	1	61.25	36.75
Receiver - Ash	986624	1	2.00	1.20
Reflector - Red Reflex - 4"	985223	1	1.58	.95
Rest Arm - Door - Comm. & Truck	986154	1	3.90	2.34
Rest Arm - Door (Pair) Model 1509 (Handyman) Only	986909	Pair	8.85	5.31
Rest Arm - Door (Pair) - Pass.	986809	Pair	8.85	5.31
Ring - Wheel Trim 15" - (Set of 5)	986258	5	10.75	6.45
Ring - Wheel Trim 15" - Single	986259	1	2.70	1.62
Safetylight & Mirror - W/L.H. Bracket - Pass.	986626	1	22.25	13.35
Safetylight W/L.H. Bracket - Comm. & Trk.	986173	1	18.95	11.37
Shaver - Electric 110 V-AC-DC - 6 V-DC	986418	1	24.95	14.97
Shield - Door Handle (Set of 4)	986886	4	2.95	1.77
Shield - Gravel Front Fender (Pair)	986782	Pair	6.70	4.02
Sidewall Trim - White 15" Wheel - (Set of 4)	986269	4	11.00	6.60
Sidewall Trim - White 15" Wheel - Single	986297	1	2.77	1.66
Signal - Direction-Dbl. Face Unit - C&T.	986636	1	31.00	18.60
Signal - Direction-Dbl. Face Unit - C&T.	986881	1	25.95	15.57
Signal - Direction-Single Face Unit - C&T	986551	1	26.10	15.66
Signal - Direction-Single Face Unit - C&T	986880	1	24.55	14.73
Signal - Parking Brake Electric	986903	1	3.95	2.37
Speaker - Rear Seat Radio	986694	1	11.54	7.04
Spotlight - Hand Portable	986555	1	7.95	4.77
Ventshade - Truck - (Pair)	986623	Pair	5.25	3.15
Ventshade - Coupe except Sport Coupe	986658	Pair	5.00	3.00
Ventshade - Two Door - All.	986659	Set	10.00	6.00
Ventshade - Four Door - All.	986661	Set	10.00	6.00
Viewer - Traffic Light	986550	1	2.65	1.59
Visor - R.H. Sun - Comm. & Truck	986155	1	3.21	1.93
Visor - R.H. Sun - Model 1509 (Handyman) Only	986940	1	5.13	3.08
Visor - R.H. Sun - Inside 150 Series	986696	1	5.13	3.08
Visor - Outside All Pass. Except Sport Coupe, Sedan Del., Sta. Wagon & Conv't.	986674	1	22.00	13.20
Visor - Outside - Sport Coupe.	986675	1	22.00	13.20
Visor - Outside - Comm. & Truck	986877	1	22.00	13.20
Washer - Windshield Foot-Operated - Comm. & Truck	986527	1	6.77	4.06
Washer - Windshield Foot-Operated - Pass., Comm. & Truck	986776	1	6.77	4.06
Washer - Windshield - Pass.	986650	1	7.25	4.35
Wire Wheel Cover (Set of 4)	986908	4	79.50	47.70

SERVICE ACCESSORIES

Description	Part No.	List Price	Net Price
Anti-Freeze - W/S Washer (12-6 oz. Bottles)	986180	7.20	4.32
Anti-Freeze - W/S Washer (12-6 oz. Bottles) New York City Only	986775	7.20	4.32
Anti-Freeze - Zerex (24-1 qt. Cans)	986645*	24.00	16.08
Anti-Freeze - Zerex (6-1 Gal. Cans)	986646*	22.50	15.06
Anti-Freeze - Zerone (24-1 qt. Cans)	986647*	9.00	6.30
Anti-Freeze - Zerone (6-1 Gal. Cans)	986648*	9.00	5.88
Anti-Freeze - Zerone (54 Gal. Drum)	986649*	81.00	48.60
Caroma - Evaporator Unit (12 Vials)	983715	3.60	2.16
Cleaner Unit Fabric (12-16 oz. Cans)	986076	6.60	3.96
Cleaner Fabric (1 Gal.)	986285	3.25	1.95
Cleaner Sponge (12)	986225	5.88	3.12
Cleaner Unit Glass (12-10 oz. Cans)	986193	5.40	3.24
Cleaner - Cooling System (12 Cans)	986052	12.00	6.72

Description	Part No.	Unit	List Price	Net Price
Cloth Unit - Polishing (12 Cloths)	986077		6.00	3.60
Compound Valve Grinding (36-4 oz. Cans)	986078		9.00	5.04
Flush Unit Radiator (12-16 oz. Cans)	986079		5.88	3.12
Injector - Static Eliminator Powder	986033		1.25	.75
Lock-Ease (12-4 oz. Cans)	986434		4.20	2.80
Lubricant Stick Door-Ease (12 Sticks)	985093		1.20	.68
Oil Unit - Dripless Penetrating (36-4 oz. Cans)	986082		9.00	4.68
Oil Unit - General Use (36-4 oz. Cans)	986054		9.00	4.68
Polish Unit Chromium (12-8 oz. Cans)	986084		4.20	2.52
Polish Unit Triple Action (12-16 oz. Cans)	986085		9.00	5.40
Polish Triple Action (1 Gal.)	985888		3.15	1.89
Polish Luster Seal #1 (12-12 oz. Bottles)	986945		40.20	24.00
Polish Luster Seal #2 (12-12 oz. Bottles)	986946		40.20	24.00
Polish Luster Seal Haze Cream (24-8 oz. Bottles)	986947		24.00	14.40
Porcelainize Liquid (24-8 oz. Bottles)	986175		105.60	60.00
Porcelainize Wash Cream (24-8 oz. Bottles)	986176		14.40	8.64
Porcelainize Cleaner (1 Gal. Can)	986363		NL	4.75
Powder Unit - Static Eliminator (12 Envelopes)	986087		4.80	2.88
Preventive Unit Rust (24-4 oz. Cans)	986086		6.00	3.60
Ru-Glyde (1 Gal.)	986047		3.60	2.15
Sealer Unit - GM Chrome Protective (12)	986680		15.00	9.00
Sealzit Unit - Glass Sealer (12-2 oz. Bottles)	986199		10.20	6.12
Spot Remover Unit (12-8 oz. Cans)	986075		6.00	3.60
Stop Leak Unit Radiator (12-10 oz. Cans)	986088		5.88	3.12
Undercoating (54 Gal. Drum)	986359		NL	46.44
Undercoating (44 Drum Truckload)	986653		NL	1,782.00
Undercoating (80 Drum Carload)	986548		NL	3,110.40
Undercoating (54 Gal. Drum) Pacific Coast Region only	986635		NL	46.44
Undercoating (44 Drum Truckload) Pacific Coast Region only	986654		NL	1,782.00
Undercoating (80 Drum Carload) Pacific Coast Region Only	986638		NL	3,110.40
Undercoating (54 Gal. Drum) - Water Base New York City only	986800		NL	46.44
Undercoating (44 Drum Truckload) - Water Base New York City only	986801		NL	1,782.00
Undercoating (80 Drum Carload) - Water Base New York City only	986802		NL	3,110.40
Wax Unit - Auto Liquid (12-16 oz. Cans)	986072		9.00	5.40

*Prices shown are subject to the provisions of the Fair Trade Acts of those States having such laws.

For driving comfort in any weather

Ventshades. Stainless Steel sun shades permit windows to be lowered in any weather for better ventilation and comfort.

Right-Hand Sun Visor. Matches the left-hand visor inside automobile; increases the driving comfort of passengers.

Outside Sun Visor. Reduces sun glare and protects windshield from snow and ice. All metal, chrome trimmed. Finished in the same color as the automobile.

G. M. Sav-A-Battery Caps. When caps are filled with water they keep the battery water at the proper level. A real time saver. Freezing will not affect the caps. A real battery saver.

For your lighting needs

Courtesy Lights. Useful, convenient lamps for increased safety. Automatically places two beams of light on floor when either front door is opened.

Underhood Lamp. Automatic: operates with the raising and closing of the hood. Ideal, convenient for night inspections under the hood.

Safetylight and Mirror. Powerful, sealed-beam light and mirror mounted on the left front door panel and controlled from inside of automobile.

Portable Spotlight. A powerful sealed-beam light. Can be used all around the automobile and to read around the car and to read road signs. Useful trouble lamp.

Tool Kit contains basic tools for most road emergencies. Complete with durable container.

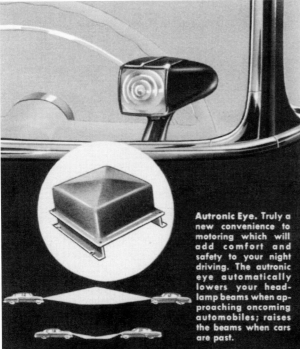

Autronic Eye. Truly a new convenience to motoring which will add comfort and safety to your night driving. The autronic eye automatically lowers your headlamp beams when approaching oncoming automobiles; raises the beams when cars are past.

The new 1954 Chevrolet Bel Air 4-Door Sedan. With three great series, Chevrolet offers the most beautiful choice of models in its field.

This is what's new about
the beautiful new 1954 Chevrolet...

New beauty is only the beginning. There's much more power. Much finer performance. And new economy, too—with money-saving gas mileage. In every way, this 1954 Chevrolet is the finest ever.

Here are some of the new advantages you get in the lowest-priced line in the low-price field.

Thrifty new power in all models. Finer performance with money-saving gasoline mileage, too! That's what Chevrolet gives you with new power in two great, high-compression valve-in-head engines—the "Blue-Flame 125" in Powerglide models and the "Blue-Flame 115" in gearshift models.

New styling that stays new. Fresh, new 1954 styling outside and in makes Chevrolet even more of a stand-out. And there's an exciting choice of rich new colors that harmonize with the new and more colorful interiors.

New automatic window and seat controls. A touch of a button adjusts front windows and seat to your liking. (Optional on Bel Air and "Two-Ten" models at extra cost.)

Powerglide for all models, and a new low price on Power Steering. Now Powerglide, the *smooth, economical* automatic transmission, is available for all models. And you can enjoy Power Steering at a saving. (Both features optional at extra cost.) See your Chevrolet dealer. . . . Chevrolet Division of General Motors, Detroit 2, Michigan.

Powered for Performance!
Engineered for Economy!

SYMBOL OF SAVINGS
CHEVROLET
EMBLEM OF EXCELLENCE

MORE PEOPLE BUY CHEVROLETS THAN ANY OTHER CAR!

The 1954 Chevrolets made their usual debut appearance on a Friday. This year it was right before the Christmas holidays got into full swing. The date was December 18, 1953. One of the choice examples happened to be this 1954 Bel Air Convertible which claimed to be the second most expensive model for the model run. This vehicle weighed 3445 pounds and delivered for $2,185. A total of 19,333 found buyers.

Chevrolet for 1954

Chevrolet announced the arrival of the 1954 models again on a Friday, only this year it was December 18th, 1953 that the new cars made their debut.

I had been in the Army all of eight days and no way was I allowed out of Fort Ord to see my favorite cars at the local Chevrolet dealer, Roller Chevrolet in Monterey, California. When finally I did see them, I was equally impressed with all as I had been with the 1953s. My favorite, again, was the Bel Air Sport Coupe in Turquoise and India Ivory. For 1954, the lineup was less than the previous year. Gone were the 210 Convertible Hardtop Sport Coupe and Club Coupe. For the "150" Models, the Business Coupe was dropped and a Utility Sedan took its place. This vehicle looked exactly the same as the 2-Door Sedan, from the outside. Interior-wise, it did not have a rear seat compartment. As for the Bel Air line, things were great in '53, so why change anything? The only difference amounted to the eight-passenger Townsman Wagon now had become a member of the Bel Air line, rather than stay in the 210 family. An addition also took place in the 210 line. It was a new model, as far as interior was concerned, and it received the title of Delray Club Coupe. The model came with a vinyl interior and full carpeting. It really looked sharp, but those hot vinyl seats sent many a suit to the cleaners more often than not.

General appearances of the 1954 Bel Air Sport Coupe were the same car as the 1953s. This example is a bare-bones vehicle for sure not even a set of whitewalls for the photo session. It weighed 3300 pounds and carried a price tag of $2,061, just $10.00 up from the previous year. A total of 66,378 were produced for the season.

The car saw a production run of 66,403 units sold. It weighed 3185 pounds and delivered for $1,782. The general model breakdown went like this: The "150" Series saw the Utility Sedan as the lowest-priced unit Chevrolet built in 1954. It sold for $1,539. The 2-Door vehicle weighed 3145 pounds and saw a production run of 10,770 vehicles. The Handyman 4-Door Wagon was the only

Things changed a bit for the 1954 models and the '54 Bel Air 4-Door Sedan was America's #1 model. The Sedan saw a production of 248,750 units. The car delivered for $1,884 and it weighed 3255 pounds. The skirts and deluxe wheelcovers were part of the standard equipment.

The Townsman Wagon was no longer part of the "210" Series, but was now Chevrolet's most expensive vehicle, excluding, of course, the Corvette. The model nomenclature was 2419. The eight-passenger, 3-seat wagon weighed 3540 pounds and carried a price of $2,283. The imitation wood trim was standard equipment on this model. Continual care was required to keep the wood trim in pristine condition. Products, such as we have today, just weren't on the market at that time.

model in the "150" Series to sell for over $2,000. Its base price was $2,020 tipping the scales at 3455 pounds.

The 210 models offered the 2-Door Sedan as the lowest priced car for $1,717, up ten dollars from the previous year. It weighed 3185 pounds leaving the most expensive model in the 210 line up to the Handyman Wagon for $2,133. It weighed 3470 pounds and had a vehicle run of 27,170 units sold making it the lowest production of 210 models for 1954. The best seller for Chevrolet again in the 210 line up was the family 4-Door Sedan. It weighed 3280 pounds sold for $1,771 and had a production run of 235,146 vehicle sales.

The Bel Air line continued to be very popular for 1954. In fact, it surpassed the 210 models in sales as far as 4-Door Sedans were concerned. The Bel Air 4-Door Sedan saw a production run of 248,750 units sold. This was an increase of 13,604 models sold over the mid-priced bread-and-butter 210 4-Door Sedan which was always Chevrolet's most popular model. The lowest production in the Bel Air line went to the newly placed Bel Air Townsman Wagon of which only 8,156 were manufactured. The Bel Air 2-Door Sedan continued to be the

Looking very similar to the 1953 Bel Air 2-Door Sedan was this Model 2402 for 1954. The model had a run of 143,573 units priced at $1,830 weighing in at 3220 pounds.

lowest priced vehicle in the series selling for $1,830. The Bel Air Hardtop Sport Coupe delivered for $2,061 to 66,378 customers. The Sport Coupe weighed 3300 pounds, down 10 pounds from the previous year. The Bel Air Convertible drew 19,383 followers for $2,185, a ten dollar increase over the 1953 models. This Model 2434 weighed 3445 pounds.

Additional optional equipment became available on the 1954 cars. New for 1954 were items like power brakes for an additional $38; power windows at $86 more; power seats for the same cost, and the proven automatic transmission was becoming increasingly more popular. It was now available in each series.

Color choices were basically the same as in 1953, with new names given to some which were very popular. The most often chosen new color combination was Turquoise bottom with India Ivory top, available only in the Bel Air line. Pueblo Tan bottom and India Ivory top also shared the limelight as a new combination choice, available only in the Bel Air series. A more yellow color than cream color to appear for 1954 was available only as a single color if the model was a convertible. If you wished it in the 210 or Bel Air line, it came in two-tone arrangement only, with Fiesta Cream bottom and Bermuda Green top. Bermuda Green was available in either top or bottom of this choice, with the contrasting Shoreline Beige to share the honors. Chevrolet claimed, among their three series, a buyer could have his choice from a total of 67 different varieties. The color confusion is just to begin! Years to follow showed very few look alikes to come down the assembly line in one day, with all the color choices and options that were now beginning to appear.

As for the Sedan Delivery units, production amounted to 8,255 vehicles delivered. The car sold for $1,632 and weighed 3195 pounds. The 1954 year was the first time a Sedan Delivery was available with the Powerglide transmission.

Mechanically, things remained pretty much the same as in 1953 with the exception that the standard transmission vehicles now came with full pressure

Still holding its own in the popularity race, but coming in second place to the Bel Air 4-Door Sedan, was this "210" 4-Door Sedan which weighed 3230 pounds and, for $1,771, went home to 235,146 customers. Since 1953 saw the start of high cost accessories in the low-priced field, such as power steering, deluxe wire wheel covers, etc., there was no reason why 1954 shouldn't offer things like electric windows for $86.00, electric seats for the same tab, and power brakes for a mere $38.00 additional. True, these items found their way onto Bel Air cars with a factory order, but were rarely ordered on a "210" model. It is doubtful if luxury equipment like this ever got to a "150" model.

lubrication. These cars saw an increase in horsepower from 108 to 115 with compression ratio increase to 7.5:1 at 3700 R.P.M. The Powerglide vehicles had an increase in power to 125 at 4000 RPMs.

As for the Corvettes in 1954, it was virtually the same package as its 1953 counterpart. New for 1954 were two additional color choices: Pennant Blue and Bolero Red. Most purchasers still preferred the Polo White. The Corvette interior was done in red to compliment the white exterior, or a beige interior went in the blue and red vehicles.

Now the Corvette went under the model designation of 2934. The unit also increased in price approximately $50 more than the 1953 cars. Few additional accessories were available for the owner to choose beyond the $145 signal-seeking radio and $91 for the heater. DeLuxe wheel covers and whitewalls were part of the regular package included for the customers. Corvette production for 1954 amounted to 3,640 units.

Virtually the same car from all external appearances was the "210" 2-Door Sedan and the "210" Delray Club Coupe. Only differences were seen on the inside where the Delray came with full carpeting and durable vinyl seats. The Delray cost $65.00 more than the "210" 2-Door, going home for $1,782. Both models weighed the same 3185 pounds. The Delrays had a production run of 66,303 while plain "210" 2-Door cars had a production of 195,498 units. The 2-Door model was a far more popular car.

Since the Motoramas were very much present again in 1954, GM chose to display more experimental cars. Among these vehicles were the dream cars, based on the Corvette fiberglass body. The fastback Coupe was called the Corvair (a name used for Chevrolet's compact, starting in 1960), and the Corvette Nomad Wagon, often referred to as the Waldorf Astoria car.

Regular Chevrolet production for 1954 consisted of a calendar year run of 1,414,352 sales while model year figures were 1,151,486 units. It will probably always be a running battle between Chevrolet and Ford aficionados, as to who

A Model 2109 better known as the "210" Handyman saw 27,175 units delivered. The vehicle only came as a six-passenger wagon selling for $2,133 and weighing 3470 pounds. The last rear window was stationary which many people complained about because ventilation was not at its best.

was first for 1954. True, Ford did produce more cars in the model year, but Chevrolet truly outsold Ford as far as calendar year sales are concerned. I prefer to keep it that Chevrolet again was Number One in sales for 1954!

This was Chevrolet's lowest-priced wagon for 1954. It was the "150" Special Handyman Wagon, Model 1509 selling for $2,020 and finding its way to 21,404 owners. The vehicle weighed 3455 pounds. The rear seat like in the "210" wagons could be folded flat for additional cargo space.

This example was very similar to the "210" 2-Door Sedan and Delray's Club Coupe in that its external features were exactly the same. The models were the "150" 1954 2-Door Sedan and the "150" Utility Sedan. The example took the place of the former Business Coupe which meant it had no rear seat. The 2-Door Sedan sold for $1,623 weighed 3165 pounds, and the Utility Sedan delivered for $1,539, weighed 3145 pounds. The 2-Door had a production run of 64,855 units, while the Utility Model 1512 saw only 10,770 vehicles produced. It was the next poorest seller to the Bel Air Townsman Wagon.

The lowest priced 1954 Chevrolet Sedan came as this 4-Door Special "150". It delivered to 32,430 customers for $1,680, and it weighed 3,210 pounds. Truly a basic transportation car with no external and for that matter no interior frills. It offered only one sun visor, no door armrests, black plastic dash knobs, no horn ring on the steering wheel, and exterior saw no stainless body trim. Only a black rubber scuff pad on the rear door.

An array of sparkling new Chevrolets on display at a 1954 G.M. Motorama. In the foreground sits the newly-introduced 1954 Chevrolet Delray Club Coupe. It sports the factory approved bumper accessory guards, whitewall tires, and a two-tone paint job. In the background are a 210 4-Door Sedan, a couple of Bel Air Sedans and the 1954 Corvette equipped with its fiberglass hardtop. To the right on the turntable is the experimental Corvair also done in a reinforced plastic body.

This is the experimental Nomad that was better known as the Waldorf Astoria car. It carried the components of the Corvette 150 horsepower engine and was fitted with the Powerglide transmission. This was the vehicle that was to give the public an inkling that a new station wagon, using this name, was just around the corner from production.

Own a Corvette now!

It packs more sheer fun into every mile than any car you've ever driven!

First of the dream cars to come true

down to the smallest detail...
MORE BEAUTY, SMARTER STYLING

The sleek new hood ornament, brightly chrome plated, accents the wide horizontal lines of your beautiful 1954 Chevrolet.

This glistening, colorful new hood emblem complements the brilliant beauty of the new Chevrolet.

Notice how the deck lid and the high crown fenders give the car a longer, lower appearance. Notice also, the new chrome hub caps and hooded tail lights.

You'll find *only* Chevrolet provides this smart, practical styling—down to the *smallest* detail. For example, the new front bumpers extend farther around fenders for greater protection. The attractive new parking lights clearly show the full width of the car and contribute to its wide appearance.

The huge trunk provides maximum room for all your luggage. And the low sill and the counterbalanced lid make it easy to load or unload.

CHEVROLET
America's First Choice Car

Crank operated ventipanes can be easily adjusted to admit just the right amount of ventilation. The chrome plated hardware is designed to *stay* beautiful for years! The new built-in arm rests in Bel Air models provide new comfort and luxury.

The slim steering wheel has deeper finger notches — providing a more comfortable and safer grip. The attractive new horn ring cap contains the smart design of the '54 hood emblem.

◄ Wheel cover panels, standard on Bel Air models, add beauty and luxury. The smart Bel Air crest lends additional styling and distinction.

Down to the smallest detail, the 1954 models offered more beauty and smart styling. The hooded taillights are displayed in the upper left photo. A wider frontal appearance was developed from the new front bumper that extended around the fenders to the attractive parking lights, as seen in the center photo. In the bottom photo, note the wheel covers which were standard equipment for the Bel Air, and added a touch of class. All this made for a nice package for the model run.

82

An array of cars, from experimental Corvair, Nomad, to the actual 1954 productioned Corvettes, seen here both with the removable fiberglass top and the more often seen top-off Corvette.

A close-up view of the grille and finely meshed screens over the headlamps are displayed for this 1954 Vette. Note the familiar coat-of-arms in the center above the grille.

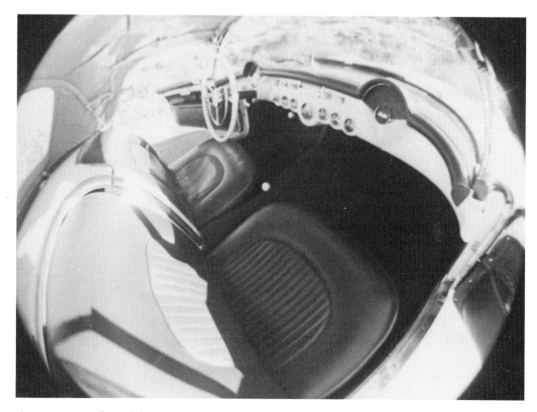

A panoramic shot of the pristine 1954 Corvette showing off all its gauges neatly arranged on the dashboard. Seat material for the car was red vinyl, making for a rather hot ride on a warm day.

Looking at the 1954 Corvette dash gauges through the steering wheel, makes for a rather unique effect. Note the signal-seeking radio placed in the center of the dash was one of the few additional-cost accessories available for the owner to purchase. It added $145 to the vehicle's cost. I can't imagine any were delivered without it, either.

This 1954 Corvette inspires an awesome effect with me. It almost looked like something from another planet when I first saw it back in those early days at the GM Motoramas. The 1954 models came with tan tops rather than just the black tops that 1953 cars offered.

1954 CHEVROLET ACCESSORIES PRICE SCHEDULE

PASSENGER CAR SECTION

Description	Part No.	Unit	Suggested List Price	Dealer Net
Adapter - Outside Visor for Station Wagon used with 986674 Visor	986998	1	.65	.39
Antenna - Fender Mounting	986627	1	6.35	3.81
Automatic H/Lamp Control - Autronic Eye	986804	1	44.25	33.19
Blade - Windshield Wiper Self-De-Icing	986882	12	2.50 ea.	1.50 ea.
Block - Junction	986630	1	1.75	1.05
Bracket - Safetylight for Station Wagon (used with 986626 Safetylight)	986950	1	1.90	1.14
Cap - Sav-A-Battery	986781	12 sets	16.68	10.00
(Single set price)			(1.39)	(.83)
Cap - Gasoline Tank Locking	986691	1	2.90	1.74
Clock - Springwind	986633	1	10.50	6.30
Clock - Electric	986971	1	18.75	11.25
Condenser - Radiator Overflow	986643	1	4.35	2.61
Compass	986995	1	5.95	3.57
Co-ordinator - Windshield Washer	986984	1	3.50	2.10
Cover - Full Wheel (Disc Type)	986944	Set of 4	22.25	14.46
Cover - Wire Wheel	986908	Set of 4	79.50	47.70
Cover - Seat - Nylon - All		1	45.00	27.00
Cover - Seat - Plastic - All		1	38.75	23.25
Cover - Seat - Fiber - All		1	27.50	16.50
Cover - Glamour Glide - Front or Rear		1	9.90	5.94
Cover - Accelerator Pedal	986325	6	7.00	4.20
(Single unit price)			(1.17) ea.	(.70) ea.
Dispenser - Tissue	986672	1	3.50	2.10
Extension - Exhaust	986885	1	3.25	1.95
Filter - Cooling System	986894	1	14.95	8.97
Filter - Cooling System - 6 Filters - 12 Filter Elements - 1 cut away filter and display cards	986760	6	87.90	52.74
Filter - Gasoline	986640	12	26.40	15.84
(Single Filter)			(2.20)	(1.32)
Frame - License Plate	986708	Pair	3.25	1.95
Glareshade - Windshield - All Sedans	986683	1	8.75	5.25
Glareshade - Windshield - Sport Coupe & Convt.	986685	1	8.75	5.25
Guard - Front Fender and Grille	986993	Set	28.50	17.10
Guard - Rear Fender	986808	Pair	24.00	14.40
Guard - Dr. Edge - 2 Dr. - Sport Coupe & Convt.	986943	Pair	3.95	2.37
Guard - Door Edge - 4 Door	986963	Set	6.95	4.17
Guard - Gasoline Filler Door	986789	6	9.90	5.94
(Single Unit Price)			(1.65)	(.99)
Heater & Defroster - Air Flow	986629	1	74.75	45.60
Heater & Defroster - Recirculating	986628	1	40.50	24.71

Description	Part No.	Unit	Suggested List Price	Dealer Net
Kit - Tool	986362	1	2.90	1.93
Lamp - Powerglide Indicator.	986999	1	3.00	1.80
Lamp - Back-Up - Conventional Transmission	986663	Pair	5.55	3.33
Lamp - Back-Up - Powerglide.	986664	Pair	5.95	3.57
Lamp - Courtesy	986806	Pair	2.75	1.65
Lamp - Luggage Compartment	986625	1	1.85	1.11
Lamp - Underhood.	986642	1	2.25	1.35
Lamp - Glove Compartment	986899	1	1.25	.75
Lighter - Cigarette	986966	1	2.95	1.77
Marker - Front Fender.	986981	Pair	5.50	3.30
Mat - Floor - Brown	986997	6	9.90	5.94
Mat - Floor - Blue.	986765	6	9.90	5.94
Mat - Floor - Red.	986766	6	9.90	5.94
Mat - Floor - Green.	986767	6	9.90	5.94
Mat - Floor - Black.	986768	6	9.90	5.94
(Single Mat Price)			(1.65)	(.99)
Mirror - Rear View - Outside - Clamp-On	986641	1	3.15	1.89
Mirror - Rear View - Outside - Rain Deflector	986692	1	3.00	1.80
Mirror - Rear View -Outside - Remote Control	987092	1	7.95	4.77
Mirror - Rear View - Inside - Non Glare.	986948	1	3.95	2.37
Mirror - Vanity Visor.	986605	1	1.60	.96
Panel - Rear Fender (prime)	986619	Pair	16.00	9.60
Radio & Antenna - Push Button	986670	1	79.85	47.91
Radio & Antenna - Manual	986671	1	61.25	36.75
Receiver - Ash	986876	1	2.00	1.20
Rest - Arm	986969	Pair	8.95	5.37
Rest - Arm - Handyman	986973	Pair	8.95	5.37
Ring - Wheel Trim 15"	986906	Set of 5	11.75	7.05
Safetylight & Mirror	986626	1	21.95	13.17
Shaver - Electric - 6 V. - 110 V. A.C.-D.C.	987090	1	29.50	17.70
Spotlight - Hand Portable (12 ft. cord)	986555	1	7.95	4.77
Shield - Door Handle	986886	Set of 4	2.95	1.77
Shield - Front Fender Gravel	986782	Pair	6.75	4.05
Signal - Electric Parking Brake	986903	1	3.95	2.37
Speaker - Rear Seat	986694	1	11.45	6.87
Ventshade - Utility Sedan	986658	Pair	4.75	2.85
Ventshade - All Two Door Sedans	986659	Set of 4	8.75	5.25
Ventshade - All Four Door Sedans	986661	Set of 4	8.75	5.25
Viewer - Traffic Light	986550	1	2.65	1.59
Visor - Outside Metal - All Sedans.	986674	2	22.00 ea.	13.20 ea.
Visor - Outside Metal - Sport Coupe	986675	2	22.00 ea.	13.20 ea.
Visor - R.H. Sun (150 Series)	986968	1	5.50	3.30
Visor - R.H. Sun Handyman	986972	1	5.50	3.30
Washer - Windshield - Vacuum Type.	986650	1	7.25	4.35
Washer - Windshield - Foot Operated	986983	1	7.25	4.35

1954 CHEVROLET ACCESSORIES PRICE SCHEDULE

TRUCK & COMMERCIAL SECTION

Description	Part No.	Unit	Suggested List Price	Dealer Net
Adapter - Gasoline Filter	986621	6	3.60	2.16
(Single Unit Price)			(.60)	(.36)
Antenna - Cowl Mounting.	986772	1	7.25	4.35
Bracket - Rear View - Inside (used with 986948 Mirror)	986898	1	1.25	.75
Cover - Wheel 16" (Full Disc)	986992	Set of 4	21.25	13.81
Cover - Seat - Fiber Multi-Color Stripe	986976	1	13.50	8.10
Cover - Seat - Plastic Multi-Color Plaid	986994	1	15.95	9.57
Flap - Mud - Dual Wheel.	986904	2 pr.	16.50 pr.	9.90 pr.

Description	Part No.	Unit	Suggested List Price	Dealer Net
Flap - Mud - Single Wheel	986905	2 pr.	12.75 pr.	7.65 pr.
Guard - Grille - Commercial	986949	1	22.75	13.65
Guard - Grille - Truck	986957	1	31.50	18.90
Guard - Bumper - Truck	986978	Pair	9.50	5.70
Heater & Defroster - Air Flow	986895	1	64.75	40.15
Heater & Defroster - Recirculating	986896	1	38.25	22.95
Housing - Clock used with 986633 Clock	986960	1	3.75	2.25
Horn - High Note	986893	1	6.25	3.75
Lamp - Fog	986942	Pair	15.95	9.57
Lamp - R.H. Tail	986907	1	7.35	4.41
Lamp - Glove Compartment	986899	1	1.25	.75
Lighter - Cigarette	986965	1	2.95	1.77
Mirror - Outside Rectangular Rear View With Extension Arm	986985	1	6.25	3.75
Mirror - Head Rectangular	986986	1	1.65	.99
Ornament - Hood	986982	1	7.95	4.77
Radio & Antenna - Manual	986770	1	69.00	41.40
Reflector - Red Reflex 4"	985223	1	1.75	1.05
Rest - Arm	986769	1	3.90	2.34
Safetylight	986173	1	18.95	11.37
Signal - Direction - Single Face Front & Rear	986878	1	23.15	13.89
Signal - Direction - Double Face Front & Single Face Rear	986902	1	24.35	14.61
Signal - Direction - Single Face Front & Flush Rear	986951	1	22.65	13.59
Signal - Direction - Double Face Front & Flush Rear	986964	1	23.85	14.31
Signal - Direction - Pick-Up	986937	1	17.50	10.50
Signal - Direction - Panel	986938	1	24.00	14.40
Step - Rear Platform	986980	1	9.50	5.70
Ventshade	986623	Pair	5.25	3.15
Visor - R.H. Sun	986773	1	3.20	1.92
Visor - Outside Metal (Prime)	986936	2	22.00 ea.	13.20 ea.
Washer - Windshield - Foot Operated	986983	1	7.25	4.35

1954 CHEVROLET ACCESSORIES PRICE SCHEDULE

SERVICE ACCESSORIES SECTION

Description	Part No.	Unit	Suggested List Price	Dealer Net
Anti-Freeze - W/S Washer - 6 oz. Bottles	986180	12	7.20	3.60
(Single Bottle)			(.60)	(.30)
Anti-Freeze - W/S Washer - 6 oz. Bottles (N.Y.)	986775	12	7.20	3.60
(Single Bottle)			(.60)	(.30)
Anti-Freeze - G.M. Permanent Type - Gal. Cans	986952	6	17.70	11.82
(Single Gallon)			(2.95)	(1.97)
Anti-Freeze - G.M. Permanent Type - Qt. Cans	986953	24	19.20	12.48
(Single Quart)			(.80)	(.52)
Anti-Freeze - G.M. Methanol Type - Gal. Cans	986954	6	9.00	5.64
(Single Gallon)			(1.50)	(.94)
Anti-Freeze - G.M. Methanol Type - Qt. Cans	986955	24	9.60	6.12
(Single Quart)			(.40)	(.26)
Anti-Freeze - G.M. Methanol Type - 54 Gal. Drum	986956	1	81.00	46.44
(Single Gallon)			(1.50)	(.86)
Caroma Evaporator - Unit	983715	12	3.60	2.16
(Single Unit)			(.30)	(.18)
Cleaner - Sponge	986225	12	5.88	3.12
(Single Sponge)			(.49)	(.26)
Cleaner - Cooling System	986052	12	12.00	6.72
(Single Can)			(1.00)	(.56)
Cloth - Polishing	986077	12	8.28	4.96
(Single Polishing Cloth)			(.69)	(.41)
Door-Ease - Stick Lubricant - Utility Size	986897	6	2.40	1.44
(Single Stick)			(.40)	(.24)

Description	Part No.	Unit	Suggested List Price	Dealer Net
Element - Cooling System.	986706	6	11.10	6.66
(Single Unit)			(1.85)	(1.11)
Grinding Compound - Valve - 4 oz. Cans.	986078	36	9.00	5.04
(Single Can)			(.25)	(.14)
Inhibitor - Corrosion - Cool. Sys. - 16 oz. Cans	986977	12	6.00	3.60
(Single Can)			(.50)	(.30)
Lockease - Lubricant - 4 oz. Cans.	986434	12	4.20	2.80
(Single Can)			(.35)	(.23)
Luster Seal #1 - 12 oz. Plastic Bottle	986945	12	40.20	24.00
(Single Bottle)			(3.35)	(2.00)
Luster Seal #2 - 12 oz. Plastic Bottle	986946	12	40.20	24.00
(Single Bottle)			(3.35)	(2.00)
Luster Seal Haze Cream - 8 oz. Plastic Bottles.	986947	24	24.00	14.40
(Single Bottle)			(1.00)	(.60)
Oil - Dripless Penetrating - 4 oz. Cans.	986082	36	9.00	4.68
(Single Can)			(.25)	(.13)
Polish - Chromium - 8 oz. Cans.	986084	12	4.20	2.52
(Single Can)			(.35)	(.21)
Polish - Triple Action - 16 oz. Cans.	986085	12	9.00	5.40
(Single Can)			(.75)	(.45)
Polish - Triple Action - Gallon	985888	1	3.15	1.89
Powder - Static Eliminator - Envelopes	986087	12	4.80	2.88
(Single Envelope)			(.40)	(.24)
Porcelainize - Liquid - 8 oz. Bottles.	986175	24	105.60	60.00
(Single Bottle)			(4.40)	(2.50)
Porcelainize - Wash Cream - 8 oz. Bottles.	986176	24	14.40	8.64
(Single Bottle)			(.60)	(.36)
Porcelainize - Cleaner - Gallon Can	986363	1	No List	4.75
Porcelainize - Fastac - 8 oz. Bottles.	986961	24	30.00	18.00
(Single Bottle)			(1.25)	(.75)
Ruglyde - Rubber Lubricant & Cleaner - Gal. Can.	986047	1	3.60	2.15
Sealzit - Glass Cleaner - 2 oz. Bottles	986199	12	10.20	6.12
(Single Bottle)			(.85)	(.51)
Spot Remover - 8 oz. Cans.	986075	12	6.00	3.60
(Single Can)			(.50)	(.30)
Stopleak - Radiator - 10 oz. Cans.	986088	12	5.88	3.12
(Single Can)			(.49)	(.26)
Tipon Touch-Up Paint - 1954 Chevrolet Colors - 32 Assorted Colors	986991	32	32.00	19.20
(Single Tube)			(1.00)	(.60)
Tipon Touch-Up Paint - 1954 Chevrolet Colors - Dealers Choice of Colors	986990	12	12.00	7.20
(Single Tube)			(1.00)	(.60)
Tipon Touch-Up Paint - 1953 Chevrolet Colors - Dealers Choice of Colors	986959	12	12.00	7.20
(Single Tube)			(1.00)	(.60)
Undercoating - 54 Gallon Drum	986359	1	No List	46.44
Undercoating - Truckload	986653	44	No List	1,782.00
Undercoating - Carload.	986548	80	No List	3,110.40

PACIFIC COAST ONLY:

Description	Part No.	Unit	Suggested List Price	Dealer Net
Undercoating - 54 Gallon Drum	986635	1	No List	46.44
Undercoating - Truckload	986654	44	No List	1,782.00
Undercoating - Carload.	986638	80	No List	3,110.40

NEW YORK CITY ONLY:

Description	Part No.	Unit	Suggested List Price	Dealer Net
Undercoating - 54 Gallon Drum	986800	1	No List	37.80
Undercoating - Truckload	986801	44	No List	1,591.92
Undercoating - Carload.	986802	80	No List	2,764.80

The "Two-Ten" Handyman—one of Chevrolet's four
beautiful new Station Wagons with Body by Fisher.

**<u>Never</u> have you seen Station Wagons
as wonderful as the new Chevrolets!**

**They're <u>handsome</u> (just look!). They're
<u>handy</u> (new seat fold provides nearly
11 inches more cargo deck!).**

**Two doors or four, V8 or 6, three modern
transmissions—and a wagonload of other
new things you want.**

You <u>can</u> have your cake and eat it, too—with Chevrolet's spanking-new line of Station Wagons! For here is sophisticated big-city style (and the longest look of any Chevrolet) . . . plus pack-horse performance and astonishing new utility features. Now, both the rear seat cushion and the backrest fold flush with the floor to give almost <u>11 inches more cargo space</u>. <u>Curved rear quarter windows</u> combine with the deep Sweep-Sight Windshield to give visibility unlimited. With this two-in-one versatility you get all of Chevrolet's great engineering advances—the 162-h.p. "Turbo-Fire V8" or the two new "Blue-Flame" 6's, the smoothness of Glide-Ride front suspension, the stability of outrigger rear springs, Anti-Dive braking control, 12-volt electrical system and new Synchro-Mesh transmission. Plus your choice of extra-cost options such as Powerglide automatic transmission or Overdrive, Power Steering, Power Brakes—even Air Conditioning (on V8 models). How versatile can a car be? Why not call your Chevrolet dealer and see? . . . Chevrolet Division of General Motors, Detroit 2, Michigan.

More than a new car  *a new* ***concept*** *of low-cost motoring*

The lowest priced 1955 Chevrolet Sedan was the "150" 4-Door Sedan that sold for $1,827 as a 6-cylinder model. The car drew 29,898 sales for the season. The vehicle weighed 3125 pounds.

Chevrolet for 1955

Wow, what a change! As good looking as the 1954 cars were, the 1955 models were as different as night and day. It was often remarked, about the only thing interchangeable trim-wise between a 1954 and 1955 Chevrolet were the inside door handles. Body styles were completely new. The egg crate grille styling was something that had to grow on you, the special two-tone paint combinations with a cap and deck paint scheme really sent heads turning. Wild combinations of Shadow Gray and Coral, Shoreline Beige and Gypsy Red, to name just a couple, were the start of an entirely new era for Chevrolet as far as paint combinations did go. People were ready for something new and Chevy had it!

The new models for 1955 retained the 115-inch wheelbase from the previous year, but now were 195.6 inches in overall length while the wagons came with a 197-inch length. A new frame was employed given more stability to the car and offered a much better ride.

Under the hood, big news was also part of the surprise package for the year. Chevy had its first V-8 since the days of the not too popular 1917-1919 Chevrolet V-8. The company offered the standard 265 cubic-inch overhead V-8 that gave a 3.75 x 3 bore and stroke. The compression ratio was 8:1. The engines developed 162 horsepower at 4400 RPM in regular fashion or as many people were out for all the power they could get ordered the souped up "Power Pak"

87

Drawing the most sales in the "150" lineup was the 2-Door Sedan Model 1502 with 66,416 cars delivered. This unit weighed 3080 pounds and sold for $1,784. Looking exactly the same from the exterior was Model 1512, the 2-Door Utility Sedan. Seeing no back seat, was the main difference. The car was excellent for salesmen who generally needed this area for carrying their sales supplies. However, the car had limited appeal with the public and sold only 11,196 units for the year. It weighed 3,055 pounds and carried a price tag of $1,692 making it the lowest priced car Chevrolet offered for the year.

The Handyman 2-Door Wagon in the "150" Series was referred to as Model 1529. It weighed 3260 pounds and 17,936 units were delivered to customers for $2,129 each.

In the mid-range line, again, were two models looking exactly the same from the exterior. This example is the "210" Delray Club Coupe Model 2124 with its vinyl and carpeted interior. As a 6-cylinder, it weighed 3115 pounds and sold for $1,934. A total of 115,584 were delivered for the model run. Its twin was the "210" 2-Door Sedan Model 2102, coming with a cloth interior and rubber floors. This was the lowest priced car in the "210" line with a tab of $1,874. It tipped the scale at 3,115 pounds, and saw a production run of 249,105 units delivered.

for an additional $95.00 raising the horsepower to 180 at 4600 RPM. This version consisted of a 4-barrel carburetor with dual exhausts. An easy means of detecting these 1955 models, if parked at the curb, were the small "V"s placed under the taillights. If you heard the engine running, you would know it obviously wasn't the famous 6-cylinder engine which you'd grown to appreciate. Now, for just a minute devoted to the 6-cylinder engine — an owner had a choice of two 6s. The 123 horsepower version was employed in conventional and overdrive cars with the 235.5 cubic-inch engine offering a 3.56 bore, 3.97 stroke. The compression ratio was 7.5:1. The vehicles equipped with Powerglide came with bore, stroke, and compression ratings the same, but did develop 136 horsepower from the power plant. This same 6-cylinder engine was still available in the remaining 1955 Corvettes. Most Corvettes came with the new V-8 set up, however. Their form of detection whether 6 or V-8 came from the front fender nameplate. If the Vette was an 8, the "V" in the word "Chevrolet" was elongated so that a passerby knew it wasn't from the dark ages. The Vette saw 674 units for 1955 weighing 2650 pounds and delivering for $2,934.

Also new for 1955, and first to have it among the Big Three, was a 12-volt electrical system which made cranking the new V-8s an easy chore.

A mid-season offering was the return of the 210 Hardtop Coupe. Chevrolet felt they'd try it one more time to see how successful it might be on this popular new body style. The car weighed 3158 pounds and delivered as a V-8 for $1,959. The factory found 11,675 owners for this model.

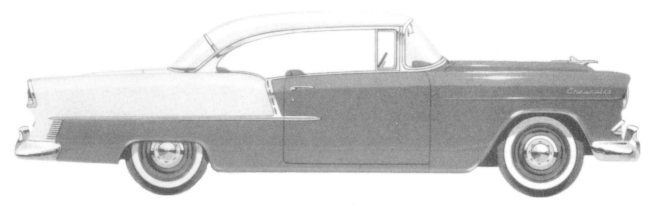

A mid-season offering to be tried once again, and hoping for better results than it offered when introduced in 1953, was the 1955 "210" Sport Coupe. This vehicle shared the body with the fashionable Bel Air Sport Coupe, but minus all the trim. It came with a less-expensive interior color-keyed floor mats and, exterior-wise, saw small hub caps and less stainless side trim than the Bel Air.

For a general rundown of the 1955 cars, the "150" Series offered the Utility Sedan as the lowest priced vehicle selling for $1,593. This model weighed 3070 pounds and found only 11,196 purchasers. A total of four models in this series made the Handyman Wagon, the most expensive selling for $2,030 for 17,936 owners. The most popular in the 150 Series was the 2-Door Sedan which weighed 3145 pounds and sold to 66,416 families for $1,685. The 150 4-Door Sedan found 29,898 owners for $1,728.

In the 210 lineup, a total of six models were available ranging in price from $1,775 for the 2-Door Sedan for 249,105 customers, to a 4-Door Townsman Wagon weighing 3355 pounds, selling for $2,127 to 82,303 owners. Besides these models, a person had his choice of the Delray Coupe for $1,835, 4-Door Sedan for $1,819 being the most popular.

The public had its widest choices of color to date with the 1955 line. They were in the following single-tone colors:

       Onyx Black
       Sea Mist Green
       Neptune Green
       Skyline Blue
       Glacier Blue
       Copper Maroon
       Harvest Gold (yellow)
       Shoreline Beige
       Autumn Bronze
       India Ivory
       Shadow Grey
       Gypsy Reel
       Regal Turquoise
       Coral (Convertible only)

Two-tone versions were:

Top	Bottom
Sea Mist Green	Neptune Green
Neptune Green	Shoreline Beige
India Ivory	Skyline Blue
Skyline Blue	Glacier Blue
Autumn Bronze	Shoreline Beige
Shoreline Beige	Autumn Bronze
India Ivory	Sea Mist Green
India Ivory	Shadow Gray
India Ivory	Onyx Black
Glacier Blue	Shoreline Beige
Glacier Blue	Skyline Blue
India Ivory	Regal Turquoise
Shoreline Beige	Neptune Green
Shoreline Beige	Glacier Blue
Onyx Black	India Ivory
Shadow Gray	Coral
India Ivory	Coral
Neptune Green	Sea Mist Green
India Ivory	Harvest Gold
India Ivory	Navajo Tan
Regal Turquoise	India Ivory
India Ivory	Gypsy Red
Shoreline Beige	Gypsy Red

A total of 37 choices were made available, to help confuse the customer.

This is the 1955 "210" 2-Door Wagon Model 2129 which weighed 3300 pounds and sold for $2,178. Sales were not as great as the 4-Door version with only 28,918 units being sold. The interior in this example, as in the other wagons, was chiefly done in vinyl.

This was the best seller, as far as the 1955 wagons were concerned. The example is the Model 2109 4-Door Townsman wagon which drew 82,303 customers for $2,236. The wagon weighed 3340 pounds.

The 1955 Bel Air Beauville Model 2409, a six-passenger wagon that weighed 3355 pounds and delivered for $2,361, had a production run of 24,313 for the year. A choice of four solid colors were available, as were the same number of two-tone combinations.

The Model 2402 Bel Air 2-Door Sedan was the lowest priced car in the top of the line series. It sold for $1,987 to 168,313 customers. This 2-Door model weighed 3125 pounds. Most examples came as two-tone models with what they referred to as a "cap and deck" paint combination meaning roof and trunk were done in a different color from the front of the car.

Always a favorite with me have been hard-top coupes by all manufacturers and certainly Chevrolet should be no exception. This is the popular Model 2454 Bel Air Sport Coupe which saw a production of 185,562 examples. The unit weighed 3,165 pounds and carried a price tag of $2,166.

Often seen in many publications — but why not show it one more time? — is the 50 millionth car produced by General Motors. It is the 1955 Bel Air Sport Coupe coming off the assembly line on November 23, 1954. The gentleman standing in the forefront is the late Harlow H. Curtice, then president of General Motors. In the background are many G.M. executives and well-wishers to the firm.

The Model 2403 Bel Air 4-Door Sedan was classed as the luxury version of the 4-door models. It weighed 3170 pounds and delivered for $2,031 to 345,372 customers. Most people were preferring the V-8 examples to the 6-cylinder models in this particular model.

Showing off its fashionable rear view is this 1955 Bel Air Convertible, Model 2434. Note the small "V" emblems under the taillight housing. This told the whole story. Either you were driving a power bomb or, if the emblem was missing, you knew it was a dependable, less powerful 6-cylinder example. Very few ordered this model in 6-cylinder style. As a V-8, it delivered for $2,305 with a weight of 3355 pounds.

Being that this was the first V-8 offered by Chevrolet since the ill-fated 1917-18 venture, the car was a hot item for the public to view. It was an instant success and was the chosen car to pace the track at Indianapolis on May 30, 1955. The Pace Car came in Shoreline Beige and Gypsy Red, a very popular color for this model.

Coming to dealerships in mid-1955 was the most popular Station Wagon Chevrolet had ever offered. The model naturally was the Nomad six-passenger. It was available only in 2-door style selling 8,386 examples making it next to the lowest production model for the year. The wagon weighed 3270 pounds and was the most expensive model for the year, delivering for $2,571. Note the chrome brows over the headlight area. A feature only seen on this model. The tailgate featured seven ribbed stainless moldings which have been tell-tale features to easily distinguish it from other Chevy wagons.

Exterior Colors

14 SOLID COLORS	"150"			"210"				BEL AIR			
	2-4-Door Sedans	Utility Sedan	Handyman	2-4-Door Sedans	Club Coupe	4-Door Townsman	2-Door Handyman	2-4-Door Sedans	Sport Coupe	Convertible	4-Door Beauville
Onyx Black	•	•		•	•			•	•	D	
Sea-Mist Green	•	•	•	•	•			•			
Neptune Green	•	•	•	•	•	•	•	•	•		•
Skyline Blue	•	•		•				•			
Glacier Blue	•	•		•	•	•	•	•			
Copper Maroon	•	•		•				•			
Shoreline Beige	•	•		•	•	•	•				
Autumn Bronze	•	•	•	•		•	•				
India Ivory	•	•		•				•			
Shadow Gray	•	•		•				•			
Gypsy Red										C	
Regal Turquoise											•
Coral										D	
Harvest Gold										•	

21 TWO-TONE COMBINATIONS

UPPER	LOWER	"150"			"210"				BEL AIR			
		2-4-Door Sedans	Utility Sedan	Handyman	2-4-Door Sedans	Club Coupe	4-Door Townsman	2-Door Handyman	2-4-Door Sedans	Sport Coupe	Convertible	4-Door Beauville
Sea-Mist Green	Neptune Green	•	•		•			•	•	•		
Skyline Blue	Glacier Blue	•	•		•							
Neptune Green	Shoreline Beige									•		
India Ivory	Skyline Blue	•	•		•	•			•	•		
India Ivory	Shadow Gray	•	•		•				•			
Autumn Bronze	Shoreline Beige						•	•				
India Ivory	Sea-Mist Green					•	•					
Shoreline Beige	Autumn Bronze				•	•			•		C	•
Glacier Blue	Shoreline Beige				•	•						
India Ivory	Onyx Black				•							
India Ivory	Gypsy Red				•							
Glacier Blue	Skyline Blue								•	•	B	
India Ivory	Regal Turquoise									•	•	D
Shoreline Beige	Neptune Green	•	•		•				•	•		
Shoreline Beige	Glacier Blue					•	•		•			•
Shoreline Beige	Gypsy Red								•		C	
Onyx Black	India Ivory								•			
Shadow Gray	Coral								•	•		
Neptune Green	Sea-Mist Green										A	•
India Ivory	Coral										D	
India Ivory	Harvest Gold							•		•	•	D

Remember... THERE'S NO VALUE LIKE CHEVROLET VALUE!

LITHO IN U.S.A.

DECEMBER, 1954

CONVERTIBLE TOP COLORS:
A—GREEN B—BLUE C—BEIGE D—WHITE

CHEVROLET MOTOR DIVISION
GENERAL MOTORS CORPORATION
DETROIT 2, MICHIGAN

Shown here are the variety of 1955 single-tone and two-tone paint combinations that were available.

A slightly different aspect of the 1955 Bel Air Sport Coupe interior. The seat material was very perishable and didn't take any rough-housing. Today, the material is available looking the same, but of a much more durable cloth.

What a car! From any view, the 1955 Nomad really is a looker. This view shows off the rear of the tailgate best of all, with its seven ribbed stainless bars which became a trademark of the vehicle.

This gives a good example of the 1955 Chevrolets, along with the availability of the factory-approved accessories the customer had his choice in ordering.

Protection and Glamour, Too

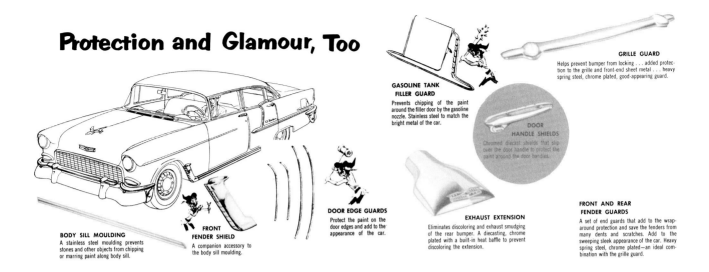

GASOLINE TANK FILLER GUARD
Prevents chipping of the paint around the filler door by the gasoline nozzle. Stainless steel to match the bright metal of the car.

GRILLE GUARD
Helps prevent bumper from locking . . . added protection to the grille and front-end sheet metal . . . heavy spring steel, chrome plated, good-appearing guard.

DOOR HANDLE SHIELDS
Chromed diecast shields that slip over the door handle to protect the paint around the door handles.

BODY SILL MOULDING
A stainless steel moulding prevents stones and other objects from chipping or marring paint along body sill.

FRONT FENDER SHIELD
A companion accessory to the body sill moulding.

DOOR EDGE GUARDS
Protect the paint on the door edges and add to the appearance of the car.

EXHAUST EXTENSION
Eliminates discoloring and exhaust smudging of the rear bumper. A diecasting, chrome plated with a built-in heat baffle to prevent discoloring the extension.

FRONT AND REAR FENDER GUARDS
A set of end guards that add to the wrap-around protection and save the fenders from many dents and scratches. Add to the sweeping sleek appearance of the car. Heavy spring steel, chrome plated—an ideal combination with the grille guard.

Mirrors-so you may see all around

SAFETYLIGHT AND MIRROR
A large optically clear mirror concaved into the head of the safetylight . . . can be adjusted from inside the car. Ideal for families where each driver must readjust the mirror.

BODY MOUNT MIRROR
Adds additional safety to rear vision when pulling away from curb or passing on the open highway . . . can be mounted to either right or left hand doors. Optically clear glass, nickle-chrome finish mirror.

VANITY VISOR MIRROR
Ideal make-up mirror for that last minute grooming. An optically clear mirror, clips to either the right or left sun visor.

INSIDE NON-GLARE REARVIEW MIRROR
A rearview mirror that reduces eyestrain from bright headlights in mirror . . . a flip of the tab subdues the bright lights and still permits full vision of traffic to the rear.

REMOTE CONTROL MIRROR
An entirely new type mirror with no gears or friction drive to slip or strip. A direct-drive type that can be set to any position from inside the car. Truly a new, modern mirror.

Lights for Every Need

BACK-UP LAMPS
Light automatically when car is shifted into reverse . . . assist in backing into or out of dark areas or driveways.

UNDERHOOD LAMP
Automatically casts a flood of light over the entire engine compartment when hood is raised . . . ideal for night engine inspections.

COURTESY LAMPS
Automatically floods floor with light when either front door is opened . . . adding safety and convenience at night.

PORTABLE SPOTLAMP
A powerful Sealed Beam light with 12-foot cord . . . plugs into cigarette lighter . . . ideal trouble lamp.

ELECTRIC BRAKE SIGNAL
Flashes red warning when ignition is turned on until brake is released.

LUGGAGE COMPARTMENT LAMP
Lights automatically when trunk lid is raised . . . leaving hands free to load or unload the trunk.

SAFETYLIGHT AND MIRROR
A powerful Sealed Beam light . . . casts a ray of light up to 1000 feet . . . can be directed in all directions from inside the car . . . ideal for reading house numbers, highway and street markers.

99

For All Weather Visibility

FOOT-OPERATED WINDSHIELD WASHER
Depressing a foot-button automatically sprays water on windshield and starts wiper blades. When button is released, wipers stop.

TRAFFIC LIGHT VIEWER
Optically clear prism viewer . . . permits driver to see overhead traffic lights in true color when view of light is blocked by top of car.

SELF DE-ICING WINDSHIELD WIPER BLADE
A rubber hood over the blade prevents ice and snow from freezing on blade . . . assures clean no-streak wipe.

OUTSIDE SUN VISOR
A chrome-trimmed all-metal visor . . . reduces sun glare . . . helps prevent ice and snow from accumulating on windshield . . . painted to match the car.

VENTSHADES
Permit windows to be lowered a few inches when driving in rain or when car is parked . . . for improved ventilation . . . help to reduce sun glare . . . help reduce window fogging.

WINDSHIELD WASHER—VACUUM
The vacuum washer can be made completely automatic with the co-ordinator . . . then when the button is depressed for several seconds, water is sprayed on the glass, the wipers are started. When glass is clean, washer automatically stops and wiper blades return to normal position.

WINDSHIELD WASHER SOLVENT
A solvent to prevent freezing in winter . . . ideal for summer use to remove road film, grime and insects, for better vision.

For that Continental Sports Car Look

CONTINENTAL WHEEL CARRIER
A wheel carrier that gives the car a Continental sports car look . . . gives additional trunk space . . . sturdy, rattle free, easy to operate.

◄ **WHEEL COVERS—DISC**
Attractive stainless-steel wheel covers to add the sports car look, smartness and beauty to the wheels; in sets of four.

WHEEL RINGS ►
Extra-wide highly polished stainless steel rings that snap into the wheel flange to give luxury appearance to the wheels; in sets of five.

AUTOMATIC TOP RAISER
Owners of convertibles can park with top down and not worry about the inside of the car getting wet. The first drop of rain automatically causes the top to be raised.

For that Showroom Look

ACCELERATOR PEDAL COVER
Fits snugly and securely over accelerator pedal . . . helps prevent foot slipping from pedal . . . increases life of floor mat.

RUBBER FLOOR MATS
Large colorful mats that help keep that new-car look by protecting the regular mats . . . easy to clean . . . ideal kneeling pad to change tires.

PORCELAINIZE
A paint treatment that gives a high lustre with depth and brilliance that last. (Must be machine applied.)

POLISHING CLOTH
A large wax-treated flannel cloth for keeping that new-car shine . . . also for household use. Won't scratch the finest finishes. Can be washed when soiled without damaging the polishing qualities.

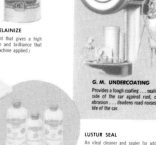

G. M. UNDERCOATING
Provides a tough coating . . . sealing the underside of the car against rust, corrosion and abrasion . . . deadens road noises . . . lasts the life of the car.

LUSTUR SEAL
An ideal cleaner and sealer for adding a high lustre to the car. (Must be machine applied.)

Chevrolet Accessories For 1955

DEALER LIST AND NET PRICE SCHEDULE

Effective March 15, 1955

ALL PRICES SUBJECT TO CHANGE WITHOUT NOTICE

The "List Prices" shown in this schedule are suggested prices for sales to consumers.

Description	Part No.	Part No. Per Pkg.	Suggested List Price	Dealer Net
Antenna-Fender Type R.H.	987100	1	6.35	3.81
Automatic Headlamp Control (Autronic Eye)	987310	1	44.25	33.19
Blade - Windshield Wiper - Self De-Icing	986882	12	2.50 ea.	1.50 ea.
Block - Wiring Junction	987094	1	1.90	1.14
Brake Unit - Power	987260	55-P, All	47.50	28.50
Brake Unit - Power	987215	54-53-Pass	47.50	28.50
Brake Unit - Power	987214	52-51-Pass	47.50	28.50
Cap - Locking gasoline tank	986691	1	2.90	1.74
Carrier - Wheel - Continental	987222	1	118.00	76.70
Carrier - Wheel - Continental - Pacific Coast only	987265	1	126.00	81.90
Clock - Electric	987093	1	17.50	10.50
Compass - Illuminated	987137	1	5.95	3.57
Co-ordinator - Use with 987105 Windshield Washer	987200	1	3.50	2.10
Cover - Seat - Nylon	All	Set	39.90	23.94
Cover - Seat - Nylon - Spring Line	All	Set	42.50	25.50
Cover - Seat - Plastic	All	Set	34.90	20.94
Cover - Seat - Plastic - Spring Line	All	Set	37.50	22.50
Cover - Seat - Fiber	All	Set	26.90	16.14
Cover - Seat - Fiber - Station Wagon	All	Frt Only	15.95	9.57
Cover - Glamour Glide - Nylon - Dacron	All	Set	19.90	11.94
Cover - Glamour Glide - Nylon - Spring Line	All	Set	19.90	11.94
Cover - Accelerator Pedal	987107	6	1.17 ea.	.70 ea.
Cover - Wheel Disc - 15" Wheel Set of 4	987184	1	19.00	12.35
Cover - Full Wheel - Set of 4	987268	1	14.95	8.97
Dispenser - Auto Tissue	987134	1	3.85	2.31
Extension - Exhaust	987116	1	3.25	1.95
Frame - License - Pair	986708	1	3.25	1.95
Glareshade - W/S - 2D. Sta. Wag.Spt. Cpe.	987139	2	8.00 ea.	4.80 ea
Glareshade - W/S - All Sedans	987115	3	8.00 ea.	4.80 ea.
Guard - Grille	987095	1	11.50	6.90
Guard - Front & Rear Fender	987221	1	39.00	23.40
Guard - Door Edge - 4 Door	987128	3	6.25 ea.	3.75 ea.
Guard - Door Edge - 2 Door	987129	3	3.45 ea.	2.07 ea.
Guard - Door Edge - Spt. Cpe, * Conv.	987130	3	3.45 ea.	2.07 ea.
Guard - Gasoline Filler Door	987099	6	1.65	.99 ea.
Heater & Defroster - Recirculating	987185	1	42.00	29.40
Heater & Defroster - Deluxe	987186	1	65.00	45.50
Kit - Tool	987322	1	2.90	1.73
Kool Kooshion - Green	987323	6	4.40	2.64
Kool Kooshion - Blue	987324	6	4.40	2.64
Kool Kooshion - Tan	987325	6	4.40	2.64

Description	Part No.	Part No. Per Pkg.	Suggested List Price	Dealer Net
Lamp - Back-Up - All	987113	1	5.85	3.51
Lamp - Courtesy	987138	1	2.75	1.65
Lamp - Luggage Compartment	987082	1	1.95	1.17
Lamp - Underhood	987082	1	1.95	1.17
Lamp - Glove Compartment	987118	1	1.10	.66
Lighter & Lamp - Cigarette	987089	1	3.00	1.80
Mat - Rubber Floor - Brown	987210	6	1.75 ea.	1.05 ea.
Mat - Rubber Floor - Blue	987206	6	1.75 ea.	1.05 ea.
Mat - Rubber Floor - Black	987209	6	1.75 ea.	1.05 ea.
Mat - Rubber Floor - Green	987208	6	1.75 ea.	1.05 ea.
Mat - Rubber Floor - Red	987207	6	1.75 ea.	1.05 ea.
Mirror - Outside R.V. Body Mount	987124	1	3.60	2.16
Mirror - Remote Control	987220	1	6.95	4.17
Mirror - Inside R.V. Non Glare	986948	1	3.95	2.37
Mirror - Visor Vanity	936605	1	1.60	.96
Moulding - Body Sill	987122	3	7.00 ea.	4.20 ea.
Radio & Antenna - Push Button	987101	1	84.50	50.70
Radio & Antenna - Manual	987102	1	62.00	37.20
Radio & Antenna - Signal Seeker	987103	1	105.00	68.25
Raiser - Automatic Tap	987223	1	34.00	22.10
Receiver - Ash	987120	1	2.00	1.20
Rest - Arm - Green	987144	1	9.25	5.55
Rest - Arm - Gray	987108	1	9.25	5.55
Rest - Arm - Straw	987109	1	9.25	5.55
Ring - Wheel trim - 15"	986906	1	11.75	7.05
Safetylight & Mirror	987224	1	24.50	14.70
Seat & Back Rest - Sacro-Ease	987338	1	19.75	11.85
Spotlamp - Hand portable	987112	1	7.95	4.77
Shaver - Electric A.C. - D.C	987119	1	29.50	17.70
Signal - Electric Parking Brake	987121	1	4.25	2.55
Shield - Door Handle	987204	1	2.80	1.68
Shield - Front Fender	987133	1	6.75	4.05
Speaker - Rear Seat	987117	1	12.00	7.20
Ventshade - 2 Door Sedan	987136	1	8.75	5.25
Ventshade - 4 Door Sedan	987135	1	8.75	5.25
Visor - Outside - All Sedans & Station Wagons	987110	2	19.90 ea.	11.94 ea.
Visor - Outside - Sport Coupe	987111	2	19.90 ea.	11.94 ea.
Visor - R.H. Sun Gray	987141	1	5.75	3.45
Visor - R.H. Sun Straw	987142	1	5.75	3.45
Visor - R.H. Sun Green	987143	1	5.75	3.45
Viewer - Traffic Light	987273	1	2.90	1.74
Washer - W/S Vacuum	987105	1	7.05	4.77
Washer - W/S Foot	987280	1	7.50	4.50

1955 Chevrolet Accessories Price Schedule
TRUCK AND COMMERCIAL SECTION

Description	Part No.	Units	Suggested List Price	Dealer Net
Antenna - Fender - Mounting	987188	1	7.25	4.35
Blade - Windshield Wiper - Self De-Icing	Same as Passenger			
Block - Wiring Junction	Same as Passenger			
Bracket - Mirror - Inside - Rear View				
Used with 986948 Non Glare Mirror	987179	1	1.55	.93
Cover - Seat - Fiber	987267	1	14.25	8.55
Condenser - Radiator - Overflow	986643	1	4.35	2.61
Cover - Full Wheel Set of 4 - 15"	Same as Passenger			

Description	Part No.	Part No. Per Pkg.	Suggested List Price	Dealer Net
Compass - Illuminated ....Same as Passenger				
Flap - Mud - Dual Wheel	987226	2	9.90	5.94
Bracket - Mud Flap - Dual Wheel	987228	1	6.90	4.14
Flap - Mud - Single Wheel	987227	2	6.50	3.90
Bracket - Mud Flap - Single Wheel	987229	1	6.60	3.96
Guard - Bumper - Commercial (Chrome)	987270	1	12.50	7.50
Guard - Bumper - Commercial (Painted)	987177	1	9.50	5.70
Guard - Bumper - Truck	987219	1	10.75	6.45
Guard - Grille - Commercial - Brush Type	987212	1	29.90	17.94
Guard - Grille - Truck - Brush Type	987213	1	32.00	19.20
Guard - Door-Edge	987205	1	3.45	2.07
Guard - Gas Tank Filler Door	987247	1	1.75	1.05
Heater & Defroster - Deluxe	987216	1	67.50	41.85
Heater & Defroster - Recirculating	987218	1	45.00	27.00
Horn - High Note	987211	1	6.35	3.81
Kit - Tool ....Same as Passenger				
Lighter - Cigarette	987190	1	3.25	1.95
Lamp - Tail R.H.	987202	1	7.60	4.56
Lamp - Fog	987263	1	17.75	10.65
Lamp - Back-Up	987225	1	11.00	6.60
Lamp - Glove Compartment ....Same as Passenger				
Lamp - Underhood ....Same as Passenger				
Mirror - Outside - Rear-View - With Bracket	987230	1	7.75	4.65
Mirror - Outside - Rear-View - Head Only	987262	1	2.75	1.65
Mirror - Inside Rear-View - Non-Glare ....Same as Passenger				
Mats - Rubber - Floor 5 Colors ....Same as Passenger				
Ornament - Hood	987242	1	8.50	5.10
Radio & Antenna - Manual	987189	1	69.50	41.70
Rest - Arm	987181	1	3.90	2.34
Reflector - Red Reflex	985223	1	1.75	1.05
Safetylight - With Mirror	987243	1	22.50	13.50
Seat & Back Rest - Sacro-Ease ....Same as Passenger				
Shaver - Electric AC-DC ....Same as Passenger				
Shield-Door Handle	987245	1	2.95	1.77
Spotlamp - Hand - Portable ....Same as Passenger				
Signal Direction - Front - Single Face				
Rear-Bracket Mount	987238	1	24.50	14.70
Signal Direction - Front - Double Face				
Rear-Bracket Mount	987239	1	26.00	15.60
Signal Direction - Front - Double Face				
Rear - Flush Mount	987240	1	26.00	15.60
Signal Direction - Front - Single Face				
Rear - Flush Mount	987241	1	24.50	14.70
Signal Direction - Pick-Up	987250	1	19.50	11.70
Signal Direction - Panel	987251	1	26.00	15.60
Signal Direction - Deluxe Pick-Up	987252	1	18.00	10.80
Signal - Parking, Brake	987237	1	4.75	2.85
Step - Rear Platform	986980	1	9.50	5.70
Visor - Sun - Outside - Metal	987182	1	13.75	8.25
Visor - Sun - R.H.	987183	1	3.25	1.95
Ventshade	987203	1	5.25	3.15
Viewer - Traffic-Light ....Same as Passenger				
Washer - Windshield	987257	1	7.50	4.50

1955 Chevrolet Accessories Price Schedule
SERVICE ACCESSORIES SECTION

Description	Part No.	Units	Suggested List Price	Dealert Net
Anti-Freeze - W/S Washer - 6 oz. bottles	986180	12	7.20	3.60
(Single Bottle)			(.60)	(.30)
Anti-Freeze - W/S Washer - 6 oz. bottles (N.Y.)	986775	12	7.20	3.60
(Single Bottle)			(.60)	(.30)
Anti-Freeze - G.M. Permanent Type - Gal. Cans	986952	6	17.70	11.82
(Single Gallon)			(2.95)	(1.97)
Anti-Freeze - G.M. Permanent Type - Qt. Cans	986953	24	19.20	12.84
(Single Quart)			(.80)	(.535)
Anti-Freeze - G.M. Methanol Type - Gal. Cans	986954	6	9.00	5.64
(Single Gallon)			(1.50)	(.94)
Anti-Freeze - G.M. Methanol Type - Qt. Cans	986955	24	9.60	6.12
(Single Quart)			(.40)	(.26)
Anti-Freeze - G.M. Methanol Type - 54 Gal.Drum	986956	1	81.00	46.44
(Single Gallon)			(1.50)	(.86)
Caroma Evaporator - Unit	983715	12	3.60	2.16
(Single Unit)			(.30)	(.18)
Cleaner - Sponge	986225	12	5.88	3.12
(Single Sponge)			(.49)	(.26)
Cleaner - Cooling System	986052	12	12.00	6.72
(Single Can)			(1.00)	(.56)
Cloth - Polishing	986077	12	8.28	4.96
(Single Polishing Cloth)			(.69)	(.41)
Compound - Gasket Sealer - 16 oz. cans	987266	6	13.50	8.10
(Single Can)			(2.25)	(1.35)
Door-Ease - Stick Lubricant - Utility Size	986897	6	2.40	1.44
(Single Stick)			(.40)	(.24)
Element - Cooling System	986706	6	11.10	6.66
(Single Unit)			(1.85)	(1.11)
Inhibitor - Corrosion - Cool. Sys -16oz.Cans	986977	12	6.00	3.60
(Single Can)			(.50	(.30)
Lockease - Lubricant - 4 oz. Cans	986434	12	4.20	2.80
(Single Can)			(.35)	(.23)
Luster Seal #1 - 12 oz. Plastic Bottle	986945	12	40.20	24.00
(Single Bottle)			(3.25)	(2.00)
Luster Seal #2 - 12 oz. Plastic Bottle	986946	12	40.20	24.00
(Single Bottle)			(3.35)	(2.00)
Luster Seal #1 Machine - I Gal. Can	987284	1	28.50	17.00
Luster Seal #2 Machine - 1 Gal. Can	987285	1	28.50	17.00
Luster Seal Haze Cream - 8 oz. Plastic Bottles	986947	24	24.00	14.40
(Single Bottle)			(1.00)	(.60)
Mitt - Angora - Washing - Dusting	987269	12	19.80	11.88
(Single Unit)			(1.65)	(.99)
Oil - Dripless Penetrating - 4 oz. Cans	986082	36	9.00	4.68
(Single Can)			(.25)	(.13)
Polish - Chromium - 8 oz Cans	986084	12	4.20	2.52
(Single Can)			(.35)	(.21)
Polish - Triple Action - 16 oz Cans	986085	12	9.00	5.40
(Single Can)			(.75)	(.45)
Polish - Triple Action - Gallon	985888	1	3.15	1.89
Porcelainize - Liquid 8-oz. Bottles	986175	24	105.60	60.00
(Single Bottle)			(4.40)	(2.50)
Porcelainize - Wash Cream - 8 oz. Bottles	986176	24	14.40	8.64
(Single Bottle)			(.60)	(.36)
Porcelainize - Cleaner - Gallon Can	986363	1	No List	4.75

Description	Part No.	Units	Suggested List Price	Dealert Ne
Porcelainize - Fastac - 8 oz. Bottles	986961	24	30.00	18.00
(Single Bottle)			(1.25)	(.75)
RuGlyde - Rubber Lubrican & Cleaner - Gal Can	986047	1	3.60	2.15
Sealzit - Glass Sealer - 2 oz. Bottles	986199	12	10.20	6.12
(Single Bottle)			(.85)	(.51)
Spot Remover - 8 oz. Cans	986075	12	6.00	3.60
(Single Can)			(.50)	(.30)
Stopleak - Radiator - 10 oz. Cans	986088	12	5.88	3.12
(Single Can)			(.49)	(.26)
Tipon Touch-Up Paint - 1954 Chevrolet Colors				
32 Assorted Colors	986991	32	32.00	19.20
(Single Tube)				
Tipon Touch-Up Paint - 1954 Chevrolet Colors				
Dealers Choice of Colors	986690	12	12.00	7.20
(Single Tube)			(1.00)	(.60)
Tipon Touch-Up Paint - 1953 Chevrolet Colors				
Dealers Choice of Colors	986959	12	12.00	7.20
(Single Tube)			(1.00)	(.60)
Tipon Touch-Up Paint - 1955-54-53 Chevrolet				
Colors - Dealers Choice of (6)	987261	6	6.00	3.60
(Single Tube)			(1.00)	(.60)
Tipon Touch-Up Paint - 1955 Chevrolet Truck				
32 Assorted Colors	987321	32	32.00	19.20
Undercoating - 54 Gallon Drum	986359	1	No List	46.44
Undercoating - Truckload	986653	44	No List	1782.00
Undercoating - Carload	986548	80	No List	3110.40

Pacific Coast Only:

Description	Part No.	Units	Suggested List Price	Dealert Ne
Undercoating - 54 Gallon Drum	986635	1	No List	46.44
Undercoating - Truckload	986654	44	No List	1782.00
Undercoating - Carload	986638	80	No List	3110.40

New York City Only:

Description	Part No.	Units	Suggested List Price	Dealert Ne
Undercoating - 54 Gallon Drum	986800	1	No List	37.80
Undercoating - Truckload	986801	44	No List	1591.92
Undercoating - Carload	986802	80	No List	2764.80

The new Bel Air Convertible with Body by Fisher — one of 20 new Chevrolet beauties.

Man, that Chevy's really got it!

What's the younger generation coming to? New Chevrolets, that's what. Because Chevrolet, too, speaks the language of youth!

Ever notice how quickly teen talk changes? We'll admit, for example, that we don't know exactly, word for word, what the younger generation is saying about the new Chevrolet these days. "Real cool!" maybe, or "It's the greatest!" More likely, though, it's some brand-new phrase in the language of youth.

But one thing's sure—Chevrolet's in solid with the young set. It's a young kind of car. Fresh and frisky and fun-loving, but with a both-feet-on-the-ground kind of stability.

That's why Chevy's *your* kind of car. It brings you horsepower ranging up to 225, a sweet-feeling sureness of control—and all the other road car qualities that make for safer, happier driving.

Any teenagers you know could probably tell you all about the new Chevrolet. But if you don't "dig" the latest language, better stop by your Chevrolet dealer's. You'll see what they mean! . . . Chevrolet Division of General Motors, Detroit 2, Michigan.

THE HOT ONE'S EVEN HOTTER

America's Favorite —by a Margin of 2 Million Cars!

This is the 1956 Chevrolet Model 1503, or also known as the "150" 4-Door Sedan. This example is fairly well equipped with a two-tone paint combination whitewalls and, the "V" on the hood tells us it is equipped with a V-8 engine not too often employed on a low-priced model. This example weighed 3,186 pounds, sold for $1,968 and delivered to 51,544 customers.

Chevrolet for 1956

For 1956, Chevrolet gave its public a very attractive car once again. Those who preferred the more conventional grille design usually weren't big followers of the 1955 front end design. I was also in that group, for I liked the 1956 cars the best of the three-year styling.

Just out of the service and back to school for my last semester of schooling, I had my heart set on working for General Motors. Hopefully, there might be an opening in the Los Angeles Chevrolet Zone Office, upon graduating in January. Fortunately, the position was open and my life-long dream of working for my favorite car manufacturer became a reality. During that semester of school, I pestered many Chevrolet dealers in the Los Angeles area to see what was new for the 1956 cars. When I actually saw the first one, a Dune Beige and Matador Red Bel Air Sport Coupe at the Angelus Chevrolet Company in Highland Park (a suburb of Los Angeles), I wondered, "How can I trade my '53 2-door for this new car?" Great thoughts went through my mind on a trade for a car that, for the last three years, had been such a struggle to meet the payments on. Now that it's paid for, I wanted to again burden myself with another car payment for three more years! Well, I kind of came to my senses, realizing the '53 would do me for a while longer — at least until I became a little more solvent.

Then the long-awaited date of February 1, 1956 arrived, and my big day of joining the work force of "Big Business" had come. My boss, Fred Donnelly, the best boss anyone ever could have had, was the person I had to answer to. I will never forget. I was there probably all of three weeks and learning the ropes of New Car Distribution. My job was filling orders for the 144 Chevrolet dealers in the Los Angeles Zone. Being a believer that a 6-cylinder engine was as good as a V-8, I was filling orders sending a good portion of the allotment of 6-cylinder cars to the Van Nuys assembly plant to be put in Bel Air Coupes, Convertibles, and Nomads. Fred called me into his inner office and I'll never forget his patient way of asking me, "Jim, are you the one sending these original orders to the factory to build 6-cylinder cars in our premium line of vehicles?" My response was, "Oh, sure! I've done it." He cringed and said, "Holy Toledo! this is bad merchandise to dispose of, especially when equipped with electric windows, electric seats, padded dash, etc., etc., which many of these cars are equipped with. Don't ever send another unit out of here equipped like this. You've used up our allotment of 6-cylinder production, 'til June!"

Years later, after moving to Santa Barbara, I spotted a 1956 Bel Air Sport Coupe done in India Ivory and Dawn Gray that was built as a 6-cylinder. Upon closer inspection, I saw it had a padded dash, electric windows, and power steering. I eventually purchased the car and one day, while working on it, I pulled the clock out and here was a date for assembly of 2-1-56. This was my first day on the job! I'm sure it must have been one of my first "goof cars." What a dependable car it was, as I had it for about seven years of great transportation. Today, it's in the hands of an Alan Feinstein in Studio City, California.

Now, getting back to one of my favorite years for Chevrolet of the fifties, the famous slogan of "The Hot Ones Even Hotter," was seen in much advertising for 1956. The two-tone paint treatment was an instant success, especially in the Bel Air line where nearly all models came with this treatment giving an appearance of motion while standing still. The 35-millionth production car to come from Chevrolet was a Bel Air Sport Coupe.

"ONE-FIFTY" SERIES SPECIAL TWO-TONE

A late addition to the "One-Fifty" models is the special two-tone treatment illustrated above. The new "One-Fifty" chrome styling for '56 makes this two-toning possible.

Chevrolet offered twelve single-tone color choices for the 1956 model run (Figure 1).

SERIES AND MODELS	Crocus Yellow	Nassau Blue	Pinecrest Green	Matador Red	Onyx Black	Tropical Turquoise	Sherwood Green	Dusk Plum	Calypso Cream	Harbor Blue	India Ivory	Inca Silver
BEL AIR SPORT SEDAN	●	●	●	●	●	●	●	●		●	●	●
BEL AIR SPORT COUPE	●	●	●	●	●	●	●	●		●	●	●
BEL AIR 4-DOOR SEDAN	●	●	●	●	●	●	●	●		●	●	●
BEL AIR 2-DOOR SEDAN	●	●	●	●	●	●	●	●		●	●	●
BEL AIR CONVERTIBLE	●	●	●	●	●	●	●	●		●	●	●
BEL AIR BEAUVILLE	●	●	●	●	●	●	●	●			●	●
BEL AIR NOMAD					●							●
210 SPORT SEDAN	●	●	●	●	●	●	●	●		●	●	●
210 SPORT COUPE	●	●	●	●	●	●	●	●		●	●	●
210 4-DOOR SEDAN	●	●	●	●	●	●	●	●		●	●	●
210 2-DOOR SEDAN	●	●	●	●	●	●	●	●		●	●	●
210 DELRAY COUPE	●	●	●	●	●	●	●				●	●
210 BEAUVILLE	●	●	●	●	●	●	●				●	●
210 4-DOOR STATION WAGON	●	●	●	●	●	●	●				●	●
210 2-DOOR STATION WAGON	●	●	●	●	●	●	●				●	●
150 4-DOOR SEDAN		●	●	●	●	●	●		●		●	
150 2-DOOR SEDAN		●	●	●	●	●	●		●		●	
150 UTILITY SEDAN		●	●	●	●	●	●		●		●	
150 2-DOOR STATION WAGON		●	●		●		●		●		●	

1956 CHEVROLET COLORS (Figure. 1)

Single tones were not too popular at this time. The colors were:

        Onyx Black
        India Ivory
        Pinecrest Green
        Sherwood Green
        Harbor Blue
        Nassau Blue
        Dusk Plum
        Matador Red
        Twilight Turquoise (early year color)

        Spring Colors
        Tropical Turquoise
        Crocus Yellow
        Calypso Cream
        Inca Silver

The two tone varieties were far more popular with 80 percent of purchasers preferring these choices (see Figure 2):

Top	Bottom
India Ivory	Sherwood Green
India Ivory	Pinecrest Green
Onyx Black	Calypso Cream
Onyx Black	Crocus Yellow
Nassau Blue	Harbor Blue
India Ivory	Nassau Blue
Adobe Beige	Sierra Gold
India Ivory	Dusk Plum
India Ivory	Matador Red
Adobe Beige	Matador Red
Calypso Cream	Grecian Gold (spring color)
India Ivory	Onyx Black
Sherwood Green	Pinecrest Green
Crocus Yellow	Laurel Green
India Ivory	Tropical Turquoise (spring color)
Imperial Ivory	Inca Silver (spring color)

A total of 16 tastefully combined combinations from which Chevrolet prospects had to select.

SERIES AND MODELS	India Ivory / Sherwood Green	Onyx Black / Crocus Yellow	Imperial Ivory / Inca Silver	Nassau Blue / Harbor Blue	India Ivory / Nassau Blue	Adobe Beige / Sierra Gold	India Ivory / Matador Red	Onyx Black / Calypso Cream	Calypso Cream / Grecian Gold	India Ivory / Pinecrest Green	India Ivory / Dusk Plum	India Ivory / Onyx Black	Adobe Beige / Matador Red	Sherwood Green / Pinecrest Green	Crocus Yellow / Laurel Green	India Ivory / Tropical Turquoise
BEL AIR SPORT SEDAN	●	●	●	●	●	●			●	●	●	●	●	●	●	●
BEL AIR SPORT COUPE	●	●	●	●	●	●			●	●	●	●	●	●	●	●
BEL AIR 4-DOOR SEDAN	●	●	●	●	●	●	●		●	●	●	●		●	●	●
BEL AIR 2-DOOR SEDAN	●	●	●	●	●	●			●	●	●	●		●	●	●
BEL AIR CONVERTIBLE	●	●	●	●	●	●	●		●	●	●	●			●	●
BEL AIR BEAUVILLE		●	●		●	●			●	●	●	●	●		●	●
BEL AIR NOMAD	●		●	●	●	●			●	●	●	●	●	●		●
210 SPORT SEDAN	●	●	●	●	●		●		●	●	●	●		●	●	●
210 SPORT COUPE	●	●	●	●	●		●		●	●	●	●		●	●	●
210 4-DOOR SEDAN	●	●	●	●	●		●		●	●	●	●		●	●	●
210 2-DOOR SEDAN	●	●	●	●	●		●		●	●	●	●		●	●	●
210 DELRAY COUPE	●	●	●		●		●		●	●	●	●		●	●	●
210 BEAUVILLE	●	●	●		●	●			●	●	●	●		●	●	●
210 4-DOOR STATION WAGON	●	●	●		●	●	●		●	●	●	●		●	●	●
210 2-DOOR STATION WAGON	●	●	●		●	●	●		●	●	●	●		●	●	●
150 4-DOOR SEDAN					●		●	●	●	●			●		●	
150 2-DOOR SEDAN					●		●	●	●	●			●		●	
150 UTILITY SEDAN					●		●	●	●	●			●		●	
150 2-DOOR STATION WAGON	●				●	●		●	●	●			●		●	

1956 CHEVROLET COLORS (Figure 2)

110

A 1956 Chevrolet Model 1502 2-Door Sedan appearing the same as the Model 1512 Utility Sedan at least as far as its exterior is concerned. The 2-Door Sedan drew 82,384 customers for $1,925. It weighed 3144 pounds while the Utility Sedan, weighing 3107 pounds, had a production run of only 9,879 units built. Its delivered price as a 6-cylinder car was $1,833. The Utility Sedan basically was a three-passenger car with a large capacity area where normally a back seat was employed in the 2-Door Sedan.

The 1956 "150" Series 2-Door Wagon commonly called Model 1529 Handyman. The popularity of this model wasn't overpowering, as it could be ordered for only a few dollars more in the "210" lineup. However, for those choosing it, it was available for $2,270 weighing 3,289 pounds. The production amounted to 13,487 units. Most noticeable trim difference between it and a "210" model was the absence of body stainless trim on the rear quarter panel.

Coming back in popularity after losing it for a couple of seasons to the Bel Air line is this Model 2103 "210" 4-Door Sedan. It had a production of 283,125 vehicles for the year. The two-tone paint that this example wears cost an additional $68.00 and most customers preferred it.

Here, again, take your pick. This example could be either a "210" 2-Door Sedan Model 2102, or it might be a "210" Delray Club Coupe Model 2124. As stated in the past two chapters, the 1954-1955 2-Door models in the "210" line were exactly the same exterior-wise. As a 2-Door Sedan, this unit sold for $2,011, weighed 3157 pounds and found 205,545 customers. As a Delray example the car delivered for $2,070, weighed 3162 pounds and found 56,382 homes. Proving again not to be as popular as the 2-Door Sedan.

Many trim changes were employed in addition to the new grille styling which made an enhancement in all models. The wheelbase remained 115 inches, while the wagons grew 3.7 inches overall to 200.8 inches. The remaining models increased only 1.9 inches to an overall length of 197.5 inches.

Each series, "150," "210," and Bel Air, had their own distinctive trim differences for instant identification. The 150 cars had a single bar running from the headlight area going halfway into the rear door of the Sedans or halfway into the rear quarter panel on 2-door vehicles. The 210 cars saw the trim molding going the full length from front fender edge to the rear bumper going in a sloping fashion. Both 150 and 210 cars had the Chevrolet nameplate placed at the upper level of the rear quarter panel. On Bel Air models, the trim consisted of a double bar of stainless trim beginning at the front edge of the front fender with the lower molding continuing downward to meet the edge of the rear bumper. Most models came with the contrasting paint leading from the trunk and rear quarter panel into the narrow front portion of front fenders. Bel Air cars had the nameplate affixed to the upper rear quarter panel.

Engine-wise, the V-8 models continued with the same 265 cubic-inch engine that 1955 cars offered. The standard transmission cars developed a 162 horsepower at 4400 R.P.M., with an 8:1 compression ratio. If the owner chose the Powerglide transmission the horsepower was raised to 170 at the same R.P.M.. Also available was the Power Pak option which consisted of dual exhausts, dual 4-barrel carburetor and a 9:25 compression ratio. The engine then developed 205 horsepower at 4600 R.P.M.

Seen now for its second year in this 1955 to 1957 body style is Model 2154 "210" Hardtop Sport Coupe. This example shows less chrome trim than its brother, the Bel Air Sport Coupe. The main differences were lack of Bel Air wheel covers, no clock, rubber floor carpeting, and upholstery not as luxurious as seen in the top-of-the-line cars. It delivered for $2,162 weighed 3184 pounds and found 18,616 customers.

The companion car to the "210" Sport Coupe was this "210" Sport Sedan which made its debut for the first time. It was referred to as Model 2113 seeing a production run of only 20,021 units. The vehicle weighed 3242 pounds and sold for $2,216. As a "six", it was $99.00 less.

The 1956 Model 2109 was a "210" 4-Door Station Wagon. This model was a six-passenger and was the most popular model wagon Chevrolet built for 1956. A total of 113,656 were produced at $2,362. This example weighed 3361 pounds. It was also another one of those models that, when looking at it from the outside, was exactly the same as a similar body style. In this case, it was the Beauville Model 2119 nine-passenger wagon which drew only 17,988 customers. It weighed in at 3480 pounds.

Playing a game of competition with its cousin the "210" 4-Door Sedan, again for the popularity race, was this 2403 Bel Air 4-Door Sedan. With a production of 269,798 units delivered, the second place for popularity was given to this model. The Bel Air Sedan weighed 3211 pounds and sold for $2,167.

As for the faithful 6-cylinder models, the 235.5 cubic-inch displacement now had a compression ratio of 8:1 with a developed horsepower of 140 at 4200 R.P.M. The Powerglide transmission in both 6 and V-8 cars was an additional $189. If the customer was more economy minded and preferred an Overdrive transmission, it cost him an extra $108.

The 1956 Bel Air Beauville 4-Door Station Wagon Model 2419 saw even fewer produced than the Beauville in the "210" Series. A total of 13,279 were built at a price of $2,581. This unit weighed in at 3496 pounds. There was no six-passenger 4-Door Wagon offered in the Bel Air line for 1956.

This would be the final year for 15-inch rims for Chevrolet in the 1950 era. All cars came with 6:70 x 15 inch tires. The regular 4-ply tires were used on all models except for the nine-passenger station wagons which employed 6-ply tires.

Chevrolet's new model, the 4-Door hardtop, was available in both the 210 and Bel Air line. The style wasn't a huge success in the 210 series with only 20,021 units produced, however, it was an instant success in the Bel Air line with 103,602 manufactured. If a person was looking for a 4-door with a sportier design, this was the answer. With all the windows in the down position, this made a sharp looking Sedan. The 210 cars were referred to as Model 2113, and Bel Airs were classed as Model 2413.

The 1956 Corvette did not appear with the regular line of cars. It was an early 1956 introduction coming only as a V-8. The overall length was 168 inches, the wheelbase measured 102 inches. You still knew it was a Corvette, even though revisions had been made. Most noticeable was the roll-up windows and the then to become popular concave side panels. The removable hardtop could be purchased for an additional $200 and a power operated unit could be purchased for an extra $100 on soft top versions. All Corvettes came with the standard V-8 of 210 horsepower at 5200 R.P.M. The compression ratio was 9:25 to 1. If a customer desired, he could order the 225 horsepower engine with dual 4-barrel carburetors for an additional $160.00.

Color combinations bloomed aplenty for the first time on Corvettes. Available were the traditional white and, in addition to this, were black, red, blue, turquoise, green and copper. The fender panel insert could be ordered with a contrasting color such as silver or beige, to name just a couple. Interior choices

Seen here is my 1956 Bel Air Hardtop Sport Coupe which was discussed in the text. This was one of 128,382 units produced. The fender skirts were nice looking items, but not considered part of Chevrolet's factory accessories as many people are led to believe.

were either red or beige, depending on the exterior color. Top material was a choice of white, black, or beige, again depending on the exterior color. Corvette production for 1956 amounted to only 3,467 units, and the vehicle sold for $3,149. Sales were down partially due to late year introduction. In the long run, however, it was beneficial because of their production, it has become a highly collectable car, today.

Chevrolet's production figures for 1956 were 1,574,740 units for the model run which, again, helped them hold the number one sales position.

A clean, frontal appearance is what the 1956 models had to offer as this example portrays the neat two-tone paint arrangement was accepted by nearly everyone. It has been stated that the 1956 cars with this paint treatment gave the appearance of a look of motion while standing still. The Bel Air Sport Coupe had a base price of $2,275 and weighed in at 3212 pounds.

A beautiful Model 2434, Bel Air Convertible had a production run of 41,268 units sold for $2,443 per copy. I always felt the forward spear-like setting of the side panels was one of Chevrolet's most desirable looking cars.

This was the car which changed my whole lifestyle, at that time. It's the 1956 Bel Air Sedan which caused the accident in which I was involved. Still, I've always liked the crisp lines of the 1956 models and have owned four of them at different times.

New for the year and an instant success was the Bel Air 4-Door Sport Sedan. This model weighed 3260 pounds and sold for $2,329. The year saw 103,002 units delivered to proud customers.

A real look of spaciousness and airiness was what the new Sport Sedan tried to convey. They surely succeeded, too, with the lack of a pillar.

Close-up views of the two 1956 Chevrolets, in passing, furnish testimony to the vehicle's clean lines. Note how the bolder grille and lamp treatment tend to lower the model's appearance.

Chevrolet introduced its lineup of 1956 cars to the public on Friday, November 4, 1955. Newspapers announced the new cars to be more rugged than ever, offering a lower longer look. New colors unique two-toning and tasteful interiors gave each series its own marque of distinction. Note how in the above photo the front end has a fleeter look. The grille, bumpers, guards, headlamps and ornamentation are of a new design.

As a single-tone car, the 1956 Bel Air Sport Sedan doesn't have quite the appeal that was offered on the two-tone models. This would be the final year for the 6.70 x 15-inch tires to be seen on Chevrolets.

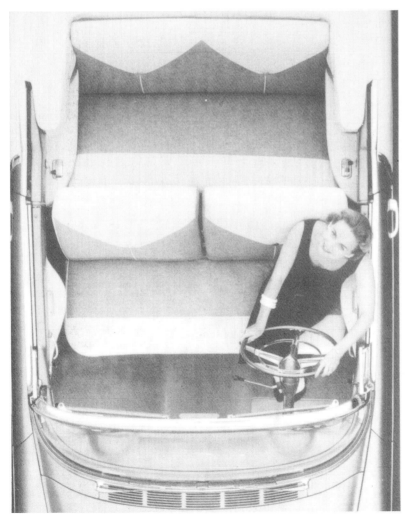

A view of the 1956 Convertible interior styling presented a tasteful combination of ribbed fabric and leather grained vinyl with vinyl welting and plastic silver buttons.

"210" conventional models, Sport Sedans as well as Sport Coupes sparkled with starry frosted bolsters and ribbed pattern cloth done in nylon.

Boy, how well I remember cars at the Los Angeles Zone Office decked out like this. All the accessories you could get on a car was generally the story. This was the way Parts and Accessories Reps and Zone District Managers got rid of their allotted merchandise.

Hello 1956 Owners . . .

Christmas is coming, which means gift buying for the family and friends. We believe we can be of help to 1956 Chevrolet owners because we have some very attractive 1956 Accessories left in stock.

Most merchants would have an after-Christmas Bargain Sale, but we're going to be different and have ours before Christmas. We are offering 1956 Chevrolet owners these attractive accessories at greatly reduced prices—accessories that will add to your driving pleasure.

Pictured are a few examples of these accessories. These and other items are available in a price range that fits every purse. Each has a useful purpose that the whole family can enjoy.

Please accept our invitation to make our dealership headquarters for all your automotive needs.

P.S.   The early shopper, like the early bird, has the widest range of choice.

EXHAUST EXTENSION—Durable chrome exhaust extension deflects fumes from rear bumper and painted metal . . . adds a smart look to tail pipe . . . prevents hard-to-remove exhaust dirt on rear end of your Chevrolet.

WAS $3.25   NOW $1.95

FRONT FENDER AND GRILLE GUARD—The front fender and grille guard will give your Chevrolet the new look. Heavy-gauge chromed steel will protect your front end (one dented fender or damaged grille costs more than guard), and add styling and front end insurance to your '56 Chevrolet.

WAS $39.80   NOW $18.50

WIRE WHEEL COVERS—High luster chrome wire wheel covers which give the running wheels the wire wheel look. . . . Usable on all models . . . good buy for any smart-looking Chevrolet.

WAS $39.50   NOW $19.90

WHEEL CARRIER—A wheel carrier that gives your Chevrolet a continental sports car look . . . this eye catcher also gives additional trunk space . . . can be operated by any member of the family . . . fits all passenger car models except Corvette.

WAS $123.00 NOW $84.50

This folder sheet I've had in my literature collection ever since 1956. I get a kick out of the way dealers who were overstocked with accessories were trying desperately to dispose of them. Look at some of those prices. A 1956 Continental Kit reduced in price to $84.50, and wire wheel covers discounted to $19.90. Wouldn't we like to have a few sets of N.O.S. pieces lying around the garage today?

Chevrolet was in the fleet business like always to police departments, large corporations, taxi companies, etc. Here is an example often chosen by taxi companies. This is a "210" 4-Door Sedan. engine choices were both 6-cylinder or V-8. For economical reasons, the 6 seemed to be the choice of most taxi companies. Note the absence of the "V" emblem on the hood of this unit tells us the 6-cylinder engine is used.

A completely restyled Corvette made its debut in early 1956. Features of the new model included a power operated top to the most powerful (225 H.P.) engine built thus far by Chevrolet. The new model offered this top as an option bit of equipment. Also available was a floor-mounted manual shift for those preferring this type of transmission to the regular automatic Powerglide.

A Chevrolet Bel Air Convertible is displayed with a unique geared mechanism which tilted the vehicle to a full 90-degree angle in either direction. This display was featured at the 1956 Chicago Auto Show. The young lasses in the car are considered Community Queens of the show from outlying cities of Chicago.

The first 24 Corvettes to reach the San Francisco area. These units were shipped to the Bay Area for the 1956 Motorama in San Francisco. These vehicles here are displayed with dealers behind the wheel who took the mass delivery of the first units and drove them to the courtyard of California's Palace of the Legion of Honor.

The first Impala to make the scene was the experimental five-passenger 2-Door Sedan seen at Motoramas in 1956. Features of the two-toned blue dream car consisted of molded styling lines using chrome sparingly. Interior padding was designed with special safety and comfort. The vehicle was devoid of center side pillars. The vehicle was 6 inches lower and 4 1/2 inches longer than a regular 1956 Model. The front seats were on a sliding rack. The engine compartment claimed a 225 horsepower V-8 with a 9.25 to 1 compression ratio four barrel carburetor with twin exhausts. The 116.5-inch wheelbase car had an overall length of 202 inches.

Another Motorama Show car for 1956 came as this Biscayne 4-Door Sedan. The vehicle came with a fiberglass body for light-weightedness, and a stratospheric windshield swept over the driver's head to form part of the roof. The upper portion of glass was tinted to help defray glare from the roof line. Projectile front fenders incorporated the parking lamps with the grille being part of the front bumper. Concave panels on the body sides permitted the use of trim profile light doors. The engine that was used was an experimental V-8, developing 215 horsepower with dual exhausts and four barrel carburetor, and the transmission was Powerglide. The name "Biscayne" was used two years later to replace the "210" series of cars which was adopted in 1953.

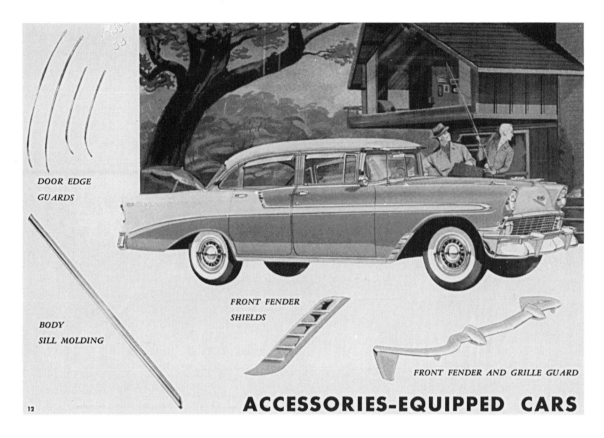

DOOR EDGE
GUARDS

BODY
SILL MOLDING

FRONT FENDER
SHIELDS

FRONT FENDER AND GRILLE GUARD

ACCESSORIES-EQUIPPED CARS

12

A couple of views of an artist's conception of well-dressed 1956 models. On the top is a Bel Air Sedan, and on the bottom is a rear view of a Bel Air Sport Coupe with all but the "kitchen sink".

FRONT FENDER
TOP MOLDING

DOOR
HANDLE SHIELDS

EXHAUST
EXTENSION

REAR FENDER GUARDS

ADD MORE *pleasure* **TO LIVING**

13

Chevrolet Accessories For 1956

DEALER LIST AND NET PRICE SCHEDULE

Effective February 1, 1956

ALL PRICES SUBJECT TO CHANGE WITHOUT NOTICE

The "List Prices" shown in this schedule are
suggested prices for sales to consumers.

PASSENGER CAR SECTION

Description	Part No.	Part No. Per Pkg.	Suggested List Price	Dealer Net
ADAPTER-Rear Fender Antenna	987449	1	3.50	2.10
ADAPTER UNIT-Seat Belt (Corvette)	987492	1	3.95	2.37
AIR CONDITIONER ONLY (For cars w/Dlx. Heaters) 8 Cyl.	987494		405.00	307.80
AIR CONDITIONER Complete 8 Cylinder	987534		425.00	323.00
AIR CONDITIONER ONLY (For cars not to be equipped with Heaters) 8 Cylinder	987496		410.00	311.00
AIR CONDITIONER ONLY (For cars w/Dlx. Heaters) 6 Cyl.	987495			
AIR CONDITIONER ONLY (Complete) 6 Cylinder	987535			
AIR CONDITIONER ONLY (For cars not to be equipped with Heaters) 6 Cylinder	987497			
HEATER DELUXE, DEFROSTER & OUTLET (For use with Air Conditioner 987497 and 987496)	987536			
ANTENNA-Fender Type R.H.	987100	1	6.35	3.81
AUTOMATIC HEADLAMP CONTROL (Autronic Eye)	987310	1	44.25	33.19
BELT-Seat	987480	1	10.95	6.57
BLADE-Windshield Wiper-Self De-Icing	986882	12	1.65 ea.	.99 ea.
BLOCK-Wiring Junction	987419	1	2.85	1.71
BRACKET-R.H. Safetylight	987328	1	2.45	1.47
BRAKE UNIT-Power	987260	56-55-P.All	47.50	28.50
BRAKE UNIT-Power	987215	54-53-Pass	47.50	28.50
BRAKE UNIT-Power	987214	52-51-Pass	47.50	28.50
CAP-Locking gasoline tank	987347	1	2.90	1.74
CARRIER-Wheel-Continental	987327	1	123.00	79.95
CARRIER-Wheel-Continental-Pacific Coast only	987352	1	131.00	85.15
CLOCK-Electric	987372 or 987468	1	17.65	10.59
COMPASS-Illuminated	987137 or 987473	1	5.95	3.57
COVER-Seat-Fiber	All	Set	29.95	17.97
COVER-Seat-Nylon	All	Set	42.50	25.50
COVER-Seat-Plastic	All	Set	39.95	23.95
COVER-Seat-Terry Cloth 2 door-3 Sets-1 each				
Blue, Green, Yellow	987506	3		
COVER-Seat-Terry Cloth 4 door-3 Sets-1 each				
Blue, Green, Yellow	987507	3		
COVER-Glamour Slide-Nylon	All	Set	19.90	11.94
COVER-Accelerator Pedal	987107	6	1.17 ea.	.70 ea.
COVER-Wheel Disc-15" Wheel Set of 4	987361	1	19.00	12.35
COVER-Wheel Disc-15" Wheel Set of 4	987268	1	--	4.60
COVER-Full Wheel-Set of 4	987353	1	15.95	10.37
COVER-Wire Wheel	987463	1	39.50	23.70
DISPENSER-Auto Tissue	987348	1	3.95	2.37

EXTENSION-Exhaust	987116	1	3.25	1.95
FILTER UNIT-Gasoline All Exc (3400, 3500, 3700)	987500	1	2.35	1.41
FRAME-License	987359	1	4.50	2.70
GLARESHADE-W/S-2D. Station Wagon Sport Coupe	987139	2	8.00 ea.	4.80 ea.
GLARESHADE-W/S-All Sedans	987115	3	8.00 ea.	4.80 ea.
GUARD-Front Fender and Grille	987351	1	39.80	23.88
GUARD-Rear Fender	987329	1	10.90	6.54
GUARD-Door Edge-4 Door	987411	3	6.25 ea.	3.75 ea.
GUARD-Door Edge-2 Door	987129	3	3.45 ea.	2.07 ea.
GUARD-Door Edge-Sport Coupe & Convertible	987130	3	3.45 ea.	2.07 ea.
GUARD-Door Edge-Sport Sedan	987339	3	6.25 ea.	3.75 ea.
HARNESS SHOULDER (To be used with 987480 Seat Belt)	987491	1	9.50	5.70
HEATER & DEFROSTER-Recirculating	987413	1	42.00	29.40
HEATER & DEFROSTER-Deluxe	987415	1	65.00	45.50
HORN UNIT-Vibrator	987490	1	7.90	4.74
KIT-Tool	987322	1	3.10	2.07
KOOL KOOSHION-Blue	987370	6	4.40 ea.	2.64 ea.
KOOL KOOSHION-Green & White	987452	6	4.40 ea.	2.64 ea.
LAMP-Back-up-All	987360	1	6.25	3.75
LAMP-Courtesy	987136	1	2.75	1.65
LAMP-Luggage Compartment	987083	1	1.95	1.17
LAMP-Underhood	987442	1	1.95	1.17
LAMP-Glove Compartment	987436	1	1.10	.66
LIGHTER & LAMP-Cigarette	987337	1	3.25	1.95
MAT-Deluxe Contour-Black	987435	1 pr.	6.95	4.17
MAT-Deluxe Contour-Blue	987432	1 pr.	6.95	4.17
MAT-Deluxe Contour-Copper	987461	1 pr.	6.95	4.17
MAT-Deluxe Contour-Green	987434	1 pr.	6.95	4.17
MAT-Deluxe Contour-Red	987433	1 pr.	6.95	4.17
MAT-Deluxe Contour-Turquoise	987437	1 pr.	6.95	4.17
MAT-Rubber Floor-Blue	987206	6	1.75 ea.	1.05 ea.
MAT-Rubber Floor-Black	987209	6	1.75 ea.	1.05 ea.
MAT-Rubber Floor-Green	987208	6	1.75 ea.	1.05 ea.
MAT-Rubber Floor-Red	987207	6	1.75 ea.	1.05 ea.
MAT-Rubber Floor-Copper	987477	6	1.75 ea.	1.05 ea.
MAT-Rubber Floor-Turquoise	987478	6	1.75 ea.	1.05 ea.
MIRROR-Outside R.V. Body Mount	987460	1	4.35	2.61
MIRROR-Outside R.V. Remote Control	987220	1	6.95	4.17
MIRROR-Inside R.V. Non Glare	987338	1	4.50	2.70
MIRROR-Visor Vanity	986605	1	1.60	.96
MOULDING-Body Sill	987281	3	8.15	4.89
MOULDING-Front Fender Top	987362	1	5.85	3.51
RADIO & ANTENNA-Push Button	987369	1	85.00	51.00
RADIO & ANTENNA-Manual	987367	1	63.50	38.10
RADIO & ANTENNA-Signal Seeker	987365	1	105.00	68.25
RAISER-Automatic Top	987223	1	34.00	22.10
REST-Arm-Green	987335	1 pr.	9.50	5.70
REST-Arm-Black	987334	1 pr.	9.50	5.70
SAFETYLIGHT & MIRROR	987224	1	24.50	14.70
SCREEN-Radiator Insect	987350	1	.95	.57
SPOTLAMP-Hand Portable	987112	1	7.95	4.77
SHAVER-Electric A.C.-D.C. 12 Volt	987474	1	31.50	18.90
SIGNAL-Electric Parking Brake	987441	1	4.25	2.55
SHIELD-Door Handle	987204	1	2.80	1.68
SHIELD-Front Fender	987286	1	6.95	4.17
SPEAKER-Rear Seat	987363	1	12.00	7.20
VENTSHADE-2 Door Sedan	987136	1	8.75	5.25
VENTSHADE-4 Door Sedan	987135	1	8.75	5.25
VISOR-Outside-All Sedans & Station Wagons	987110	2	19.90 ea.	11.94 ea.

Description	Part No.	Part No. Per Pkg.	Suggested List Price	Dealer Net
VISOR-Outside-Sport Coupe	987111	2	19.90 ea.	11.94 ea.
VISOR-Outside-Sport Sedan	987444	2	19.90 ea.	11.94 ea.
VISOR-R.H. Sun Gold 1500 Series exc. 1508-29	987332	1	5.95	3.57
VISOR-R.H. Sun Gold used on 1508 & 1529	987333	1	5.95	3.57
VIEWER-Traffic Light	987273	1	2.90	1.74
WASHER-W/S Coordinated	987465	1	9.95	5.97
WASHER-W/S Foot Operated	987410	1	6.75	4.05

TRUCK AND COMMERCIAL SECTION

Description	Part No.	Part No. Per Pkg.	Suggested List Price	Dealer Net
ADAPTER-Radiator Grille Guard (8,000, 10,000)	987438	1	6.35	3.81
ANTENNA-Fender-Mounting	987188	1	7.25	4.35
BLADE-Windshield Wiper-Self De-Icing . . . . Same as Passenger				
BLOCK-Wiring Junction	987094-987455	1	1.90	1.14
BRACKET-Mirror-Inside-Rear View				
Used with 987338 Non Glare Mirror	987179 or 987481	1	1.55	.93
COVER-Seat-Fiber	987471	1	15.75	9.45
COVER-Wheel Disc Deluxe Do-Nut Type	987268	1		4.60
COMPASS-Illuminated . . . . Same as Passenger				
FLAP-Mud-Dual Wheel	987226	2 sets	9.90 set	5.94 set
BRACKET-Mud-Flap-Dual Wheel	987228	1	7.25	4.35
FLAP-Mud-Single Wheel	987227	2 sets	6.50 set	3.90 set
BRACKET-Mud Flap-Single Wheel	987229	1	6.80	4.08
BRACKET-Mud Flap-Single Wheel 1955-56	987516	1		
GUARD-Bumper-Commercial (Chrome)	987270	1	12.50	7.50
GUARD-Bumper-Commercial (Painted)	987177	1	9.70	5.82
GUARD-Bumper-Truck	987219	1	10.75	6.45
GUARD-Grille-Commercial-Brush Type	987212	1	35.00	21.00
GUARD-Grille-Truck -Brush Type	987213	1	37.00	22.20
GUARD-Door-Edge	987205	1	3.45	2.07
GUARD-Gas Tank Filler Door	987247	1	1.75	1.05
FILTER-Gasoline (Use with 8,000, 9,000, 10,000)	987500	1	2.35	1.41
HEATER & DEFROSTER-Deluxe	987216	1	68.50	42.47
HEATER & DEFROSTER-Recirculating	987218	1	43.50	26.10
HORN-High Note	987211	1	6.50	3.90
KIT-Tool . . . . Same as Passenger				
LIGHTER-Cigarette	987190	1	3.50	2.10
LAMP-Tail-R.H.	987202 or 987458	1	7.60	4.56
LAMP-Fog	987263	1	17.75	10.65
LAMP-Back-up	987225 or 987454	1	11.00	6.60
LAMP-Glove Compartment . . . . Same as Passenger				
LAMP-Underhood	987442	1	1.95	1.17
MIRROR-Deluxe Rear View, Full View (All Trucks)	987479	1	14.95	8.97
MIRROR-Outside-Rear-View-With Bracket	987230	1	7.75	4.65
MIRROR-Outside-Rear-View-Heat Only	987262	1	2.75	1.65
MIRROR-Inside-Rear-View-Non Glare . . . . Same as Passenger				
MATS-Rubber-Floor-6 Colors . . . . Same as Passenger				
ORNAMENT-Hood	987242	1	9.95	5.97
RADIO & ANTENNA-Manual	987189	1	69.50	41.70
REST-Arm (All Trucks exc 3124 & Deluxe Equipment)	987470	1	3.90	2.34
REFLECTOR-Red Reflex	985223	1	1.75	1.05
SAFETYLIGHT-With Mirror	987243	1	22.50	13.50
SCREEN-Radiator Insect . . . . Same as Passenger				
SHAVER-Electric AC-DC . . . . Same as Passenger				
SHIELD-Door-Handle	987245	1	2.95	1.77
SPOTLAMP-Hand-Portable . . . . Same as Passenger				
SIGNAL DIRECTION-Front-Single Face Rear-Bracket Mount	987238	1	24.50	14.70

Description	Part No.	Qty	List	Net
SIGNAL DIRECTION-Front-Double Face Rear-Bracket Mount	987239	1	26.50	15.90
SIGNAL DIRECTION-Front-Double Face Rear-Flush Mount	987240	1	26.50	15.90
SIGNAL DIRECTION-Front-Single Face Rear-Flush Mount	987241	1	24.50	14.70
SIGNAL DIRECTION-Pick-Up	987250 or 987457	1	19.50	11.70
SIGNAL DIRECTION-Panel	987251	1	26.50	15.90
SIGNAL DIRECTION-Deluxe Pick-Up	987252	1	18.50	11.10
SIGNAL UNIT-Double Face Direction "Class A" (Front Lamps and Switch Assy. Only)	987514	1		
SIGNAL UNIT-Single Face Direction "Class A" (Front Lamps and Switch Assy. Only)	987515	1		
SIGNAL-Parking, Brake	987237	1	4.75	2.85
STEP-Rear Platform	986980	1	9.50	5.70
TRAY UNIT-Utility (All Comm. Trucks)	987493	1		
VISOR-Sun-Outside-Metal	987182	1	14.90	8.94
VISOR-Sun-R.H.	987469	1	3.25	1.95
VENTSHADE	987203	1	5.25	3.15
VIEWER-Traffic-Light	Same as Passenger			
WASHER-Windshield	987459	1	6.75	4.05

1956 Service Accessories Section

Description	Part No.	Qty	List	Net
ANTI-FREEZE-W/S Washer-6-6-2 oz.				
Envelopes per Package	987462	6	7.50	4.50
(Package of 6-2 oz. Envelopes)			(1.25)	(.75)
ANTI-FREEZE-G.M. Permanent Type-Gal. Cans	986952	6	19.50	13.02
(Single Gallon)			(3.25)	(2.17)
ANTI-FREEZE-G.M. Permanent Type-Qt. Cans	986953	24	20.40	13.62
(Single Quart)			(.85)	(.568)
ANTI-FREEZE-G.M. Methanol Type-Gal. Cans	986954	6	9.60	6.42
(Single Gallon)			(1.60)	(1.07)
ANTI-FREEZE-G.M. Methanol Type-Qt. Cans	986955	24	10.32	6.84
(Single Quart)			(.43)	(.285)
ANTI-FREEZE-G.M. Methanol Type-54 Gal Dr.	986956	1	86.40	53.46
(Single Gallon)			(1.60)	(.99)
CAROMA EVAPORATOR-Unit	983715	12	3.60	2.16
(Single Unit)				
GLASS NU KIT (Consists of 1.24 oz. Glass Nu and 13" Felt Wheel)	987502	1	--	17.25
CLEANER-Cooling System	986052	12	12.00	7.20
(Single Can)			(1.00)	(.60)
CLEANER-White Side Wall Tire	987475	6	6.00	3.60
(Single Bottle)			(1.00)	(.60)
CLEANER-Leather-All	987476	6	6.00	3.60
(Single Bottle)			(1.00)	(.60)
CLOTH-Polishing	986077	12	9.00	5.40
(Single Polishing Cloth)			(.75)	(.45)
COMPOUND-Gasket Sealer-16 oz. Cans	987266	6	13.50	8.10
(Single Can)			(2.25)	(1.35)
DOOR-EASE-Stick Lubricant-Utility Size	986897	6	3.00	1.80
(Single Stick)			(.50)	(.30)
INHIBITOR-Corrosion-Cool. Sys-16 oz. Cans	986977	12	9.00	5.40
(Single Can)			(.75)	(.45)
KAR KLEEN-28 OZ. Cans	987456	6	12.00	7.20
LOCKEASE-Lubricant-4 oz. Cans	986434	12	6.00	3.60
(Single Can)			(.50)	(.30)
LUSTER SEAL #1-12 oz. Plastic Bottle	986945	12	40.20	24.00
(Single Bottle)			(3.35)	(2.00)
LUSTER SEAL #2-12 oz. Plastic Bottle	986946	12	40.20	24.00
(Single Bottle)			(3.35)	(2.00)
LUSTER SEAL #1 Machine-1 Gal. Can	987284	1	28.50	17.00
LUSTER SEAL #2 Machine-1 Gal. Can	987285	1	28.50	17.00

Description	Part No.	Qty	List	Net
LUSTER SEAL HAZE CREAM-8 oz Plastic Bottles	986947	24	24.00	14.40
(Single Bottle)			(1.00)	(.60)
MITT-ANGORA-Washing-Dusting	987269	12	19.80	11.88
(Single Unit)			(1.65)	(.99)
OIL-Dripless Penetrating-4 oz. Cans	986082	36	9.00	4.68
(Single Can)			(.25)	(.13)
POLISH-Chromium-8 oz. Cans	98608	12	6.00	3.60
(Single Can)			(.50)	(.30)
POLISH-Triple Action-16 oz. Cans	986085	12	12.00	7.20
(Single Cans)			(1.00)	(.60)
POLISH-Triple Action-Gallon	985888	1	4.00	2.40
PORCELAINIZE-Liquid-8 oz. Bottles	986175	24	105.60	60.00
(Single Bottle)			(4.40)	(2.50)
PORCELAINIZE-Wash Cream-8 oz. Bottles	986176	24	14.40	8.64
(Single Bottle)			(.60)	(.36)
PORCELAINIZE-Cleaner-Gallon Can	986363	1	No List	4.75
PORCELAINIZE-Fastac-8 oz. Bottles	986961	24	30.00	18.00
(Single Bottle)			(1.25)	(.75)
PLASTIC SOLDER Repair Kit	987511	1		
RESIN KIT	987341	1	No List	21.50
CLOTH-Fiberglass-3-1/2 Yds.	987342	2	No List	6.65
RESIN-2 lb. Can	987343	1	No List	5.25
HARDENER-1 lb. Can	987344	1	No List	2.75
FILLER-1/2 lb. Can	987345	1	No List	1.15
FIBERGLASS-Chopped, Roving-1/2 lb.	987346	1	No List	1.70
KERODEX-#55 1 lb. Jar-Hand Cream	987447	1	No List	2.65
KERODEX-#71-1 lb. Jar-Hand Cream	987448	1	No List	2.65
RUGLYDE-Rubber Lubricant & Cleaner-Gal. Can	986047	1	3.60	2.15
RUGLYDE KIT-(1 Service Kit 2-1 gal. cans)	987340	1	No List	7.60
SEALZIT-Glass Sealer-2 oz. Bottles	986199	12	10.20	6.12
(Single Bottle)			(.85)	(.51)
SPOT REMOVER-8 oz. Cans	987272	12	9.00	5.40
(Single Can)			(.75)	(.45)
STOPLEAK-Radiator-10 oz. Cans	986088	12	9.00	5.40
(Single Can)			(.75)	(.45)
TIPON TOUCH-UP PAINT-1956-55-54-53				
Chevrolet Colors-Dealers Choice of (6)	987261	6	6.00	3.60
(Single Tube)			(1.00)	(.60)
TIPON TOUCH-UP PAINT-1955 Chevrolet Truck				
32 Assorted Colors	987321	32	32.00	19.20
UPHOLSTERY TINT (Used Cars) Blue (1 Pkg. of 2, 2 oz. env.)	987482	1	No List	1.40
UPHOLSTERY TINT (Used Cars) Green (1 Pkg. of 2, 2 oz. env.)	987483	1	No List	1.40
UPHOLSTERY TINT (Used Cars) Taupe (1 Pkg. of 2, 2 oz. env.)	987484	1	No List	1.40
UPHOLSTERY TINT (used Cars) Brown (1 Pkg. of 2, 2 oz. env.)	987485	1	No List	1.40
UPHOLSTERY TINT (Used Cars) Grey (1 Pkg. of 2, 2 oz. env.)	987486	1	No List	1.40
UPHOLSTERY TINT (Used Cars) Yellow (1 Pkg. of 2, 2 oz. env.)	987487	1	No List	1.40
UPHOLSTERY TINT (Used Cars) Turquoise (1 Pkg. of 2, 2 oz. env.)	987488	1	No List	1.40
UPHOLSTERY TINT (Used Cars) Red (1 Pkg. of 2, 2 oz. env.)	987489	1	No List	1.40
UNDERCOATING-Drum	986359	1	No List	42.75
UNDERCOATING-Truckload	986653	44	No List	1606.00
UNDERCOATING-Carload	986548	80	No List	2760.00
PACIFIC COAST ONLY:				
UNDERCOATING-Drum	986635	1	No List	42.75
UNDERCOATING-Truckload	986654	44	No List	1606.00
UNDERCOATING-Carload	986638	80	No List	2760.00

A pair of 1956 Chevrolet Bel Air Sport Coupes that I owned at the same time. The one on the left is the famous "goof car", as I called it when I mentioned in the text how it employed the 6-cylinder engine. The other was an Inca Silver India Ivory Bel Air Sport Coupe equipped with the 265 cubic-inch V-8. Actually, the 6-cylinder car was a far better machine than this V-8 unit.

The late Tom McCahill took this 1956 Chevy 150 2-Door Sedan on one of his famous road tests back when new and gave it top honors agreeing with the slogan, "The Hot One is Even Hotter," and that the '56 Chevy design had "clicked with the public." He felt the V-8 engine was the best in the U.S., to that date.

A close-up shot of the Continental Kit on the Bel Air vehicle. Today these units bring big bucks, especially if you find a N.O.S. piece. The part number was 987327 and carried a retail price of $123.00 but, for some strange reason in California, carried a price of $131.00 and was available under part number 987352.

The Continental Wheel Carrier. A wheel carrier that gave Chevrolet a continental sports car look.

Gave additional trunk space and did not interfere with jacking-up the car.

Sturdy, rattle free, and could be operated by anyone.

THREE GREAT ENGINES...

Two V8's ... and a husky Six

Top:
205-H.P. "Super Turbo-Fire V8"

Middle:
170-H.P. "Turbo-Fire V8"

Bottom:
140-H.P. "Blue-Flame 140"

The magnificent heart of every Chevrolet was its engine - and for 1956 you could choose from three of the most brilliant and advanced powerplants ever created.

There was the ultra-compact 170-h.p. "Turbo-Fire V8" (162-h.p. with SynchroMesh or Overdrive) that set the standard for all V8's in its field ... its performance mate, the astonishing 205-h.p. "Super Turbo-Fire V8" with four-barrel carburetor and dual exhausts ... and, for supreme economy and durability, Chevrolet created the new 140-h.p. "Blue Flame 140" the pinnacle of more than a quarter-century's experience building valve-in-head six-cylinder engines.

full of spunk...

but beautifully behaved . . . the '57 Chevy!

It doesn't just <u>look</u> sweet, smooth and sassy . . . it is! And you get sports car control behind the wheel . . . a solid, sure-footed feel on the road, smooth and easy response to every command.

That's why you get more of a lift out of driving a '57 Chevy. Its pep and easy handling make it fun. Safer, too. It's spacious inside, daring in design outside. But still it's a stickler for tradition, and in the grand Chevrolet manner it's known to be as trouble-free as that totem pole!

Drive a new Chevy, one with the exact power you prefer (h.p. goes up to 245*). With triple-turbine Turboglide, too, the newest and smoothest of all automatic drives (an extra-cost option). Your dealer will gladly arrange it. . . . Chevrolet Division of General Motors, Detroit 2, Michigan.

CHEVROLET

1 USA
'57 CHEVROLET

270-h.p. high-performance V8 also available at extra cost. Also Ramjet fuel injection engines with up to 283 h.p.

The new Bel Air 2-Door Sedan with Body by Fisher—one of 20 new Chevrolets.

Similar to the 210 4-Door Sport Sedan in lack of popularity was this 210 2-Door Hardtop, commonly known as the 210 Sport Coupe. A total of only 22,631 were manufactured for the year. The vehicle weighed 3256 pounds and, equipped with a 6-cylinder engine, sold for $2,204. If the V-8 were installed, it went home for $2,304. The main external differences, between this model and the Bel Air Sport Coupe, were lack of rocker molding trim, full wheel covers, gold trim nameplates, and gold insert grilled bars.

Chevrolet for 1957

The year everyone looks back on as being "The year for Chevrolet." It emphasized this as the car that was "Sweet, Smooth and Sassy." Actually, with all the fanfare, 1957 wasn't all that great of a year for Chevrolet sales. Possibly it was two great years preceding this that flooded the market, and also this was a facelift year at Chevrolet that kept many potential buyers from wanting to purchase a body style that was now in its third year. One more big deterrent was that those, who were not truly loyal to the make, chose Ford and Plymouth who offered new clean lines for 1957. I recall, when I purchased a 1958 Impala in the spring of 1958, that our local dealer in Pasadena, California had 1957s coming out his ear. They just couldn't get rid of them. He was selling brand new 1957s for under $2500. I purchased a new 1957 Bel Air Sport Coupe in the fall of 1956 while working for the Los Angeles Zone Office. Try and get rid of it at the end of 1957 without taking a big loss. The only person out there to take it off my hands was my sister, as she needed a car. I recall telling her whatever

137

The lowest-priced 1957 Chevrolet was this example, a Series 150 2-Door Sedan, Model 1502, delivering for $2,096. Most of this style were 6-cylinder vehicles with a production run of 70,774 units for the model run.

the price tag was on a used '57 Sport Coupe that we looked at, just for comparison sake, I'd sell her my car without interest being due. We agreed on $2,395. Wouldn't it be nice to find a '57 with only 6000 miles on it, today for that figure?

In the previous chapter, I expressed my feelings for the 1956 cars. I felt that, as long as the 1957s weren't in for major changes, it would appear almost the same as the '56 model.

This particular car saw many stock car events during the year which helped Chevrolet's image for the season. It, however, carried the V-8 power plant with fuel injection. This Model 1512, or its near look-alike, were the examples more often used for general track competition.

Shown here is the least expensive 4-Door Chevrolet produced in 1957. The 3232-pound car sold for $2,048 if equipped with its dependable 6-cylinder engine. If a V-8 were chosen, it sold for $100 additional. A good percentage of 150 models came with the two-tone paint combination which did help its overall appearance. Chevrolet produced 52,266 of this model. Very few are seen today.

When all Zone employees attended the dealer and factory new car showing at the Long Beach Auditorium on September 12, 1956, I was truly disappointed. Knowing I wanted a new car and there wasn't any reason to look for a new leftover 1956, since I was in a position to purchase the 1957 at dealer cost, it only made sense that the 1957 was the way to go. About the only thing I truly liked was the turquoise and white color combination. When they unveiled the Sport Coupe, the band played, "See the U.S.A. in your Chevrolet . . ." A great

The 150 Handyman 2-Door Wagon, classed as Model 1529, delivered for $2,407 and weighed 3402 pounds. The model wasn't received as well as the 210 versions and only 14,740 saw production for the model run.

A 1957 Chevrolet 210 2-Door Sedan equipped with Bel Air wheel covers and the accessory bumper guard equipment is being put through the paces as seen in these photos.

Chevy called it a bounce curve as it took the tightest turns with ease. The Glide Ride front suspension cushions the shocks and outrigger springs provided that extra margin of stability for better safety. In this second photo, Chevy stole the show in a star-pattern cornering event. Ball-Race steering, which was exclusive for Chevy in its class, made it easy for obstacles that spelled trouble for cars even in a higher price range.

A 1957 Chevrolet that really didn't get to the streets. I recall seeing only one of these in Las Vegas in November 1956 at the Community Chevrolet Agency. The 210 4-Door Sedan, in Dusk Pearl and India Ivory, was having the side trim replaced with the correct stainless moldings. It made the side appearance look much better than what had originally been planned.

applause was given by the true diehard dealers and salesmen. Later in the day, we all had the opportunity to view the model more closely. Even more disappointed when I looked inside and saw the black insert upholstery. Ugh! Then the bomb sights on the hood, small 14-inch wheels, and gold bits of trim all over the car. As a friend of mine said, shortly after I got my car, "It looks like rather than give a gold watch to those men who are retiring from Chevrolet, they let them have fun putting little gold 'do-dads' all over the body." It was a zinger hurt, but he was right. The 1957 models have grown on me through the years and I've owned four Sport Coupes at different times but, I must admit, there are other years I have preferred. So wait for the next chapter.

This '57 Sport Coupe, Model 2454 was purchased on November 17, 1956 from the Guaranty Chevrolet Company in Santa Ana, California. I paid $2,874 for it, on a two-year contract. It was basically a plain car, just to hold the price down. The vehicle was equipped with Powerglide, Wonderbar radio, recirculating heater, E-Z Eye Glass whitewalls, bumper guards and side view mirror. When my sister bought it from me, she put skirts on it, which really added to the appearance. These were after-market items, as Chevrolet did not offer skirts on their cars at this time.

On April 20, 1957, I was involved in a very serious auto accident, which I briefly mentioned in the introduction of this book. So for a time, the 1957 Bel Air Sport Coupe saw little action. It really wasn't until the time that my sister owned the car that I began to appreciate it. Then she sold it and, for a few years, I kept in contact with the couple who owned it. One day, the wife telephoned me and asked if I was interested in purchasing the car from her. It had deteriorated and, now with over 80,000 miles on it, I decided against it. I'm sure that, by today, it's been recycled into some other form of steel.

The final decision of what the 1957 210 4-Door Sedan, Model 2103 finally appeared with that extra piece of quarter panel stainless. Most models coming as a two-tone vehicle saw a rear quarter panel with a color the same as the roof. This example was the most popular car for Chevrolet in 1957 seeing 260,401 units delivered. The sedan weighed 3,266 pounds and sold for $2,275.

Now, for the actual 1957 cars in general.

As stated above, I wasn't a big booster of the 1957 design but, engine-wise, they were one of the best. If a person still preferred the 6-cylinder engine for its dependability and economy, the Blue Flame Six was ready, willing and able, and it developed 140 horsepower from the 235 cubic-inch engine. The compression ratio was 8.0:1. The carburetor consisted of a single barrel set up. The buyer had his choice of Powerglide, Overdrive, or the regular 3-speed synchromesh transmission. The newly introduced Turboglide transmission was not available in 6-cylinder cars. The engines available in V-8 fashion consisted of the Turbo-Fire 265 cubic-inch which developed 162 horsepower at 4400 R.P.M. This engine was available only in Overdrive and Standard 3-speed synchromesh driven cars. Probably the most popular V-8 for 1957 came as the 283 cubic-inch version the developed 185 horsepower. The transmission choices were either Powerglide (the more popular) or Turboglide. This engine came with 8.5:1 compression and used a 2-barrel carburetor. The 283 cubic-inch engine also came as a Super Turbo-Fire with 9.5:1 compression ratio with a single 4-barrel carburetor. This version offered 220 horsepower. These vehicles came equipped with dual exhausts. The buyer also had his choice of four transmissions: 3-speed Synchro-mesh, Overdrive, Powerglide or Turboglide. Chevrolet also offered the public an eye-opener of the 283 cubic inch engine that developed 283 horsepower. In other words, one horsepower per cubic inch! These units carried what was referred to as the "Ramjet" fuel injection. Basically, it was a bored out 265 cubic-inch engine. There was much written about this new set up back in 1957 but, as far as actual production, the units really didn't appear. Today, it seems strange to me where all of these fuel injection cars, supposedly true 1957 production units, have come from. Could some be merely doctored up versions recreated in someone's garage? I think so, and they are being passed off as true originals!

Not as popular a model as its deluxe sister, the Bel Air Sport Sedan, was this 210 4-Door Sport Sedan often referred to as a 4-Door Hardtop, or technically called Model 2113. A total of only 16,178 were produced for the year. this was the last year for this style in the middle range of Chevrolet vehicles.

This fuel-injection unit cost $675 extra for the purchaser, and very few ran as trouble-free cars. Mostly, the problems rested in the hands of the mechanics who weren't able to cope with these so-called "problem children." I recall the first one put into Zone use was driven all of three miles from a downtown Los Angeles dealership, to the Zone Office on Wilshire Boulevard in Los Angeles. The car absolutely quit on a busy downtown street! The language was rather blue from all who were trying to get this "turkey" to start. It probably took an act of Congress to get it moved off the street and towed to the dealership. The following week, the first of the Turboglide cars began to trickle into dealerships. All district managers were to start driving cars with this transmission and equipped with every conceivable accessory so they could push all this equipment on the parts departments for the public to purchase. In the first week these Turboglide cars were in service for the 12 district managers, four of them also quit running. Sitting at a signal, proudly waiting for the signal to turn green and, when it did, watch a sharp looking car just sit there. Embarrassing? I think so.

Another interesting item at this time were the number of sales that Chevrolet kept very close tabs on in their 10-day sales reports. Fearing that Ford would outsell them, we had more factory-owned cars put into use for no more than 30 days and those, in a position to obtain a new company car, would receive one. This way they were at least registering more cars to show a sales gain. There were really a lot of near new 1957s sitting on used car lots early in 1957.

It seemed, for 1957, the color choices weren't quite so garish as in the past two seasons. Maybe it was that two-tones were more subdued. Rather than the cap and deck paint schemes, the '57s if done as a two-tone, only saw the roof in a different color in all but the "150" Series. Some color choices also had now been around for awhile and there wasn't quite the appeal they offered earlier. The new colors in two tone for the year were Dusk Pearl, Canyon Coral and Coronado Yellow, while the remainder were hashed over, possibly with just a new name to a color seen before.

Looking basically the same as the Delray Coupe is this Model 2102 2-Door Sedan in strictly base form. It delivered for $2,222 and weighed 3221 pounds. Proving to be more popular than the Delray, it saw a run of 162,090 produced for the model run. Note: this example came equipped with its antenna mounted on the right rear quarter panel. Most saw the antenna placed on the front right fender.

Laurel Green
Adobe Beige
Sierra Gold
Colonial Cream
Highland Green
Surf Green
Tropical Turquoise
Larkspur Blue
Harbor Blue
Matador Red
Imperial Ivory
Inca Silver
Onyx Black

The two-tone combinations were as follows, with the first color choice denoting the roof color, while the second is for the bottom:

Imperial Ivory	Dusk Pearl
Colonial Cream	Laurel Green
India Ivory	Canyon Coral
India Ivory	Matador Red
Adobe Beige	Sierra Gold
India Ivory	Colonial Cream
Onyx Black	Colonial Cream
India Ivory	Coronado Yellow
India Ivory	Surf Green
Surf Green	Highland Green
India Ivory	Larkspur Blue
Larkspur Blue	Harbor Blue
India Ivory	Tropical Turquoise
Imperial Ivory	Inca Silver
Onyx Black	India Ivory

A total of 15 two-tone paint combinations and 13 single colors.

The Delray Coupe, as displayed here, delivered for $40 more than the 2-Door version. The only real differences in these two vehicles were the Delray vinyl interior and carpeted floors. It sold for $2,262 and weighed five pounds less than regular 2102 models coming in at 3216 pounds. A total of only 25,644 saw production for 1957.

As for the Corvette this year, it was basically the same offering that appeared in early 1956. Its standard V-8 engine was the Super Turbo-Fire 283 cubic-inch engine that developed 220 horsepower. It came with the 9.5:1 compression ratio and used the twin 4-barrel carburetor. Other versions were available such as the fuel-injected models. A total of six different 283 cubic-inch engines were available in the Corvettes for the year.

The 1957 nine-passenger Beauville Wagon, Model 2119 was available in 1957 only in the 210 Series of vehicles. The 3556-pound vehicle delivered for $2,663 to 21,083 customers. Looking exactly the same from the exterior was the six-passenger Townsmen, Model 2109 which weighed 3457 pounds, sold for $2,356 and saw a production run of 127,803 being produced. It was the most popular wagon Chevrolet produced in 1957.

The 1957 Bel Air Townsman Wagon was available only as a 6-passenger vehicle called Model 2409. The vehicle weighed 3456 pounds, the same as the Beauville nine-passenger wagon. It saw 27,375 units delivered for a base price of $2,680 equipped in V-8 fashion. The tailgate and liftgate units both opened, as this photo indicates, making for easy access to the rear compartment.

The model designation remained 2934 and a total of 6,339 saw production telling the world Corvette now was here to stay! The Corvette sold for $3,465 in base form. Optional equipment was available from the $675 fuel-injection unit previously mentioned for regular passenger cars to heavy duty racing suspension at $725. The Powerglide transmission was an additional $175; Positraction cost $45 more if the owner chose it, and the dual 4-barrel carburetors with a performance cam on the standard 283 cubic-inch engine could add an additional $170.

A very rare car today is the El Morocco which is basically a Chevrolet with a complete face lift to the point it resembles an El Dorado of that era. The El Morocco saw production of 20 vehicles in 1956 and 187 in 1957. The vehicles were produced by a Detroit promoter named Ruben Allender. In the fall of 1993, while attending the Carlisle and Hershey shows, I was privileged to see and drive the car of Wayne Hostetler of New Cumberland, Pennsylvania. The 2-Door Hardtop retailed for $4,386.00, as shown on page 158. It also came as a 4-door Hardtop and Convertible. All cars came equipped with the 283 Power Pak, Powerglide, Power Steering, and Power Brakes. When new, they carried a warranty covered by General Motors.

The 1957, models ranged in price from $1,885 for a "150" 2-door Utility Sedan that saw a production of only 8,300 vehicles, to the top of the line Nomad 2-door Wagon for $2,857 which had a production run of 6,103 cars for the year. Chevrolet sales for 1957 amounted to 1,515,177 for the model run. Figures this year are not completely clear. Some feel Ford outsold Chevy and true Chevrolet people, like myself, prefer to give the honor, once again, to Chevy. At any rate, the figures are close.

146

The sharpest-looking wagon from Chevrolet for 1957 was this 2-door version called the Nomad, Model 2429. The wagon carried a sparkle and distinction all its own. The unit weighed 3461 pounds and sold for $2,857, making it the company's most expensive car for the year. Sales weren't the greatest with only 6,103 being produced. The most noticeable mark of distinction, as had been for the previous two years, were the ribbed stainless bars on the Nomad's tailgate.

My original 1957 Bel Air Sport Coupe, shortly after delivery from Guaranty Chevrolet in Santa Ana, California. Incidentally, the company is still very much in business having moved only a few blocks down the street. As discussed in the text of this book, this car was later sold to my sister. She eventually sold it to someone else and, a few years later, I had an opportunity to buy it back. I decided against it, as the new owner had given it very hard usage.

This 1957 Sport Coupe was purchased several years ago trying to recapture the original turquoise and ivory Sport Coupe. This unit has been shown on the Automobile Quarterly poster and several Chevrolet publications, in past years.

Here is a factory press photo of a 1957 Bel Air Sport Coupe, Model 2454. In base form, the car weighed 3,274 pounds and sold for $2,399 to 166,426 customers. The 283 cubic-inch engine, which was the most popular choice with the public answered the "Sweet, Smooth and Sassy" slogan very well with the buyers. Note that this example wears the front 3-piece bumper.

Far more popular than Model 2113, 210 Sport Sedan, is Model 2413, Bel Air Sport Sedan. This example had a run of 137,672 built. It weighed 3336 pounds and delivered for $2,464. The lack of center door posts gave this vehicle a far more sporty look than the regular Bel Air Sedan Model 2403. Its roof line is lower than on regular sedan models.

For those desiring the look of a sportier car than a straight 4-Door Sedan, and not as costly as the Bel Air Sport Coupe was this Model 2402, Bel Air 2-Door Sedan. Sales were nowhere as great as with the Sport Coupe seeing only 62,751 manufactured. The vehicle weighed 3,228 pounds and sold for $2,338. All 1957 models came equipped with 7.50 x 14 inch tires, except for the Corvette which still employed 6.70 x 15 tires. The ribbed sheet of aluminum in the rear quarter panel was an exclusive Bel Air feature.

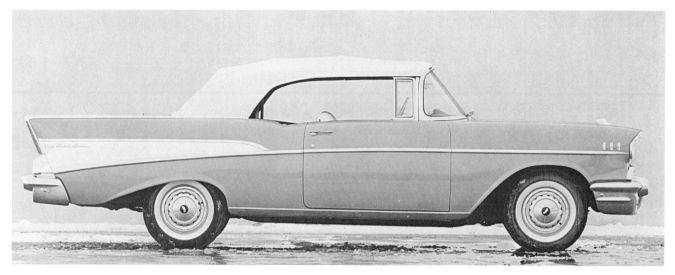

A 1957 Bel Air Convertible in the dead of winter with top in the up position. Rarely were press photos ever taken of a convertible with the top up. It just didn't show the vehicle off to its greatest expectation.

This is how convertibles should be photographed. Here sits a sharp Bel Air, Model 2413, better known as a Bel Air Convertible. The model year saw 47,562 units produced for $2,611 as a basic V-8. The vehicle weighed 3405 pounds. Convertible upholstery did not come with the black insert material, popular for 1957 Sport Coupe and Sport Sedans. A vinyl insert in an off-silver with contrasting vinyl seats matching the exterior of the vehicle, was used in the Convertible.

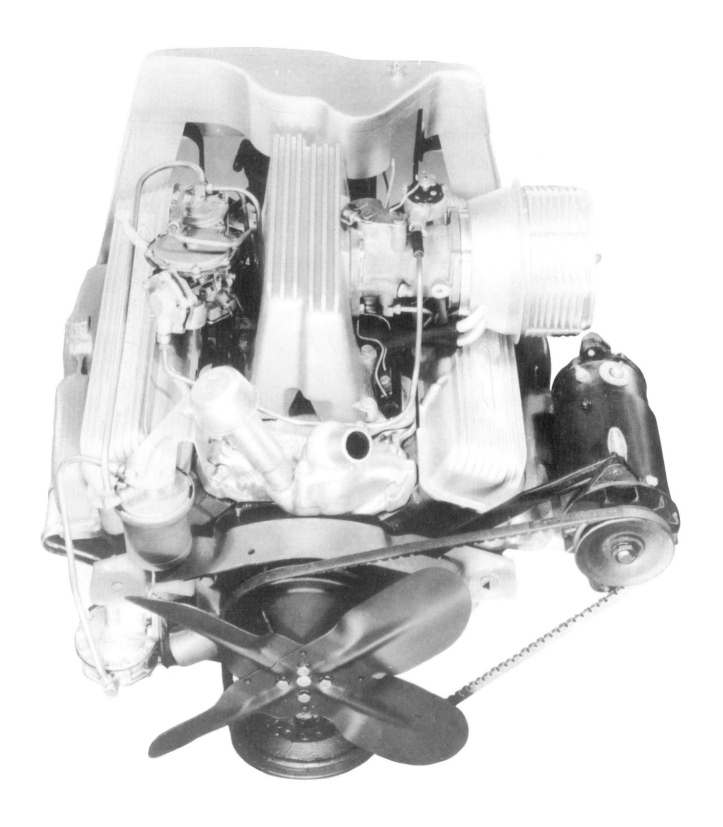

A view of the 1957 Chevrolet 283 cubic-inch engine coming as a fuel injected unit. The cost for this option was an additional $550.

A view of the newly-designed 1957 dashboard gives an uncluttered appearance. Chevrolet continued to use the idiot lights mounted next to the speedometer housing for the amps and oil-warning lights.

The 1957 2-Door Wagon in the 210 Series also referred to as a Handyman Model 2129 sold for $2,502. It weighed 3402 pounds and delivered to 17,528 customers. It, like other models in the wagon series, offered a folding rear seat making way for additional cargo.

Offered again as a model in the 150 Series was the Model 1508 Sedan Delivery. It saw a production run of only 7,273 units making it very desirable among collectors today. The vehicle weighed 3254 pounds and sold for $2,020 as a basic 6-cylinder.

The finished product as it is ready for final inspection sits this 150 model, 1502 or 1512. I wonder where this unit might be today? Is it in the hands of a collector or possibly has it been recycled? I hope not the latter.

DON'T JUST LOOK — *DRIVE IT!* '57 CHEVY

SEE YOUR AUTHORIZED CHEVROLET DEALER

Some interesting views of 1957 Chevrolets, as seen in billboard advertising. The first billboard ad tells you: DON'T JUST LOOK, DRIVE IT! — '57 CHEVY. The car shown is Model 2403 a Bel Air 4-Door Sedan.

'57 CHEVROLET
sweet, smooth, sassy!

SEE YOUR AUTHORIZED CHEVROLET DEALER

Chevrolet's advertising that caught the attention of most people in 1957, was none other than this one: SWEET, SMOOTH AND SASSY. That said it all!

Another billboard ad, not quite as eye-catching, but did the trick, was this one: TRY A TURBO FIRE V-8 — IT'S TERRIFIC. Then gave the name of the local Chevrolet dealer.

This ad I remember well on billboards showing the clock with the title, "Chevrolet — America's Best Seller. America's Best Buy." As a side note, there was one of these billboard signs about five miles from the Los Angeles Zone Office where I then worked. If I saw the clock showing 7:50, I knew I was going to be late for work that morning.

Here sits a body of a 1957 210 2-Door Sedan ready to join company with its under carriage. The vehicle apparently will have whitewall tires as long as the body descent matches up with the rest of it.

The hinged gas filler door for 1957 models posed a Chevy mystery to me the first night I owned my new 1957 Sport Coupe. Neither the gas station attendant nor I could locate it. Finally, I looked in the owner's manual and then we found it! I'm sure the dealer never put more than enough gas to get it off the lot and, at 25 cents a gallon, I probably filled the tank of this car for no more than $5.00.

An array of accessories for all 1957 Chevrolets from the 150 to the Bel Air cars. Note the printing of this 210 photo was before the cars actually came with the full stainless rear quarter trim. I'm sure very few 150s ever saw that many factory-approved accessories bedecked on their bodies.

What a beautiful car is this 1957 Chevrolet El Morocco Brougham. Too bad Chevrolet didn't decide on this rear-end design. Not that '57 Chevrolets aren't already nice, but this rear end really has a classic appearance. El Moroccos were available in 1956 and 1957. The 1956 cars totalled only 20 while 1957s amounted to 187 vehicles. The body styles were only available in the Bel Air line as 4-Door Hardtops, 2-Door Hardtops and Convertible. This example delivered for $4,386 and came equipped with automatic transmission, power steering and brakes. Also part of the package included the 283 V-8 with Power Pak. The El Moroccos carried a G.M. warranty, just the same as regular Chevrolets. The vehicles were manufactured by the Ruben Allender Company on Van Dyke Avenue in Detroit, Michigan.

The trunk emblem on the deck lid, from a distance, appeared to be the same as a '57 Chevy with gold Vee and all. Upon closer inspection, the gold Vee is there, but the nameplate tells us it's an El Morocco.

This left rear quarter view is very reminiscent of big brother El Dorado of this same period. Look at that lower stainless panel and bumper treatment. What a collector's jewel!

Chevrolet offered their vehicles for police, taxi, and Chevy fleet purposes in 1957. Shown here are examples of a 210 Police 2-Door Sedan used as the Police Cruiser, also available in the 150 Series. The 4-Door Sedans in both 210 and 150 Series were regularly used, too. Some small towns also ordered 150 and 210 Handyman Wagons and 210 Townsmans for police personnel and emergency car use such as a mini-ambulance.

Series "ONE-FIFTY" Police Cruiser

"ONE-FIFTY" 2-Door

Also shown are the choice of 150 and 210 taxicabs. Often times these examples came with a 6-cylinder engine and standard transmission chiefly due to economical reasons.

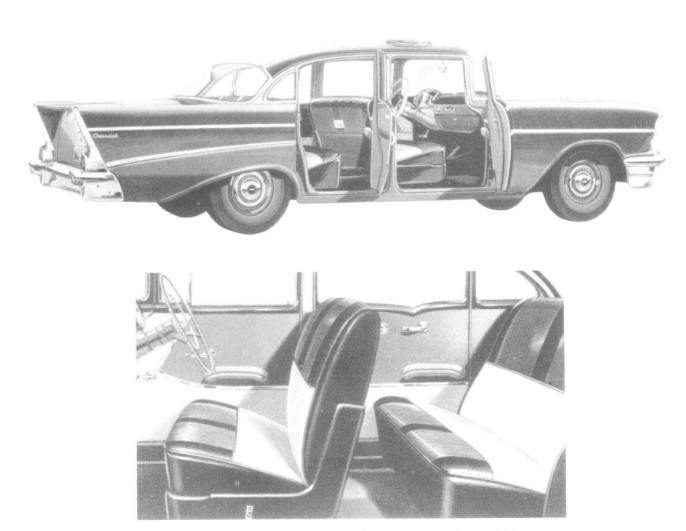

All vinyl interiors designed for rugged service - and plenty of it!

Chevrolet Accessories For 1957

DEALER LIST AND NET PRICE SCHEDULE

Effective February 1, 1957

ALL PRICES SUBJECT TO CHANGE WITHOUT NOTICE

The "List Prices" shown in this schedule are suggested prices for sales to consumers.

PASSENGER CARS AND EQUIPMENT

FACTORY INSTALLED OPTIONS

Option Number	Description	Installed Price
110	Air Conditioner	$453.53
263	Auxiliary Seat (1508)	42.37
303	Close Ratio Transmission	61.33
100	*Directional Signals	16.75
397	Electric Seats (21-2400)	44.60
426	Electric Windows (21-2400)	105.93
426	Electric Windows (2429-2434)	61.33
320	*Electric Windshield Wipers	11.71
417	Engine Positive Ventilation	13.43
398	EZI Glass	33.47
697	EZI Glass (Special)	16.73
578	Fuel Injection	501.60
579	Fuel Injection	501.60
482	Full Width Seat (1508)	80.87
338	Generator Equipment (15-21-2400) (35 Amp.)	7.83
325	Generator L.C.I. (40 Amp)	83.60
241-A	Governor (6 Cylinder)	18.96
241-H	Governor (8 Cylinder)	39.07
101B-E	Heater, De Luxe	83.80
101C-F	Heater, Recirculating	55.65
345	Heavy Duty Battery	7.83
227	Heavy Duty Clutch	5.60
216	Oil Bath Air Cleaner	5.60
315	Overdrive	111.47
237	Oil Filter (6 Cylinder)	8.97
104-A	*Oil Filter (8 Cylinder)	8.97
114	Padded Dash	16.73
412	Power Brakes	39.07
313	Powerglide	202.00
410	Power Pack	44.60
411	Power Pack (High Cams)	250.80
411	Power Pack (Regular Cams)	217.40
324	Power Steering	72.47

697	Shaded Glass	16.73
254	Springs-5 leaf (Regular Passenger)	2.80
254U	Springs (Station Wagon)	3.37
254Y	Springs-6-leaf (1529, 2109, 2159, 2409)	3.95
254X	Springs-6-leaf (1508, 2434, 2429)	4.52
254V	Springs-6-leaf (Passenger)	6.75
330	Taxi Cab Equipment (1503-2103) Cloth Trim	36.67
330	Taxi Cab Equipment (1503-2103) Vinyl Trim	44.00
465	Tires (7.50-14-4 White Walls except 2119)	42.53
466	Tires (7.50-14-6 Black Walls) (2119 Basic)	54.33
466	Tires (7.50-14-6 White Walls except 2119)	97.73
466	Tires (7.50-14-6 White Walls 2119 only)	54.33
525-559	Tu-Tone Paint	29.60
302	Turboglide	

*Factory Required Option

CHEVROLET ACCESSORIES FOR 1957
PASSENGER CARS

Description	Installed Price
ADAPTER - Seat Belt	3.95
AIR CONDITIONER - 8 cyl. with Heater	464.00
AIR CONDITIONER - 8 cyl. without Heater	449.00
AIR CONDITIONER - 6 cyl. with Heater	469.00
ANTENNA - Electric R.H. Rear Fender	35.75
ANTENNA - Manual - L.H. Front	9.60
ANTENNA - Manual - L.H. Rear	14.35
AUTRONIC EYE	54.00
BELT - Seat	14.85
BLOCK - Wiring Junction	5.35
BRACKET - Safetylight R.H.	2.55
BRAKE - Unit - Power	65.00
CAP - Locking Gas Tank	3.90
CARRIER - Wheel - Continental	169.15
CLOCK - Electric	19.15
COMPASS - Illuminated	7.90
COVER - Accelerator Pedal	1.95
COVER - Wheel Full	24.05
CUSHION - Bumper - Rubber	5.20
DISPENSER	5.70
FILTER UNIT - Gasoline	4.40
FRAME - License (one)	4.25
GLARESHADE - with Shade (All)	9.85
GUARD - Bumper - Front and Rear	31.40
GUARD - Door Edge - 4-Door	7.55
GUARD - Door Edge - 2-Door	4.10
GUARD - Door Edge - Sport Sedan	7.55
GUARD - Door Edge - Sport Coupe	4.10
HARNESS - Shoulder	10.80
HORN - 3rd Note	10.70

KIT - Tool	3.55
KOOL KOOSHION - Blue	4.55
KOOL KOOSHION - Green and Tan	4.55
KOOL KOOSHION - Black and Ivory	5.20
LAMP - Back-up	19.15
LAMP - Courtesy	4.70
LAMP - Glove Compartment	2.45
LAMP - Luggage Compartment	3.40
LAMP - Underhood	4.05
LIGHTER - Cigarette	4.65
MAT - De Luxe - Contour	6.95
MAT - Rubber, Floor	1.80
MIRROR - Inside R.V. Non-Glare	5.60
MIRROR - Outside R.V. Body Mount	6.35
MIRROR - Vanity Visor	1.65
MOULDING - Body Sill	13.55
MOULDING - Trunk Lid - Lower Edge	19.40
PAD - Instrument Panel	26.00
RADIO AND ANTENNA - Manual	78.50
RADIO AND ANTENNA - Push Button	102.50
RADIO AND ANTENNA - Wonder Bar	125.50
REST ARM	11.20
SAFETYLIGHT with MIRROR	31.00
SCREEN - Radiator Insect	.95
SHAVER - Electric - AC-DC - 12 Volt	31.50
SHIELD - Door Handle	5.85
SIGNAL - Electric Parking Brake	6.60
SPEAKER - Rear Seat	16.15
SPINNER - Wheel	13.10
SPOTLIGHT - Hand Portable	7.95
TANK - Vacuum	3.10
VENTSHADE - 4-Door Sedan	13.00
VENTSHADE - 2-Door Sedan	13.00
VIEWER - Traffic Light	3.60
VISOR - Outside (All)	29.70
VISOR - R.H. Sun	6.85
WASHER - W/S Push Button	17.15
WASHER - W/S Foot-operated	15.75

Preliminary surveys indicate, to maintain adequate operation, the following are suggested minimum prices:

PASSENGER CAR MODELS

		SIX	EIGHT
150 SERIES			
1502	2-Door Sedan	$2316.41	$2432.05
1503	4-Door Sedan	2371.06	2486.70
1508	Sedan Delivery	2348.43	2464.07
1512	Utility Sedan	2199.93	2315.57
210 SERIES			
2102	2-Door Sedan	2484.88	2600.52
2103	4-Door Sedan	2540.34	2655.98
2113	4-Door Sport Sedan	2642.59	2758.23
2124	Club Coupe	2527.51	2643.15
2154	Sport Coupe	2572.23	2687.87
BEL AIR SERIES			
2402	2-Door Sedan	2608.29	2723.93
2403	4-Door Sedan	2663.75	2779.39
2413	4-Door Sport Sedan	2742.44	2858.08
2434	Convertible	2899.11	3014.75
2454	Sport Coupe	2673.45	2789.09
STATION WAGONS			
1529	2-Door Station Wagon	2642.63	2758.27
2109	4-Door Station Wagon	2840.53	2956.17
2119	4-Door Station Wagon	2954.24	3069.88
2129	2-Door Station Wagon	2782.99	2898.63
2409	4-Door Station Wagon	2972.60	3088.24
2429	2-Door Statioln Wagon	3160.84	3276.48
CORVETTE			
2934	Convertible (2 Pass.) Manually operated soft top, Synchro 3-speed transmission, single 4-barrel carburetor		3610.32

These last few pages shown here gives prices of the various models, along with factory-installed options and passenger car accessories. These prices are basically higher than those mentioned with the photo and caption sections in this book. This is chiefly because these are considered California prices where additional taxes and freight had to be added.

A 1957 Corvette ready to take the young couple for a spin. Powerglide was available again for the 1957 Vettes. This example, with a manually operated soft top and single 4-barrel carburetor, delivered for $3,610.32.

Model 2934, or better known as the 1957 Corvette, with its removable hardtop in place. This extra-cost item proved to be very popular, especially with its drop in price. By 1957, the fiberglass top cost $215. Notice the narrow whitewall tires employed on this unit. Personally, I think the wider whitewalls looked sharper. The Vettes continued to use 6.70 x 15-inch tires on the 1957 models.

A left rear three-quarter view of the fashionable 1957 Nomad Wagon. Model 2429. This unit was delivered in the popular new color of Dusk Pearl and Imperial Ivory and equipped with factory air power brakes and steering, wonder bar radio, whitewalls and wheel spinners. Power windows and seat were deleted.

My 1957 Bel Air Sport Coupe, after my sister purchased the car from me. Note what an improvement the skirts made in the car's rear appearance. The turquoise and ivory coupe had 13,000 miles on it when I took this photo of it in 1958.

A close-view of the rear quarter panel of my first 1957 Bel Air Sport Coupe showing the rear quarter fin, the sculptured anodized aluminum panel, and the contoured fender skirts. The skirts may not have been a factory piece of equipment, but sure did add to the cars appearance.

167

The stylish new Bel Air 4-Door Sedan

The beautiful way to be thrifty!

The '58 CHEVROLET

Economy never looked, or performed, or rode like this before. But now look what the '58 Chevrolet offers you in the biggest, boldest move a car ever made!

Not in two blue moons have so many fine new things come along in a car to delight and excite you—especially a car in the low-price field..

You can see the new Chevrolet has style. It looks so ready for action that you almost expect the one above to pick up and roll off the page.

And a Chevrolet can move, all right. Its new Turbo-Thrust V8* engine pours out a sweet, all-new version of spice and spirit, guarantees your money's worth in performance. Just sample it. And for the quickest combination of silkiness and response that there is, add Chevrolet's Turbo-glide,* first and only triple-turbine transmission.

Even Chevrolet's tried-and-true Blue-Flame 6 has new spunk for 1958 —and thrifty ways!

It's for certain, too, that economy never rode like this. The new Full Coil suspension, standard with Chevrolet, is as gentle and easy as if a Chevy were striding along on tiptoe. There is also a real air ride*—and you can't have it softer than riding on air.

You'll want to sample all of Chevrolet's new features and remarkable ways—the solid ride that comes from its new body-frame design, the new smoothness in Powerglide,* the new foot-operated parking brake, the beautiful interiors!

For the super surprise, see Chevrolet's special models, the Bel Air Impala Sport Coupe and Convertible. See your Chevrolet dealer and pick *your* Chevrolet, the beautiful way to be thrifty. . . . Chevrolet Division of General Motors, Detroit 2, Michigan.   **Optional at extra cost*

THE BEAUTIFUL WAY TO BE SPORTY! New 1958 Corvette with new style, new power and new sparkle, strictly for those who speak the Corvette's special language. Get the feel in the new '58 Corvette cockpit. Sample any one of its four ultra-compact V8's (including the 290-h.p. Fuel Injection* version); and its three transmissions. You'll be driving the absolutely best road car in America.   **Optional at extra cost*

Chevrolet's lowest priced 4-Door Sedan was this Delray. It delivered for $2,262 and tipped in at 3432 pounds. This vehicle proved popular with taxi and police departments. Approximately 178,000 Delrays were built in 1958.

Chevrolet for 1958

"So low. So long. So surprisingly smart."

Remember, in the last chapter, I cautioned, "Wait until the next chapter"? Well, here is where I come to life!

I feel the 1958 Chevy is the most beautiful car Chevrolet ever built. The first night I got my '58 Impala Sport Coupe, I said, "I'll never get rid of this car." Now, some 37 years later, I still own it, and have no intention in parting with it. The Silver Blue Coupe shows 63,000 miles and is totally original, at this writing. My only complaint, which has been with me since it was new, is poor gas mileage — 9 MPG. The vehicle carries the 348 cubic-inch engine developing 250 horsepower with the Powerglide transmission. The 1958s came out on Friday, as had been their practice now for several years. This year, it was on my birthday — Halloween, October 31, 1957. Probably this car was the main thing that helped me hang in there to live. At this point in my life there wasn't a whole lot I had going for me, except that I had to own a '58 Impala! I vacillated daily between which engine, color, type of accessories, etc., that I should order on the car. My very first choice was the 283 cubic-inch V-8 developing 185 horsepower (which I should have stuck with), Powerglide, in solid Silver Blue. My second choice, very close to the blue, was Honey Beige, followed by Colonial Cream. Then it was a toss up between Glen Green and

The 1958 Chevy Sedan Delivery shown here displays a Vee on its hood telling us a V-8 engine lies under the hood. Therefore, this example was referred to as Model 1271. If it has a 6-cylinder engine then it was classed as Model 1171. This vehicle weighed 3531 pounds and sold for $2,230. The Sedan Delivery was classed in the new Delray Series and came with only one passenger seat, however, as an option, a double seat could be ordered.

Cashmere Blue. As far as color goes, my first choice was the right one. The car is nicely equipped with nothing but '58 Chevrolet accessories, from the above-mentioned, to radio, heater, power steering, power brakes, E-Z glass, twin side mirrors, inside non-glare rear view mirror, wheel spinners, door edge guards, courtesy lights, under hood lamp, and trunk lamp. A couple of small changes

A close-up view of a 1958 model in the Delray line. The vehicle is equipped with deluxe Bel Air wheelcovers and whitewalls, but lacks other finery of deluxe models. The longer hood emblem says a 6-cylinder is employed, rather than a V-8.

The side paneling of a Yeoman Station Wagon classed in the Delray Series of vehicles. The wagon line-up for 1958 chose to place the wagons with a different nomenclature from regular models in the series.

that I took the liberty of making are changing the backup lamps to the station wagon variety, which are placed right next to the license plate on the valance

This 1958 2-Door Wagon, classed as a Yeoman, was the only wagon offered in Chevrolets low-priced field. The vehicle came with either a 6 or V-8 power plant. In this series, the 6-cylinder was more popular. Its base price was $2,520 and weighed 3681 pounds. The rear compartment came with a durable linoleum for extended wear. A total of 16,590 were delivered.

A Delray 2-Door Sedan appeared exactly the same as the Model 1121 Utility Sedan except that this unit had a rear seat compartment. The Delray 2-Door Sedan sold for $2,108 in 6-cylinder version while a V-8 was approximately $100 more. The Utility Sedan delivered for $2,013 making it the lowest priced car from Chevrolet for 1958.

panel. This way, I have three red taillights in each rear quarter panel. The other change, which I shouldn't have made, is chroming some engine parts. I get points taken off every time the car is judged in a show. It's my car, and that's the way I chose to do it. It probably seems comical to young kids today that this old guy in his sixties has this chromed behemoth. The Sport Coupe delivered at Ernie Porter Chevrolet on May 5, 1958 for $3,334. "Wow, what a price! I'll never pay that kind of money again," I said then. I have repeated that same phrase many times later, whenever new cars came into the family. And I haven't paid that kind of money, again, because each next time, it was always higher.

In addition to this Coupe, I've had the privilege of owning a Honey Beige Coupe for nearly twenty years, a Snowcrest White Coupe for about five years, and a Glen Green Convertible which I restored and kept for about four years. It is one I should have kept, but it is now in Maryland and in the hands of a "Late Great Chevy" collector.

So, let's get down to the regular 1958 lineup. For 1958, Chevrolet offered another complete revision to its models. The cars were totally different in all respects, from new fresh body design, striking new interiors, X-member frame for a better ride, a new variety of engines, new model designations and an extra cost suspension system which wasn't too promising. It was referred to as Level Air, which was meant to help the car level under all conditions. This system consisted of level air bags of inflated rubber used in place of springs. The option number was 580 and cost an additional $123.75. Fortunately, not many people took advantage of this item, as they were replaced with the coil springs early on.

As for the engine compartments, the faithful 6-cylinder remained its 235.5 cubic-inches now increased to 145 horsepower with the compression ratio being 8.25:1. Next in line came the regular 185 horsepower 283 cubic-inch engine at 4600 RPM. The bore and stroke were 3.875 x 3 inches, with a compression ratio of 8.5:1. This next engine configuration proved not to be too popular. It was the Super Turbo-Fire which used the 4-barrel carburetor, a 9.5:1 compression ratio, and developed 230 horsepower. This engine option was number 410, costing only $26.90 additional. Dual exhausts were used with this engine. For an additional amount of $484.20, the engine could be ordered with the Ram-Jet fuel injection. Using hydraulic valve lifters and the 9.5:1 compression ratio, the engine could develop 250 horsepower at 5000 RPM. Another version of the 283 cubic-inch fuel injected model offered solid lifters, performance cam with a 10.5:1 compression ratio developing 290 horsepower at 6200 RPM. The version was used only in cars with a 3-speed or close ratio 3-speed transmission.

Next in the engine lineup was the one most people purchased after the regular 283 cubic-inch version. It was the new 348 cubic-inch displacement called Turbo-Thrust in base form with a 4-barrel carburetor and the same 9.5:1 compression ratio developed 250 horsepower at 4400 RPM. If the owner wished still more performance, a Super Turbo-Thrust was available with three 2-barrel carburetors, 9.5:1 compression ratio and hydraulic valve lifters. These units developed 280 horsepower at 4800 RPM. I think I've had it bad with a 9 MPG car through the years. I had a friend who owned an Impala Convertible with this engine setup. It never could be kept in tune and never did better than 7 MPG. He disposed of it two years later for a Volkswagen. Talk about an about face!

A mid-range Biscayne in the 1500 and 1600 series of vehicles replaced the 210 Series which had been around for the past five years. This 4-Door Sedan weighed 3434 pounds and sold for $2,397 in V-8 fashion. The car was nicely appointed and again was one of Chevrolet's most saleable vehicles. In the Biscayne line of cars, roughly 100,000 were built for the model run.

173

This 1958 Biscayne 2-Door Sedan was a company car belonging to my brother-in-law. The vehicle was on a two-year company-owned plan, serving him well and putting on over 40,000 miles. Shortly after buying it from the company in 1960, they found the whole rear floor compartment rusted out and the blue rubber floor mats gave way. The kids used to tease their mom about putting their feet on the pavement to stop the car. Unfortunately, this was a problem Chevy had to contend with for that model year.

Still, to top this engine, came a 3-carburetor version with a compression ratio of 11.1 solid valve lifters developing 315 horsepower at 5600 RPM.

The 1958 models were the largest Chevrolets built to date. They came on a 117.5-inch wheelbase, 209 inches overall, 77.7 inches wide and 56 inches high — that is, if you measured an Impala Coupe from floor to roof. I have a yard stick that is truly not a yard stick, but one of the promotional items given to buyers of new 1958s. This 56-inch "yardstick" was for measuring the Impala. I've held on to it, along with all the other '58 Chevy memorabilia I've acquired over the years.

Model designations changed for the year. The low-priced line took the name of Delray, a title given to the 2-door model with a fancier interior in the "210" series for the previous four years. The "210" title was dropped in favor of Biscayne. It showed only for the 4-Door Sedan and 2-Door Sedan. The name Bel Air did continue in the top of the line. It was available as a 4-Door Sedan, (pillarless 4-Door Sedan), Bel Air Sports Coupe 2-Door (pillarless 2-Door) and the 2-Door Sedan. The models with pillars were virtually the same cars as the Delray and Biscaynes except that they offered much more fancy trim, both inside and out. The Impalas were classed as a sub series in the Bel Air line offering much fancy trim and different striped upholstery. The roof line on the Impala Coupe was entirely different from the regular Bel Air Coupe having a fake air scoop located above the rear window. The Convertible did not offer this, due to the soft top configurations. One additional means of identifying an Impala against the rest of the line were the triple lights in the quarter panel. Most offered two red lights with the middle light being for backup lights except for mine and very few others, as mentioned earlier. Regular models offered only two lights with one being for a backup light, if the owner chose the $11.75 accessory. If a Station Wagon came with backup lights, it cost $17.50 as additional mounting was required. Station Wagon models offered only one taillamp in each rear quarter panel.

174

A 1958 Brookwood Station Wagon coming in the line of Biscayne models. This wagon could be purchased either as a six or nine-passenger vehicle. The six passenger models were classed as 1593 6-cylinder and 1693 8-cylinder cars. The nine-passenger vehicles were 1594 6-cylinder and 1694 8-cylinder units. The six-passenger cars sold for $2,574, while the nine-passenger models went home for $2,785. Both examples are listed as V-8 cars. Each version had rear seats which could be removed for a larger cargo area

The Station Wagon vehicles in the Delray line were called Yeomans, coming either as a 2 or 4-Door model. The Biscayne line offered a wagon which was referred to as the Brookwood. The Brookwood was available only as a 4-Door, but could seat either as a six-passenger or a nine-passenger. The top of the line wagon took the name of the past three-year luxury wagon, Nomad. It was now available only as a 4-Door model and classed in the Bel Air line, available only as a six-passenger.

The Nomad was again the top wagon from Chevy in 1958. This year, there weren't any additional wagons in the top of the line. The Nomad for 1958 came as a 4-Door model within the Bel Air line with seating for six-passengers. The model came as a 1793 6-cylinder (which very few purchased) or the common version 1893 V-8. The wagon weighed in at 3746 pounds and sold for $2,835 making it next to the most expensive car Chevrolet offered for the year, barring the Corvette from the list.

Still with us and now classed truly for the first time in passenger car fashion is the Sedan Delivery. It was catalogued in the Yeoman series and could be purchased either as a six or V-8. Prices ranged from $2,013 for a 6-cylinder Model 1121, three- passenger Delray Utility Sedan, to $2,841 for the 8-cylinder Model 1867 Impala Convertible. These prices are Detroit, Michigan, excluding all shipping destination charges.

In 1958, "Chev" offered some nice new color choices. The most popular one was an all time favorite of mine, as mentioned earlier — Silver Blue. Other new colors were Anniversary Gold, to help General Motors celebrate their 50th Anniversary, Cay Coral, Honey Beige, Aegean Turquoise, Fathom Blue, and Forest Green. The remaining shades had either been around for the past couple of years or just were given a new name to help promote the color choice. The additional shades were Snowcrest White, Colonial Cream, Cashmere Blue, Tropical Turquoise, Glen Green, Rio Red, Sierra Gold and Onyx Black. In all there were 15 single tones available. If a customer preferred a two-tone combination, he had 14 to choose from. These choices are listed below, with the first choice being the color on the roof of the car if it was the Impala Sport Coupe. All other choices were roof and lower body being the same with middle section of the car in the second selection.

Snowcrest White	Silver Blue
Arctic White	Aegean Turquoise
Arctic White	Tropic Turquoise
Arctic White	Cashmere Blue
Arctic White	Glen Green
Arctic White	Colonial Cream
Arctic White	Sierra Gold
Arctic White	Rio Red
Arctic White	Cay Coral
Arctic White	Onyx Black
Cashmere Blue	Fathom Blue
Tropic Turquoise	Aegean Turquoise
Glen Green	Forest Green
Anniversary Gold	Honey beige

Naturally, the convertible was a single-tone with the top material being a choice of Black, Ivory, Light Gray, Light Blue, Light Green, and Cream. The wheel color choices were Silver for the Impala, Bel Air and Nomad vehicles. All other models in Delray and Biscayne cars were the same as the prevailing exterior color.

Chevrolet's Corvette now received another facelift coming with quad head-lamps, a more toothy grille and in the hood department were louvers which were non-functional. A recessed side panel was still seen on the '58 Vettes with fake air vents offering three stainless bars adding that final touch to its side appearance. The '58 Corvette measured 177.2 inches overall and used its 102-inch wheelbase. The standard engine for the Corvettes was the 283 cubic-inch V-8 with 9.5:1 compression ratio, developing 230 horsepower at 4800 RPM. A Carter 4-barrel carburetor was basically employed. A second 4-barrel carburetor developing 245 horsepower could be ordered for $150.00. In addition to this, a dual 4-barrel arrangement for $183 developing 270 horsepower could also be ordered. In addition to these mentioned, fuel injection units were available to the sum of $484. They developed 290 horsepower. The 348 cubic-

The lowest priced and least popular model in the Bel Air line was the 2-Door Sedan selling for $2,493. It was classed as Model 1741 6-cylinder and 1841 8-cylinder. Appearance-wise, it looked much the same as the Delray and Biscayne 2-Door sedans except that this model came with much more bright trim and full wheel discs as standard equipment.

The rear quarter view of this Nomad wagon still carried the Nomad stainless ribbed bars like those from the previous three season. The wagon never caught on with the public as a collector's piece, like the previous Nomads did. I still thought it was a good looking car. Guess I just like station wagons!

Probably the best seller for Chevrolet in 1958 was the Bel Air 4-Door Sedan. Actual production figures per model vary in various data books, but it seems to me most people liked the dolled up version of a Delray or Biscayne enough to pay the additional fee costing the buyer $2,547 as a V-8. The sedan weighed 3440 pounds.

inch engine could not be placed in the Corvette. The transmissions available were 3-speed manual floor shift, optional 4-speed manual was available for $215 extra and the Powerglide was there for those preferring their Vette for practical city delivery for an additional $188. The Corvette in base form listed for $3,631. The model designation beginning with 1958 was 867 for these little beauties. A total of 9,168 left the St. Louis Factory during the year.

Model number designations for the 1958 line of cars were classed as 1100 Series if in the 6-cylinder Delray line and 1200 Series in 8-cylinder models. Biscayne cars equipped as 6-cylinder models were placed in the 1500 group while 8-cylinder model were in the 1600 Series, Bel Air and Impala models used the 1700 title if equipped as a 6-cylinder and 1800 title went to the 8-cylinder models. Each of the wagon models were placed within the Delray, Biscayne, and Bel Air number series

Chevrolet took top honors in the entire automobile industry for 1958. This was one of the those recession years and they managed to capture 29.5 percent of the entire market. The calendar year sales consisted of 1,255,935 units sold. As for model year production, it was 1,217,047 sales.

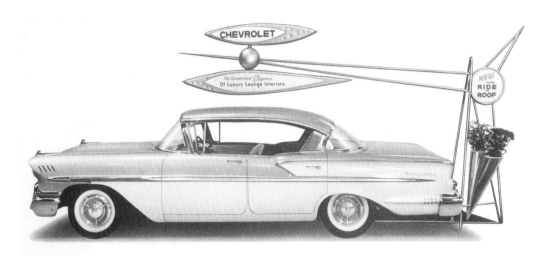

Looking virtually the same as the Bel Air 4-Door Sedan is this Bel Air Sport Sedan. The absence of the window posts and windows in the down position gives a feeling of complete airiness. This example apparently came equipped with Level Air from the display depicting its new ride. The Sport Sedan weighed 3475 pounds and delivered for $2,618. The model was classed as either a 1739 or 1839, depending on its engine.

This promotional photo states: "Down to Sea What They Can See." — J.C. Riles, H.D. Freeman, C.W. Getz and J.L. Masey, four enthusiastic skin divers, invite Colleen Emsley to join them in a below-the-surface dip in the waters of the Pacific near Pacific Beach, California. Note the Bel Air Sport Sedan carries a 1958 California license plate and the Bel Air nameplate is nicely displayed on the rear quarter panel. The background is sure reminiscent of good old Fort Ord where once I was stationed.

A total front view of an impressive car. It's the clean lines of a model in the Bel Air line. Apparently she is demonstrating the quality of steering the 1958 with center point steering. No wander over the highway.

A 1958 Impala Sport Coupe, Model 1847 coming down the line for its final inspection before being shipped to a dealership. Almost looks like its my Honey Beige Coupe, or the Snowcrest White which I used to own.

Well, here is "Blue Boy" my '58 Impala in Silver Blue. What a great car it has always been. Only problem that really irritated me were two fuel pump failures within a month of each other when it was about four years old. The garage that supposedly repaired it didn't have a clue as to how a fuel pump should be installed. The second time was in Death Valley with temperatures well over 100 when the fuel pump failed. A great highway patrolman happened along to help me limp into a wide spot in the road where it was fixed properly. To fill the tank, it cost 47 cents a gallon. I couldn't believe anyone could charge that much for gasoline!

Another view of my "pride and Joy" showing the station wagon back up lamps it wears. The car came out well-equipped from the Ernie Porter Chevrolet Agency in Pasadena, California for $3,334. Never will I spend money like that again for a car. This is something I've said every time a new car comes in the driveway. This is true, too, because they have taken a healthy increase each time.

My 1958 Impala Convertible the day I brought it home to start and restore it. What a project it was, but everything was there just in total disrepair. The owners of the car totally neglected it right from the day it was purchased when new.

After only four months of repairs, here is my 1958 Impala Convertible in like-new condition once again. I took this car for its first time out to the Harrah Car Show in Reno, Nevada back in 1977 where it took a second place award in its class.

Looking down into the interior of this 1958 Impala Convertible showing off its fashionable striped seat material. The appearance of the stripe is the same, but material is entirely different. The rear seat speaker was mounted in the center of the rear seat with the Impala emblem affixed in the center.

Note the Level Air nameplate this 1958 Impala Convertible sports. The cost of this option was $123.75 extra which didn't appear on many vehicles. This convertible in base form left the factory for $2,996 and, if Powerglide were ordered, it sold for $3,193. If the Turboglide arrangement was chosen, it went home for $3,236.

Another view of the 1958 Impala Convertible. This car has always been my favorite whether its a Delray Utility Sedan or the Convertible. This vehicle weighed 3508 pounds. A total of 55,989 Convertibles were sold for the year.

A factory photo of a 1958 Impala Sport Coupe taken on the Monterey, California Coastline. Note the license is a California plate with the same numbers of 277 which is also shown on the rear view of the Convertible. These are dealer plates also with the inscription of DLR in the center. The Sport Coupes weighed in at 3442 pounds. The base price for the model was $2,693 totally stripped of any accessories.

The late Slim Barnard, Automotive Editor of the Los Angeles Examiner, standing by his 1958 Bel Air Sport Sedan. This photo was taken on Christmas Day 1957 when he dropped by for a visit while I was recovering from my car accident of a few months earlier. Incidentally, just to stop by for a visit on Christmas Day tells what kind of a true gentleman he was.

The late Floyd Clymer, one of the early automobile publishers standing by my 1958 Impala Coupe in 1960 at his automotive publishing house on Alvarado Street in Los Angeles, California. He, too, was another great friend.

Taken at the time when I owned four 1958 Impalas. I suppose most people would be happy to own one, but I guess I'm just a little nuts, so to speak, on 1958 Chevrolets.

A small detail shot of where the front fender antenna should be mounted on all 1958 Chevrolets.

An immaculate engine compartment on a 1958 Impala. This view displays a 348 cubic-inch engine with it being clean enough to eat off of.

A popular accessory at the time was this factory approved Continental Kit. When new, the accessory sold for $182, additionally.

The same 1958 Impala with Continental Kit also shows its dual rear antennas. The right one was the one that did the work. The left antenna was a dummy which just added to the car's appearance.

This close-up view of a 1958 Impala illustrates the correct taillamp configuration with the factory exhaust ports which sold for $9.55 extra The exhaust tip is not correct and should be mounted in a bent-downward position for 1958 cars.

An assembly line view of a 1958 Bel Air, possibly a Sport Sedan, or maybe a Bel Air Sport Coupe with seats being installed. In the background appears to be a Station Wagon.

A 1958 Bel Air Sport Coupe on the assembly belt line ready to meet its front-end partner to make another beautiful model.

Santa Claus in December 1957 demonstrating the great qualities of Level Air. On the left side shows what happens when a portly Santa chooses to sit on the front right fender.

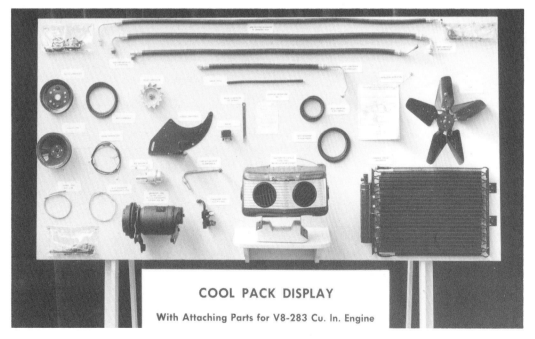

COOL PACK DISPLAY

With Attaching Parts for V8-283 Cu. In. Engine

The components which made up the Cool Pack unit that was available on 1958 models. The air conditioner was mounted directly beneath the center portion of the dashboard. It cost $268.75 list and was available for both 6 and 8-cylinder cars.

This display shows Harlow Curtice, then President of General Motors, with a young lass and her new promotional Model 1958 Impala Convertible and a Sport Sedan in the background. This was taken at a campaign that General Motors was promoting with its employees for those who wished to enter giving their feelings of what G.M. meant to them. Several first place prizes were distributed to their employees, down to G.M. Frigidaires being offered in the contest.

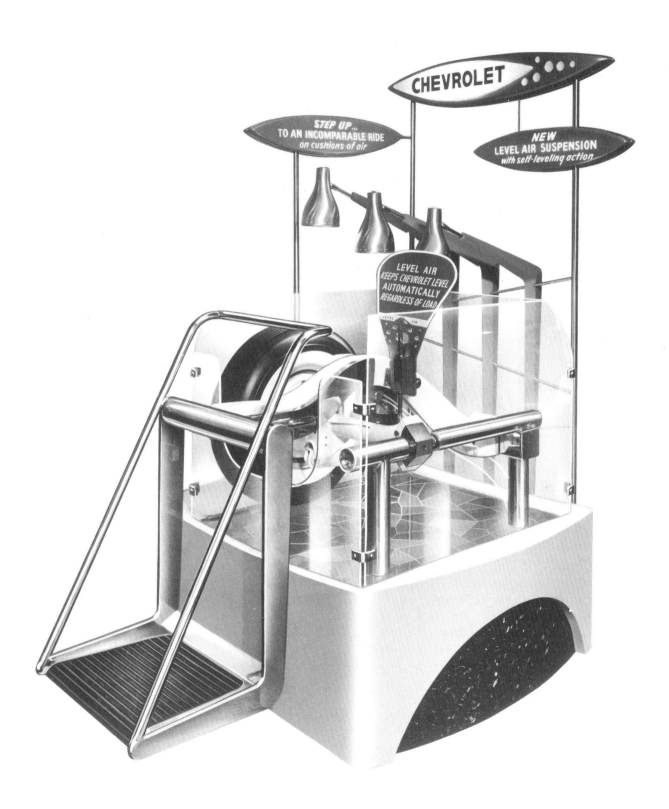

A display shown at many Chevrolet events for 1958 depicting the great qualities of the new Level Air Suspension. At least they surely tried to promote the option to the public.

Another piece of Chevrolet promotional news for 1958. This example displayed the new 250 H.P. Ramjet Fuel Injection engine being made available to the public for an additional $484.

Receiving its front-end is the 1958 Impala Sport Coupe. Note the inspection stickers placed on the windshield. In just a few minutes this vehicle will turn over on its own and be ready for a drive-away transporter. The boxes on the left state, "Packard Electric Division. Warren, Ohio." The Packard script is exactly as it appeared on Packard automobiles during previous years.

A view of my 1958 Honey Beige Impala in Colorado Springs, Colorado during the Vintage Chevrolet Club in America 15th Anniversary Meet in July 1976. The car then had 43,000 miles registered. The vehicle took a second place trophy at the show. Another real looker!

Some of the various 1958 display signs that were exhibited in Chevrolet dealerships throughout the country during that year.

A sharp looking 1958 Corvette with its removable hardtop in place. This option cost an additional $215. The vehicle, weighing 2819 pounds, delivered for $3,631. The big difference with this vehicle and its previous year was the double headlight feature.

Another view showing a left front quarter example of the '58 Corvette equipped with fuel injection according to the nameplate mounted on the front fender. Most Vettes came equipped with the contrasting side panel which added greatly to the car's appearance. The cost for this item was only $16.50 more.

The 1958 Corvette Model 867 came in six colors for the model run. Within its rakish side panel was an imitation air vent. The side panel colors available were silver or white. For 1958, the St. Louis factory produced 9,168 units.

195

The 1958 Corvette, interior view, came with new features like a tachometer and full instruments within the dash cluster. On the right was an assist bar within its own cove. In the door panels were reflectors to warn oncoming drivers that the door was open.

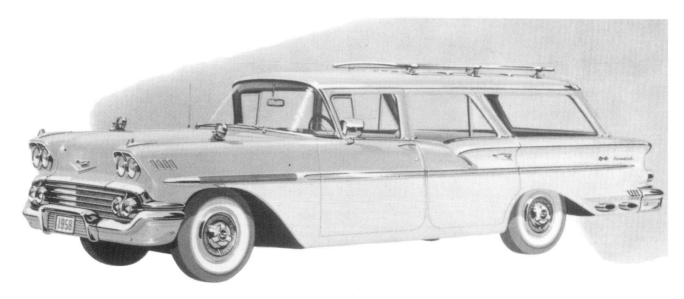

A fully bedecked 1958 Nomad illustrated with all the factory approved accessories.

Above is an artist's conception of what a fully accessorized Biscayne would have looked like if a customer chose to equip his car to the fullest. It resembles what the Los Angeles zone company cars looked like with every conceivable accessory that the vehicle could possibly manage to carry.

Promotional models aplenty. These cute little items today can bring upwards of $300 apiece. When new, often times dealers carried them in their parts department and would give one to a customer when the new car was delivered. Many body styles were offered from Impala Coupes, Convertibles to Station Wagons.

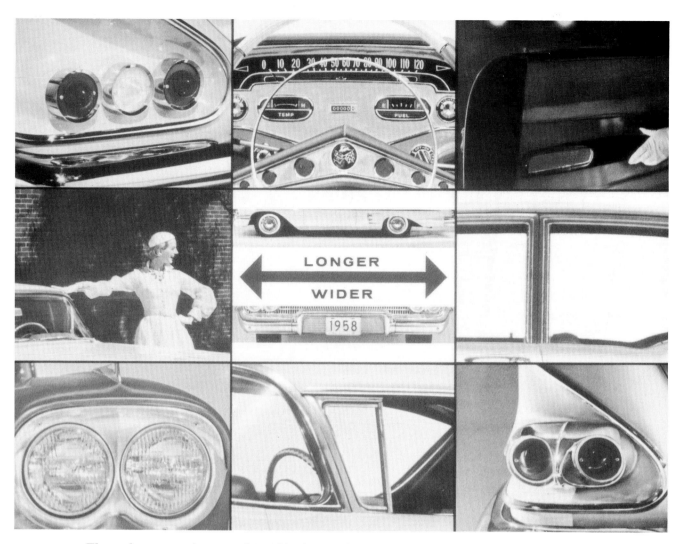

These shots were shown to the public late in the summer of 1957 to help entice the public to what was in store for them in just a short few weeks. These teaser photos sure helped hold the public for the big surprise, but didn't encourage the year end sales for 1957 models. Imagine seeing views of a longer wider Chevy with double headlights, twin taillamps, a roof line barely 56 inches high (in the Impala Sport Coupe) an anodized aluminum grille, among a host of new ideas for America's Number 1 car in 1958.

Chevrolet wasn't about to let the competition take hold in 1958. Just looking at the other two, they had nothing to fear. Take for example this Impala Sport Coupe with the Ford Skyliner and Plymouth Fury below. The Impala offered luxury trim, big-car look, feel, and ride that both Ford and Plymouth couldn't equal. The Impala was a special car, sleek and smooth with sports car spirit, yet it was priced slightly above regular Bel Air models.

Seen here are exclusive Impala features: distinctive three-tone upholstery, bright metal front-seat trim, sports-car type steering wheel, extra-long door armrests with built-in safety reflectors, color-anodized aluminum armrest panels, stainless-steel scuff protectors at door lower edges, full-length rear seat armrests with built-in ashtrays, roomy deep-cushioned rear seat with a wide center armrest that will lower into the seat cushion at an instant's notice, recessed area for exclusive rear-seat radio speaker installation that is highlighted by the Impala emblem.

For the sake of comparison, look at the 1958 Impala Convertible against the 1958 Ford and Plymouth. The clean lines of the Impala with its Impala emblem, and special quarter panel and sill moldings add distinctive accent to the sides and rear deck. The Impala Convertible was available in 15 colors with 6 top colors and sterling anodized aluminum side molding insert as standard equipment.

The Ford Convertible, as pictured here, displays a top that does not lower fully, and the top boot forms twin humps above the rear deck. Sunliner models only came in 12 solid colors with a choice of 4 convertible top colors. The contrasting color on the sides was available only with the extra-cost Styletone Ford option.

As for the Plymouth, it was basically the same vehicle as the 2-Door Fury model. It was available in 15 color choices with 4 top colors. The contrasting color between the side molding or the aluminum insert panel was available at extra cost. The special bumper and guards were also an extra-cost option.

Chevrolet offered new models that traditionally led in the field, and 1958 was certainly no exception. The entire automotive industry was expecting great things in 1958 from Chevrolet, and the car did surpass every expectation.

Shown here are some views of various models of 1958 Chevrolets, compared against a like model in the Ford and Plymouth line of vehicles.

In 1957, both Ford and Plymouth introduced new models, but really incorporated very few new ideas. These superficial changes were being offered again for 1958. Ford gave a mere facelift and Plymouth even less of a change, and they were being offered as new models. Chevrolet for 1958, with their product leadership, offered new styling, more roominess, more comfort, more conveniences and in-frame engines, suspension and power teams. There was no doubt that Chevrolet was the car of the year!

A comparison view of three sedans in the low-priced field: 1958 Bel Air Sedan, 1958 Ford Fairlane and 1958 Plymouth Belvedere.

A comparison of sedans in each series of the low-priced three:

Chevrolet Bel Air

Ford Fairlane 500

Plymouth Belvedere

Chevy's clean Bel Air lines are accented by attractive side trim at no extra cost. Anodized aluminum molding insert is standard with two-tone. Other Bel Air features include bright metal window trim, front fender ornamentation, and full rear fender outline molding. Ford Fairlane 500 does not include fender outline molding, and front fender ornaments are available only at extra cost. Plymouth does not offer bright metal window trim, and only the upper side molding shown here is standard equipment. A double molding, with either the roof color or with anodized aluminum trim between moldings, is available only as an extra-cost Sportone option on Belvedere models

Chevrolet Biscayne

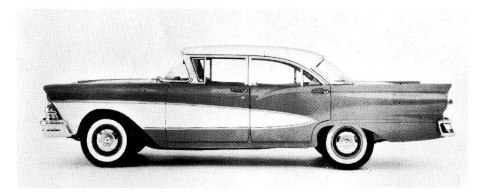

Ford Fairlane

Savoy

The popular Biscayne series features a double side molding, with sterling-anodized aluminum insert on tow-tone exteriors. Neither Ford Fairlane nor Plymouth Savory series offers anodized aluminum side trim as standard equipment, but a new extra-cost Fairlane trim option includes a small ano-dized-aluminum side panel and additional bright metal ornamentation. Fair-lane tow-tone paint area has approximately the shape of the '56 Chevrolet Corvette side panel, but without sculpturing. Solid color and two-tone Plymouth Savoys are trimmed with a plain straight line of chrome. Only with the additional-cost Sportone trim does the Savoy offer any two-tone side color treatment.

Chevrolet Delray

Custom 300

Plaza

Chevrolet's luxury-car lines are even more evident by comparison with other lowest priced models. The Delray is more than 7" longer than the Ford Custom 300, over 3" longer than the Plymouth Plaza. Neither Custom 300 nor Plaza offers the luxury look of the Delray's thin-pillar styling. Full-length body side moldings are standard on every Delray. Ford side molding shown is standard equipment, with a wider molding available at extra cost. Standard Plaza trim is a small nameplate, and the short chrome molding shown here is an extra-cost option. (Special Plaza models available in limited quantities in a few cities include a front fender molding as standard equipment.)

An interior view comparison chart of the three low-priced vehicles in each series: Bel Air, Biscayne and Delray against Ford's Fairlane 500, Fairlane and Custom 500, and same for the 1958 Plymouth Belvedere, Savoy and Plaza.

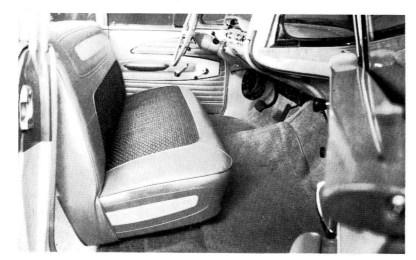

Bel Air

Fairlane 500

Belvedere

Biscaynes offer five three-tone interiors, compared with four two-tones each for Fairlane and Savoy models.

Biscayne

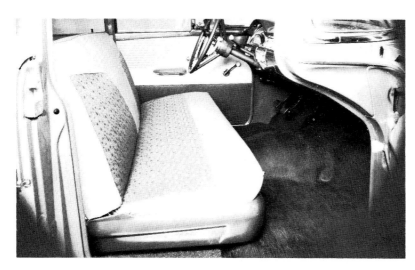

Fairlane

Savoy

Three two-tone interiors are offered in the Delray, and also in the Plaza. A two-tone gray is standard on the Custom 300, with three two-tone interiors available at extra cost, including another gray.

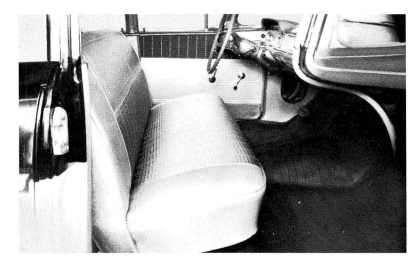

Delray

Custom 300

Plaza

In the Station Wagon field, again Chevrolet took the honors with five new wagons. Leading the list is this top of the line Nomad, followed by two Brookwood Wagons: a six-passenger vehicle, and a nine-passenger model. The low-priced series offered two Yeomans: a 2-Door six-passenger wagon, the other a 4-Door six passenger vehicle.

Nomad

Country Squire

Sport Suburan

Ford came with its top-line Country Squire, followed by a Country Sedan as either a six or nine-passenger model. The low-priced Ranch Wagon was Ford's entry as the lowest-priced wagon for the Ford Motor Company in 1958

Brookwood

Country Sedan

Custom Suburban

Plymouth gave its top-of-the-line wagon the title of Sport Suburban, followed by the mid-line version called Custom Suburban and the DeLuxe Suburban was comparable in trim to Chevrolet's Yeoman.

Yeoman

Ranch Wagon

De Luxe Suburban

In Hardtop models, Chevy led the way again. Here are the Bel Air Sport Sedan and Bel Air Sport Coupe in a comparison chart with the 1958 Ford 500 Sport Sedan and Fairlane 500 Sport Coupe. Followed by the 1958 Plymouth Belvedere Sport Sedan and Belvedere Sport Coupe.

Bel Air Sport Sedan

Fairlane 500 Sport Sedan

Belvedere Sport Sedan

The Chevrolet Bel Air Sport Sedan is the world's largest selling 4-door hardtop - and for good reasons. Chevrolet Sport Sedan and Sport Coupe combine the glamour of hardtop styling with the roominess and comfort of conventional sedans.

Bel Air Sport Coupe

Fairlane 500 Sport Coupe

Belvedere Sport Coupe

A rear view of a 1958 six-passenger Brookwood Station Wagon, Model 1693, photo-graphed here with its tailgate in the open position, showing how easy it was to place cargo in the rear compartment. This model offered up to three inches greater loading clearance than others in its field. Sometimes those three inches made the difference in a carrying load!

How'd you like to have this pair in your garage? On the left is Model 1831 Bel Air Sport Coupe that delivered for $2,554. This model was less popular than the newly-introduced Impala Sport Coupe. Next to it is another Level Air Convertible, Model 1867 V-8 Impala Convertible that has already been shown in this chapter. It's just that I don't get enough of looking at 1958 models from every angle. I guess you've figured it out by now why, in the chapter on 1957s, I said, "Wait 'til the next chapter!" Truly, this is the car I lived for.

Chevrolet Accessories For 1958

DEALER LIST AND NET PRICE SCHEDULE

Effective March 15, 1958

ALL PRICES SUBJECT TO CHANGE WITHOUT NOTICE

The "List Prices" shown in this schedule are suggested prices for sales to consumers.

"The prices shown in this schedule, under the heading 'List Prices', are suggested prices only. The prices shown in this schedule, under heading 'Dealer Prices', are the prices at which Chevrolet Motor Division, General Motors Corporation sells replacement parts to its authorized dealers. These prices are subject to change without notice."

Chevrolet Accessories Price Schedule

PASSENGER CAR OPTIONS

Description	Part No.	Part # Per Pkg.	List Price	Dealer Price
AIR CONDITIONER - basic unit	987747	1	445.00	333.75
AIR CONDITIONER - basic unit (Cool Pack) 8 cyl. pass. & trk.	987926	1	268.75	201.55
AIR CONDITIONER - basic unit (Cool Pack) 6 cyl. pass. & trk.	987297	1	268.75	201.55
ADAPTER - for V-8 engine	987743	1	4.90	3.67
ADAPTER - for V-8 engine with air suspension	987844	1	4.90	3.67
ADAPTER - for W engine	987746	1	4.90	3.67
ADAPTER - for W engine with 3 two barrel carburetors	987851	1	18.00	6.00
ADAPTER - (Cool Pack) hoses & evaporator mtg. all pass.	987880	1	28.50	21.38
ADAPTER - (Cool Pack) compressor mtg. for 283 engine	987876	1	17.75	5.82
ADAPTER - (Cool Pack) compressor mtg. for 348 engine	987877	1	17.75	5.82
ADAPTER - (Cool Pack) compressor mtg. for 348 w 3-2 barrel carburetor	987878	1	7.75	5.82
ADAPTER - (Cool Pack) compressor mtg. for 6 cyl. engine	987875	1	12.75	9.57
ADAPTER - (Cool Pack) hose & center dash evaporator mtg. truck only	987879	1	28.50	21.38
ADAPTER - (Cool Pack) hose & R.H. evaporator floor mtg. . . . . trucks only	987884	1	28.50	21.38
ANTENNA - Corvette	987861	1	7.65	4.59
ANTENNA - manual - right front fender	987732	1	6.10	3.66
ANTENNA - manual - right rear fender	987733	1	7.65	4.59
ANTENNA - dummy - left rear fender	987827	1	5.95	3.57
AUTRONIC EYE	987833	1	46.50	34.88
BELT - seat - front or rear	987777	1	10.95	6.57
BRAKE - power	987828	1	45.25	31.68
CAP - locking gasoline tank	987741	1	3.15	1.89
CARRIER - cont. wheel-Impala series - 1 piece bpr	987832	1	148.00	96.20
CARRIER - cont. wheel-all exc. Impala - 1 piece bpr.	987831	1	148.00	96.20
CARRIER - cont. wheel-Impala series - 3 piece bpr.	987704	1	137.00	89.05
CARRIER - cont. wheel-all exc. Impala - 3 piece bpr.	987702	1	137.00	89.05
CARRIER - luggage - station wagon only	987839	1	97.50	68.25

CLOCK - electric	987720	1	17.85	10.71
COMPASS - auto	987737	1	6.25	3.75
CONTAINER - litter	987799	6	3.15	1.89
COVER - accelerator pedal	987760	6	1.35	.81
COVER - wheel - set of four	987761	1	21.90	14.23
CUSHION - (Air Ride)	987899	3	6.95	4.17
DISPENSER - tissue	987800	1	4.40	2.64
FRAME - deluxe license - diecast - pair	987716	1	9.50	5.70
FRAMES - stainless steel license - pair	987815	1	2.50	1.50
GUARD - door edge - 4 door sedan - all	987801	3	6.25	3.75
GUARD - door edge - 2 door sedan - sta. wag. -sdl.	987802	3	3.45	2.07
GUARD - door edge - sport coupe and convertible	987803	3	3.45	2.07
GUARD - door edge - 4 door station wagon	987804	3	6.25	3.75
HARNESS - shoulder	987778	1	10.50	6.30
HEATER & DEFROSTER - deluxe	987742	1	71.50	49.33
HEATER & DEFROSTER - recirculating	987744	1	46.00	31.74
KIT - tool	987322	1	4.35	2.61
LAMP - ash tray	987820	1	1.35	.81
LAMP - back-up all except Impala sta. wagon & sdl.	987783	1	6.25	3.75
LAMP - back-up station wagon & sdl	987784	1	12.00	7.20
LAMP - courtesy	987736	1	2.85	1.71
LAMP - glove compartment	987604	1	1.15	.69
LAMP - luggage compartment	987721	1	2.25	1.35
LAMP - underhood	987738	1	2.25	1.35
LIGHTER - cigarette - with lamp	987683	1	3.35	2.01
MAT - contour - front - blue - pair	987792	1	6.95	4.17
MAT - contour - front - green - pair	987793	1	6.95	4.17
MAT - contour front - turquoise - pair	987794	1	6.95	4.17
MAT - contour front - gunmetal - pair	987795	1	6.95	4.17
MAT - contour front - red - pair	987846	1	6.95	4.17
MAT - contour rear - blue - pair	987852	1	7.25	4.35
MAT - contour rear - green - pair	987853	1	7.25	4.35
MAT - contour rear - turquoise - pair	987854	1	7.25	4.35
MAT - contour rear - gunmetal - pair	987855	1	7.25	4.35
MAT - contour rear - red - pair	987856	1	7.25	4.35
MAT - universal - front or rear - blue - single	987788	6	1.80	1.08
MAT - universal - front or rear - green - single	987789	6	1.80	1.08
MAT - universal - front or rear - turquoise -single	987790	6	1.80	1.08
MAT - universal - front or rear - gunmetal -single	987791	6	1.80	1.08
MAT - universal - front or rear - red - single	987847	6	1.80	1.08
MIRROR - body mount outside rear view - single	987768	1	4.40	2.64
MIRROR - deluxe outside front fender rear view	987845	1	7.95	4.77
MIRROR - non glare inside rear view	987701	1	4.95	2.97
MIRROR - Vanity Visor	986605	1	1.70	1.02
MOULDING - body sill - pair	987739	3	11.75	7.05
ORNAMENT - front fender - pair	987814	1	3.90	2.34
PORT - Exhaust - pair	987779	1	8.90	5.34
RADIO & ANTENNA				
Corvette wonder bar Corv. shielding unit - std. carb	987857	1	135.00	93.15
RADIO & ANTENNA				
wonder bar - Corvette shielding unit w/fuel injection	987858	1	135.00	93.15
RADIO & ANTENNA				
push button - Corvette shielding unit - standard carburetor	987859	1	104.00	71.76
RADIO & ANTENNA				
push button - Corvette shielding unit - w/fuel injection	987860	1	104.00	71.76
RADIO & ANTENNA - manual - front fender antenna	987723	1	57.25	39.50
RADIO & ANTENNA - manual - rear fender antenna	987725	1	57.25	39.50
RADIO & ANTENNA - push button - front antenna	987726	1	78.50	54.16

Description	Part No.	Per Pkg.	List Price	Dealer Price
RADIO & ANTENNA - push button - rear antenna	987728	1	78.50	54.16
RADIO & ANTENNA - wonder bar - front antenna	987729	1	116.00	75.40
RADIO & ANTENNA - wonder bar - rear antenna	987731	1	116.00	75.40
REST - arm - gray - Del Ray - pair	987837	1	6.70	4.02
REST - arm - copper - station wagon - pair	987838	1	6.70	4.02
REST - arm - blue - Del Ray, exc. station wagon & sdl. -pair	987903		6.70	4.02
REST - arm - green - Del Ray, exc. station wagon & sdl. - pair	987904		6.70	4.02
REST - arm - gold - Del Ray, exc. station wagon & sdl. -pair	987997	1	6.70	4.02
SAFETYLIGHT & MIRROR - left hand only	987773	1	28.25	16.95
SCREEN - radiator insect	987772	12	1.20	.72
SHIELD - door handle - 4 door	987796	1	3.50	2.10
SHIELD - door handle - 2 door	987797	1	1.95	1.17
SIGNAL - electric parking brake	987775	1	4.75	2.85
SPEAKER - rear seat - except Impala	987765	1	12.25	7.35
SPEAKER - rear seat - Impala	987766	1	12.25	7.35
SPINNER - wheel - set of four	987812	1	9.95	5.97
SPOT LAMP - portable hand	987112	1	7.95	4.77
SPOT LAMP - outside hand operated	987841	1	17.50	10.50
TANK - vacuum reserve	987811	1	6.20	3.72
TRAY - vacuum ash	987715	1	10.65	6.39
VENTSHADE - 4 door sedan	987806	1	9.75	5.85
VENTSHADE - 2 door sedan	987807	1	9.75	5.85
VENTSHADE - 2 door station wagon	987962		9.75	5.85
VENTSHADE - 4 door station wagon	987963		9.75	5.85
VIEWER - traffic light	987499	1	2.95	1.77
VISOR - right hand sun - Del Ray - gray	987834	1	5.25	3.15
VISOR - right hand sun - sta. wag. - sed. del. -silver	987835	1	5.25	3.15
VISOR - right hand sun - sta. wag. - sed. del. -beige	987836	1	5.25	3.15
VISOR - R.H. blue - Del Ray Series exc. sta. wag. & sdl.	987905	1	5.25	3.15
VISOR - R.H. green - Del Ray Series exc. sta. wag. & sdl.	987906		5.25	3.15
WASHER - windshield - push button - electric wipers	987808	1	10.65	6.39
WASHER - windshield - push button - vacuum wipers	987809	1	10.65	6.39
WASHER - windshield - foot operated - electric wipers	987810	1	8.25	4.95

TRUCK AND COMMERCIAL OPTIONS

Description	Part No.	Part # Per Pkg.	List Price	Dealer Price
ANTENNA - right front fender	987740	1	7.25	4.35
BELT - seat - all cabs	987480	1	11.95	7.17
BLOCK - junction	987616	1	2.20	1.32
BRACKET - inside rear view mirror	987481	1	1.55	.93
BRACKET - splash guard - dual wheel - pair	987228	1	7.95	4.77
BRAKE - power	987821	1	51.50	36.05
COVER - seat - all cabs	987872	1	15.85	9.51
COVER - wheel - set of four	987353	1	16.95	11.01
GUARD - bumper - commercial - chrome	987735	1	20.50	12.30
GUARD - bumper - commercial - painted	987734	1	12.75	7.65
GUARD - grille - commercial	987713	1	35.50	21.30
GUARD - grille - truck	987714	1	41.50	24.90
GUARD - splash - dual wheel - pair	987226	2	12.50	7.50
HEATER & DEFROSTER - deluxe	987691	1	65.50	45.19
HEATER & DEFROSTER - recirculating	987759	1	47.00	32.43
HORN - matched	987695	1	6.85	4.11
LAMP - back-up - commercial	987869	1	12.00	7.20
LAMP - fog - pair	987263	1	17.75	10.65
LAMP - right hand tail and stop exc. Fleetside	987458	1	7.85	4.71

LAMP - right hand tail & stop (Fleetside)	987870		4.75	2.85
LAMP - underhood	987442	1	1.95	1.17
LIGHTER - cigarette	987190	1	3.50	2.10
MIRROR - deluxe rear view	987479	1	14.95	8.97
MIRROR - extendible rear view	987230	1	7.90	4.74
MIRROR - head only	987262	1	2.75	1.65
MIRROR - inside non glare rear view	987615	1	5.35	3.21
RADIO & ANTENNA	987758	1	71.00	42.60
REFLECTOR - red reflex	985223	1	1.95	1.17
REST - arm - single	987771	1	3.90	2.34
SAFETYLIGHT & MIRROR - left hand only	987243	1	22.50	13.50
SIGNAL - direction - panel & cameo	987755	1	18.50	11.10
SIGNAL - direction - (Fleetside)	987871	1	19.75	11.85
SIGNAL - direction - pick-up	987754	1	20.85	12.51
SIGNAL - direction - truck - double face fronts only	987753	1	19.75	11.85
SIGNAL - direction - truck - double face front -flush rear	987752	1	28.00	16.80
SIGNAL - direction - truck - double face front -bracket rear . . .	987751	1	28.50	17.10
SIGNAL - parking brake	987237	1	4.85	2.91
SPOTLAMP - hand portable	987112	1	7.95	4.77
TRAY - utility	987493	1	8.95	5.37
VENTSHADE - All cabs & panels	987203	1	5.75	3.45
VIEWER - traffic light	987499	1	2.95	1.77
VISOR - right hand sun	987767	1	3.40	2.04
VISOR - outside sun - metal	987182	1	9.95	5.97
WASHER - windshield - push button - electric wipe	987824	1	10.65	6.39
WASHER - windshield - push button - vacuum wipers	987825	1	10.65	6.39
WASHER - windshield - foot operated - electric wipers	987826	1	8.25	4.95

1958 Chevrolet Accessories Price Schedule
SERVICE ACCESSORIES

Description	Part No.	Part # Per Pkg.	List Price	Dealer Price
ANTI-FREEZE - G.M. Permanent Type - Quart Cans (24)	986953	1	20.40	13.62
(Single Quart)			(.85)	(.568)
ANTI-FREEZE - G.M. Permanent Type - Gallon Cans (6)	986952	1	19.50	13.02
(Single Gallon)			(3.25)	(2.17)
ANTI-FREEZE - G.M. Methanol Type - Quart Cans (24)	986955	1	10.32	6.84
(Single Quart)			(.43)	(.285)
ANTI-FREEZE - G.M. Methanol Type - Gallon Cans (6)	986954	1	9.60	6.42
(Single Gallon)			(1.60)	(1.07)
ANTI-FREEZE - G.M. Methanol Type - 54 Gallon Drums	986956	1	86.40	53.46
(Single Gallon)			(1.60)	(.99)
ANTI-FREEZE - W/S Washer	987867	1	3.60	2.16
CAROMA EVAPORATOR -Unit (12)	983715	1	3.60	2.16
CHROME GARD (6)	987922		11.70	7.02
(Single Can)			(l.95)	(1.17)
CLEANER-Cooling System (12)	987418	1	12.00	7.20
(Single Can)			(l.00)	(.60)
CLEANER - Leather-All (6)	987476	1	6.00	3.60
(Single Bottle)			(1.00)	(.60)
CLEANER-White Side Wall Tire (6)	987475	1	6.00	3.60
(Single Bottle)			(1.00)	(.60)
CLOTH - Polishing (12)	987570	1	12.00	7.20
(Single Polishing Cloth)			(1.00)	(.60)
COOLING SYSTEM -Anti-Rust & water pump lub. (12)	986977		9.00	5.40
(Single Can)			(.75)	(.45)

DOOR EASE - Stick Lubricant - Utility Size (6)	986897	1	3.00	1.80
(Single Stick)			(.50)	(.30)
GASKET PASTE - Sealing Compound - 6 16 ounce Cans	987266	1	13.50	8.10
(Single Can)			(2.25)	(1.35)
G.M. CLEANER & SPRAY ON POLISH KIT	987722	1	15.80	9.48
(4 Kits Per Part No.)				
KAR KLEEN - 8 oz. Plastic Bottles (12)	987611	1	12.00	7.20
(Single Bottle)			(2.00)	(1.20)
KAR KLEEN - 28 oz. Cans (6)	987456	1	12.00	7.20
(Single Can)			(2.00)	(1.20)
KAR KWIK - Polish (1 Gallon)	987698	1	N.L.	8.00
KAR KWIK - Polish (4 Gallon)	987699	1	N.L.	32.00
KIT - Glass Nu - Consists of 1-24 oz. Glass Nu & 1-3" Ft. Wheel)	987502	1	N.L.	17.25
Glass Nu (24 oz. Can)	987503	1	N.L.	12.60
Felt Wheel (3" used with Glass Nu)	987504	1	N.L.	4.65
LOCK EASE - Lubricant - 4 oz. Cans (12)	986434	1	6.60	3.96
(Single Can)			(.55)	(.33)
LUBRIPLATE -Auto Lube Type A (12) 1-3/4 oz. tubes	987785	1	5.40	3.24
(Single Tube)			(.45)	(.27)
LUBRIPLATE - Auto Lube Type B 1-1 lb. can	987786	1	N.L.	.62
LUSTER SEAL - #1 Machine - 12 oz. Bottles (12)	986945	1	40.20	24.00
(Single Bottle)			(3.35)	(2.00)
LUSTER SEAL - #2 Machine - 12 oz. Bottles (12)	986946	1	40.20	24.00
(Single Bottle)			(3.35)	(2.00)
LUSTER SEAL - Haze Cream - 8 oz. Bottles (24)	986947	1	24.00	14.40
(Single Bottle)			(1.00)	(.60)
LUSTER SEAL - #1 Machine - Gallon Can	987284	1	28.50	17.00
LUSTER SEAL - #2 Machine - Gallon Can	987285	1	28.50	17.00
MITT-ANGORA - Washing - Dusting (12)	987269	1	19.80	11.88
(Single Unit)			(1.65)	(.99)
NUT-EZE - Rust & Corrosion - penetrant 12-8 oz. cans	987882	1	9.00	5.40
(Single Can)			(.75)	(.45)
OIL - DRIPLESS - Penetrating - 4 oz. Cans (36)	986082	1	9.00	4.68
(Single Can)			(.25)	(.13)
PAINT-RECONDITIONING - Black 1-Gallon	987680	1	N.L.	3.50
PAINT - Upholstery - Red	987666	1	N.L.	2.60
PAINT - Upholstery - Turquoise	987667	1	N.L.	2.60
PAINT - Upholstery - Taupe	987668	1	N.L.	2.60
PAINT - Upholstery - Dark Green	987669	1	N.L.	2.60
PAINT - Upholstery - Light Gray	987670	1	N.L.	2.60
PAINT - Upholstery - Dark Blue	987671	1	N.L.	2.60
PAINT - Upholstery - Light Blue	987672	1	N.L.	2.60
PAINT - Upholstery - Maroon	987673	1	N.L.	2.60
PAINT - Upholstery - Dark Gray	987674	1	N.L.	2.60
PAINT - Upholstery - Light Green	987675	1	N.L.	2.60
PAINT - Upholstery - Yellow	987676	1	N.L.	2.60
PAINT - Upholstery - Black	987677	1	N.L.	2.60
PAINT - Upholstery - Brown	987678	1	N.L.	2.60
PAINT - Upholstery - White	987679	1	N.L.	2.60
PLASTIC SOLDER - Repair Kit	987511	1	N.L.	15.75
POLISH - Chromium - 8 oz. Cans (12)	986084	1	6.00	3.60
(Single Can)			(.50)	(.30)
POLISH - Triple Action - 16 oz. Cans (12)	986085	1	12.00	7.20
(Single Can)			(1.00)	(.60)
POLISH - Triple Action - 1 Gallon Can	985888	1	4.00	2.40
PORCELAINIZE - Liquid - 6 oz. Bottles (24)	986175	1	105.60	60.00
(Single Bottle)			N.L.	(2.50)
PORCELAINIZE - Wash Cream - 8 oz. Bottles (24)	986176	1	20.00	12.00
(Single Bottle)			(.85)	(.50)

PORCELAINIZE - Cleaner - Gallon Can	986363	1	N.L.	6.10
PORCELAINIZE - Fastac - 8 oz. Bottles (24)	986961	1	30.00	18.00
(Single Bottle)			(1.25)	(.75)
RESIN KIT	987341	1	N.L.	21.50
CLOTH - Fiberglass - 3-1/2 Yds.	987342	1	N.L.	6.65
RESIN - 2 Lb. Can	987343	1	N.L.	5.25
HARDENER - 1 Lb. Can	987344	1	N.L.	2.75
FILLER - 1/2 Lb. Can	987345	1	N.L.	1.35
RUGLYDE - Rubber Lubricant & Cleaner - Gallon Can	986047	1	3.60	2.15
SEALZIT - Glass Sealer - 2 oz. Bottles (12)	986199	1	10.20	6.12
(Single Bottle)			(.85)	(.51)
SOLVENT - W/S Washer -36- 2 oz. envelopes per package	987631	1	7.50	4.50
SPOT REMOVER - 8 oz. Cans (12)	987272	1	9.00	5.40
(Single Can)			(.75)	(.45)
STOP LEAK - Radiator - Pellets (12)	987689	1	6.00	3.60
(Single)			(.50)	(.30)
STOP LEAK - Radiator - 10 Ounce Cans (12)	986088	1	9.00	5.40
(Single Can)			(.75)	(.45)
SPRAY-A-SQUEAK - Silicone Spray 6 16 oz. Cans	987883	1	8.10	4.86
(Single Can)			(1.35)	(.81)
TAR & ROAD OIL - Remover (12)	987782	1	9.00	5.40
(16 oz. Can)			(.75)	(.45)
TINT - Upholstery - (Used Cars) Blue	987482	1	N.L.	1.40
(1 pkg. of 2, 2 oz. envelopes)				
TINT - Upholstery - (Used Cars) Green	987483	1	N.L.	1.40
(1 pkg. of 2, 2 oz. envelopes)				
TINT - Upholstery - (Used Cars) Taupe	987484	1	N.L.	1.40
(1 pkg. of 2, 2 oz. envelopes)				
TINT - Upholstery - (Used Cars) Brown	987485	1	N.L.	1.40
(I pkg. of 2, 2 oz. envelopes)				
TINT - Upholstery - (Used Cars) Grey	987486	1	N.L.	1.40
(1 pkg. of 2, 2 oz. envelopes)				
TINT - Upholstery - (Used Cars) Yellow	987487	1	N.L.	1.40
(1 pkg. of 2, 2 oz. envelopes)				
TINT - Upholstery - (Used Cars) Turquoise	987488	1	N.L.	1.40
(1 pkg. of 2, 2 oz. envelopes)				
TINT - Upholstery - (Used Cars) Red	987489	1	N.L.	1.40
(1 pkg. of 2, 2 oz. envelopes)				
TOUCH-UP PAINT				
Chevrolet Colors--Dealers Choice of any (6) Colors	987865	1	6.00	3.60
(Single Tube)			(1.00)	(.60)
TOUCH-UP PAINT - 1958 20 spray cans assortment	987866	1	37.00	22.20
TOUCH-UP PAINT - (Spray) Dealers Choice (6)	987684	1	11.10	6.66
TOUCH-UP PAINT - 1958 - 24 tubes and display	987864	1	24.00	14.40
UNDERCOATING - Drum	986359	1	N.L.	40.63
UNDERCOATING - Truck Load (44)	986653	1	N.L.	1,512.72
UNDERCOATING - Car Load (80)	986548	1	N.L.	2,590.40
UNDERCOATING - Drum (P.C. Only)	986635	1	N.L.	40.63
UNDERCOATING - Truck Load (P.C. Only) (44)	986654	1	N.L.	1,512.72
UNDERCOATING - Car Load (P.C. Only) (80)	986638	1	N.L.	2,590.40

Shown on the previous pages are the 1958 suggested retail prices delivered to California along with the car option and accessory list. Some figures differ from prices under the captions.

The first day I owned my 1958 Impala, I took this shot of the taillight ensemble. Then I replaced it with the three red lights, placing the station wagon units next to the license.

Basically, this car looks the same as my Honey Beige '58 Impala Sport Coupe. However, this example, is done in Snowcrest White and its main difference consists of a factory safety light and mirror which cost an additional $28.95. The part number for this accessory was 987773. It was really a rather useless piece of equipment as it was difficult to see anything in the side mirror, and how often does one really put a spotlight to work?

When the 1958 Silver Blue Impala was about one-month old. The car looks the same today with 63,000 miles registered on the odometer.

With all windows down the car really gave a care-free appearance to an already beautiful car. The one big problem that many of us weren't even aware of living in Southern California was all that SMOG on a hot summer day! How we've grown accustomed to being in an air-conditioned car.

My 1958 Chevrolet Impala. Car had about 2900 miles when picture was taken in January of 1960.

Check out all the great lines of the 1958 Chevrolet. Just looking at one reminds me why the 1958 Chevrolet was my favorite of all the Chevrolets of the fifties.

'59 Corvette with new polished performance.

CHEVY'S GOT A CAR THAT LEADS YOUR KIND OF LIFE!

Chevy's come up with a combination for '59 that'll gladden anyone's heart. Fine, fresh styling that's as practical as it is handsome! Beneath that Slimline design you'll find new engineering that goes down deep. There's new roominess, new riding stability, a new Hi-Thrift 6 that stretches the distance between gas stops. For '59 you'll find more good reasons for going Chevy than ever before.

The '59 Chevy's a natural for on-the-go people who want practicality in a car as well as fresh new style. It offers a roomier Body by Fisher with vast new areas of visibility.

And there's new feel, new efficiency beneath that beauty—bigger brakes, a smoother ride, new handling ease, safer, stronger Tyrex cord tires. Chevy offers a peppery new 6 that can knock as much as 10% off gas costs—or vim-packed V8's. And has a

finish that keeps its luster for up to three years without waxing or polishing. You can choose from 14 beautiful models, including five wonderfully versatile wagons. There's also the '59 edition of America's only authentic sports car, the incomparable Corvette.

All at your Chevrolet dealer's! Stop by and see him soon. He's got a car that leads *your* kind of life! . . . Chevrolet Division of General Motors, Detroit 2, Michigan.

'59 CHEVROLET

What America wants,
America gets in a Chevy!

New 9-passenger Kingswood with rear-facing third seat. Chevy also offers 2- and 4-door 6-passenger wagons.

Chevrolet's lowest-priced offering for 1959 was this Biscayne Utility Sedan known as Model 1121, if equipped with a 6 cylinder engine. If the V-8 was chosen, the model then became a 1221. The Utility Sedan weighed 3480 and delivered for $2,160. Looking exactly the same from the exterior was the more popular Biscayne 2-Door Sedan which tipped the scale at 3535 pounds and as a 6-cylinder sold for $2247.

Chevrolet for 1959

Planned obsolescence was General Motors' plot at this time and they couldn't have proven it better than the differences between their 1958 and 1959 cars. It appears to me that, if you liked the 1958 cars, chances are you didn't care for the 1959 models. In my case, this was pretty much the truth and yet, with only a facelift, I liked the 1960s.

The 1959 Chevrolets increased their wheelbase once again and now rode on 119 inches with an overall length of 211 inches. Chevy was now the longest car in the low-priced field and its width was three inches wider than 1958 models.

A new model made its debut for 1959. Even though this book is basically Chevrolet passenger cars the vehicle classed as a truck I prefer to put it in the car category. It was the new El Camino pickup. The frontal appearance is that of a passenger car so that is why it rates being placed in here. Also, a change was seen in series designations for 1959. The low-priced Delray was now history and down graded one slot was the Biscayne to become the low-priced series. The top of the line Bel Air series since 1953 now was classed as the middle series and the previous year sub series to the Bel Air, the Impala, now became a series until itself as the luxury line for the year. All wagons remained as a series. The 2-Door Brookwood being the lowest priced wagon for $2,589, followed by the 4-Door Brookwood selling in 6-cylinder fashion for $2,656. The middle line of wagons included the six-passenger Parkwood for $2,767, and a nine-passenger version called the Kingswood, the heaviest wagon Chevrolet built in 1959 weighing 4015 pounds and selling for $2,970. The top of the line wagon was again the Nomad Model 1835, selling for $3,034.

Mechanically, only small changes occurred for 1959. The 6-cylinder engine decreased 10 horsepower from the previous year, but had the same 8.25:1 compression ratio at 4000 RPM. The basic V-8 of 283 cubic inches was still developing 185 horsepower for most of the V-8 production. For the optional V-8,

The Biscayne 4-door Sedan was Chevrolet's lowest-priced model in the 4-Door range. It was available either as a 6-cylinder or V-8. The 6-cylinder was more popular in this series of models. It weighed 3605 pounds going out the door for $2,301. A total of 311,800 Biscaynes were produced in all models for 1959.

Coming for the first year was the El Camino. Personally, I felt this was the best-looking model in the Chevrolet lineup for 1959. This example used the basic body shell of the 2-Door Wagon and often was referred to as a car with comfort, style, and also used as a utility vehicle. The El Camino had a load capacity of 1000 pounds. It weighed 3620 pounds and delivered for $2,470.

The middle class of Chevrolet vehicles for 1959 were now known as Bel Air models. This was the Bel Air 4-Door Sedan referred to as Model 1519 as a Six, or 1619 as a V-8. In V-8 fashion it delivered for $2,558. The 6-cylinder model sold for only $40 less, which is probably why most people spent the additional cost for a V-8.

customers were offered nine choices of engines, rather than only six choices as last year. The Super Turbo Fire 283 4-barrel produced 230 horsepower, for an additional $147. The Ram-Jet Fuel Injection 283, giving 250 horsepower, cost an additional $485 and, lastly, for the 283 cubic-inch engines, was a Ram Jet with 10.5:1 compression ratio which developed 290 horsepower at 6200 RPM. This engine was available for the same tab of $485 additional.

In the 348 cubic-inch engine compartment, the basic optional engine called Turbo Thrust, which produced 250 horsepower, was available for an additional $80.70. With an added choice of Super Turbo-Thrust being available developing 280 horsepower the customer could have it for $150 if the wallet warranted it. This engine used triple two-barrel carburetors and was not classed as an economical venture. In addition to the two above-described special Turbo Thrust engines, each were available with 4-barrel carburetors. One offered 305 horsepower with 11.1 compression. It was available for $172 extra while the other engine developed 320 horsepower with a compression ratio of 11.25:1. Each engine had a 5600 RPM rating. Its cost was $212, additionally. Next in the lineup came the Special Super Turbo-Thrust 348 requiring triple two-barrel carburetors. This block produced 315 horsepower with a compression ratio of 11.1, or if a 345 horsepower version were ordered with compression being 11.25:1 each turned over at 5600 RPM. Obviously, these engines required premium of premium fuels for them to operate efficiently. It seems strange why people today still want this type of engine when our no-lead gasoline that is available makes it very difficult for them to perform at their utmost potential. I suppose hardened valve seats would help to give them longer life. The true muscle engines and fuel injection units were ordered in a limited number for the model year.

A Bel Air 2-Door Sedan closely resembled the Biscayne 2-Door with only a little more trim on the Bel Air side panels. It weighed 3515 pounds and delivered for $2,386 as a 6-cylinder. A V-8 weighed oddly five pounds less and sold for $2,504. Models were fewer in 1959 and the production figures for Bel Air cars consisted of 447,100 units produced.

The most noticeable body changes from the 58 cars appeared in the rear quarter panel fins and cat's eye taillights. With it's complete change in appearance, the 1959 sales catalog put it this way when it stated, "Chevrolet for '59, all new all over again." The 4-Door hardtop design was entirely different from the previous year. It offered better visibility from the pillarless wrap-around rear window design. The roofline of the Hardtop Sedan carried an overhang lip to its flat roof which took a while for most to accept. Regular Sedans did not offer this feature. The Impala Sport Coupe for 1958 featured a special center armrest for rear seat passengers which added a touch of pizzazz. This, unfortunately, did not appear on the 1959 Sport Coupes. Full wheel covers were standard equipment in each of the top of the line Bel Airs from 1953 through 1958. However, for some strange reason, they became an option for the entire Impala line in 1959 and cost the owner an additional $16.05. A total of 14 models were available for 1959, coming in either a 6 or 8-cylinder style.

The color choices given to customers consisted of 13 single colors:

Frost Blue
Harbor Blue
Aspen Green
Highland Green
Classic Cream
Gothic Gold
Satin Beige
Crown Sapphire
Tuxedo Black
Snowcrest White
Roman Red
Grecian Gray
Cameo Coral

The following color schemes were available in all models except the convertible.

Bottom	Top
Frost Blue	Harbor Blue
Harbor Blue	Frost Blue
Classic Cream	Aspen Green
Highland Green	Snowcrest White
Gothic Gold	Satin Beige
Crown Sapphire	Snowcrest White
Tuxedo Black	Snowcrest White
Roman Red	Snowcrest White
Grecian Gray	Snowcrest White
Cameo Coral	Satin Beige

With complete body changes in the regular line of cars, Chevrolet did little in changing the appearance of the one year old styling of the Corvette. Quickly looking at it, it appeared virtually unchanged. Upon closer scrutiny, one would see the fake hood louvers were no longer present which I felt was a plus in giving a cleaner front-end appearance. Also not seen on the '59s were the two chrome stops placed on the trunk lid of the '58s. These small changes made it easy to tell the difference between the 1959 and 1959 Corvette.

Engine compartments continued using the 283 cubic-inch block of 230 horses. In addition, options included a $150 dual 4-barrel developing 245 horsepower and, with a higher compression ratio producing 270 horsepower, was seen later in the season. Besides these examples, two fuel injection

This is the 1959 Brookwood 2-Door Wagon which saw a production schedule of 20,766 units. It weighed 3860 pounds and delivered for $2,689. It was classified as a Model 1115 or 1215 depending which engine was under the hood. This example also was available in 2-Door style for $2,571.

Here sits a 1959 Parkwood Station Wagon. This body style came in either six-passenger or nine-passenger model. If the car was a 6-cylinder, nine-passenger model, they called it the Kingswood which sold for $2,852 weighing in at 4020 pounds. The V-8 delivered for $2,970. The Parkwood six-passenger Model 1635 weighed 3970 pounds and sold for $2,867.

The top of the line Nomad 4-Door six-passenger Wagon claimed to be the smartest, smoothest and most luxurious of all Nomads to date. I'm afraid I'll have to take issue with this. The vehicle was the most expensive Chevrolet for 1959, selling for $3,009. Generally, it sold as a V-8 which weighed 3,975 pounds. If the 6-cylinder engine were employed, it, like other wagons, would have weighed five pounds less.

examples debuted with a 250 horsepower and 290 horsepower engine being available for the young at heart. Each engine could be purchased in the $500 extra range. The 348 cubic-inch engine was not available from Chevrolet for the Corvette.

Production figures for the year list Chevrolet's model year at 1,481,071 units sold, and their calendar year sales amounted to 1,428,962 vehicles delivered. So, this was another one of those "Who's on first?" sales years. Chevrolet beat Ford for model sales, while Ford stole the show for the calendar year with 1,528,592 units delivered.

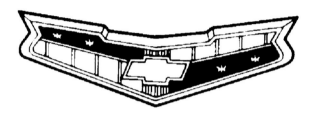

A friend from the cradle days owned this Snowcrest White 1959 Impala Convertible. It was his first brand new car and, like with any of us, was just slightly proud of it. As a V-8, which most were, weighing 3650 pounds, it delivered for $2,967.

A Chevrolet display of 1959 cars shows a variety of models from a Corvette in the foreground to a Biscayne 2-Door in the background. Note the Continental Kit Impala Sedan in the center of the display. The Continental Kit cost an additional $216 in 1959.

Two views of 1959 Impala Sport Sedans. Note the bottom photo shows the vehicle has Level Air from the nameplate at the right by the license plate. The Sport Sedan weighed 3670 pounds equipped as a V-8 and delivered for $2,782. The roof line on this model as on all G.M. vehicles for the year had its public who really liked it and others who gave it no plusses.

(Top) The rear end of 1959 Chevys was another controversial issue among diehard Chevy enthusiasts. The cat's eyes were something else again. You either loved it or hated it. One automotive publisher once said, "If anyone but Chevrolet built that car, they wouldn't have made it through the year." Others felt it was the road we were headed for with yearly body changes, basically referred to by G.M. as "Planned Obsolescence." I look at what G.M. has done in the past 15 years — in fact, the whole auto industry — and feel they were totally wrong with the Planned Obsolescence program. Today you can't tell one model from another and the public really doesn't care. How things have changed with the automotive market.

(Bottom) A close-up view of the 1959 Impala Convertible with its low-placed headlights and grille of one-piece anodized aluminum with 9 horizontal bars and 7 vertical dividers; conical projections decorated the centers of the dividers. Screened air inlets above the grille helped to cool the engine.

New car structure below belt line is essentially same for all models. In contrast with airiness of roof and windows, it is wider, longer and lower than in 1958, adding to car's fleet appearance. Distance from front of car to front wheels is less, shortening front fenders, while distance from rear wheels to rear of car is longer, increasing length of rear fenders and rear deck.

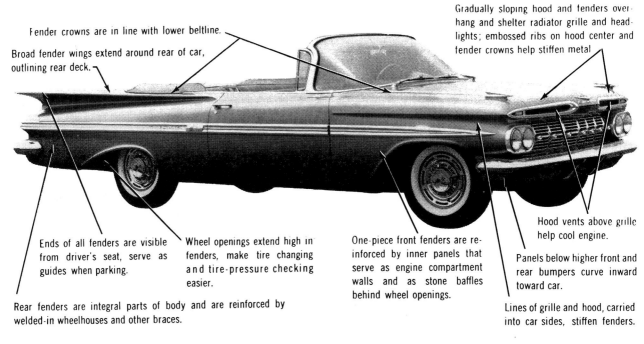

Fender crowns are in line with lower beltline.

Broad fender wings extend around rear of car, outlining rear deck.

Gradually sloping hood and fenders overhang and shelter radiator grille and headlights; embossed ribs on hood center and fender crowns help stiffen metal

Ends of all fenders are visible from driver's seat, serve as guides when parking.

Wheel openings extend high in fenders, make tire changing and tire-pressure checking easier.

One-piece front fenders are reinforced by inner panels that serve as engine compartment walls and as stone baffles behind wheel openings.

Hood vents above grille help cool engine.

Panels below higher front and rear bumpers curve inward toward car.

Rear fenders are integral parts of body and are reinforced by welded-in wheelhouses and other braces.

Lines of grille and hood, carried into car sides, stiffen fenders.

Some detailed explanations as shown on the 1959 Convertible.

A three-quarter rear view of the 1959 Impala Sport Coupe, Model 1847. This unit weighed 3580 pounds and sold for $2,717, if equipped with a V-8 engine.

One of the cleanest-looking examples for Chevrolet in 1959 was this Model 1867, or better referred to as the Impala Convertible. Wheel discs were not considered as part of the standard equipment package on its top-of-the-line models, as they had been since 1953. This year, if the buyer wished them, they cost an additional $16.05.

Still classed in the passenger car lineup, but with dwindling sales due to the popularity of the new style El Camino, is the familiar Sedan Delivery which would soon play its "swan song" at the end of the following season. The Sedan Delivery was classed as Model 1170, or 1270 if equipped as a V-8.

The spacious trunk compartment of the 1959 Impala came with a vinyl-coated jute in Impala and Bel Air models, while the Biscayne employed a black mat.

A close-up view of a well-restored 1959 Impala taken at the 1993 Hershey Car Meet. This vehicle wears its Senior badge on the grille, telling us it has had top honors bestowed upon it. The accessory grille guard cost $31.50 extra. It also sports the super deluxe wheel covers with center spinner which are fairly rare to find today.

Another close-up of the super deluxe 1959 wheel cover with the slotted openings near the outer edge admitting cool air to the brakes.

Sitting at a rakish angle is this 1959 Impala Sport Coupe equipped well with factory accessories. This vehicle was displayed at the 1993 Hershey Car Meet.

The fender skirt treatment added greatly to the appearance of this 1959 Impala Sport Coupe. However, fender skirts were not part of the factory approved accessories for the year. Truly the last factory skirts offered by Chevrolet was in 1954 and would not return as a factory piece of equipment until 1967.

Impala Series interiors were completely new and bigger for 1959. Chevrolet's most luxurious interiors feature: New seat materials, enhanced by bright metal front seat end panels in sports models.

Chevrolet Accessories For 1959

DEALER LIST AND NET PRICE SCHEDULE

Effective October 16, 1958

ALL PRICES SUBJECT TO CHANGE WITHOUT NOTICE

The "List Prices" shown in this schedule are suggested prices for sales to consumers.

EIGHT CYLINDER

IMPALA SERIES	Turboglide	Powerglide	Standard
1819 - 4 Dr. Sedan	$3098.35	$3055.35	$2856.25
1837 - Spt. Cpe.	3105.35	3062.35	2863.25
1839 - Spt. Sedan	3170.35	3127.35	2928.25
1867 - Convertible	3362.85	3319.85	3120.75
BEL AIR SERIES			
1611 - 2 Dr. Sedan	2892.35	2849.35	2650.25
1619 - 4 Dr. Sedan	2946.35	2903.35	2704.25
BISCAYNE SERIES			
1221 - Utility Sdn	2666.35	2623.35	2424.25
1211 - 2 Dr. Sedan	2753.35	2710.35	2511.25
1219 - 4 Dr. Sedan	2807.35	2764.35	2565.25
STATION WAGON SERIES			
1215 - 2 Dr. "Brkwd." - 6 Pass.	3084.85	3041.85	2842.75
1235 - 4 Dr. "Brkwd." - 6 Pass.	3151.85	3108.85	2909.75
1635 - 4 Dr. "Prkwd." - 6 Pass.	3262.85	3219.85	3020.75
1645 - 4 Dr. "Kngwd." - 9 Pass.	3365.85	3322.85	3123.75
1835 - Nomad	3404.85	3361.85	3162.75
CORVETTE - (867)			
Man. Top - Single 4 Bbl		4220.35	4021.25

SIX CYLINDER

IMPALA SERIES	Turboglide	Powerglide	Standard
1719 - 4 Dr. Sedan	2980.35	2937.35	2738.25
1737 - Spt. Cpe.	2987.35	2944.35	2745.25
1739 - Spt. Sedan	3052.35	3009.35	2810.25
1767 - Convertible	3244.85	3201.85	3002.75
BEL AIR SERIES			
1511 - 2 Dr. Sedan	2774.35	2731.35	2532.25
1519 - 4 Dr. Sedan	2828.35	2785.35	2586.25
BISCAYNE SERIES			
1121 - Utility Sdn	2548.35	2505.35	2306.25
1111 - 2 Dr. Sedan	2635.35	2592.35	2393.25
1119 - 4 Dr. Sedan	2689.35	2646.35	2447.25
STATION WAGON SERIES			
1115 - 2 Dr. "Brkwd." - 6 Pass.	2966.85	2923.85	2724.75
1135 - 4 Dr. "Brkwd." - 6 Pass.	3033.85	2990.85	2791.75
1535 - 4 Dr. "Prkwd." - 6 Pass.	3144.85	3101.85	2902.75
I545- 4 Dr. "Kngwd." - 9 Pass.	3247.85	3204.85	3005.75
1735 - Nomad	3286.85	3243.85	3044.75

Shown here are the 1959 suggested retail prices for Chevrolet cars delivered to California, along with the 1959 car options and accessories. Some figures are different from quoted prices under the caption list.

Option No.	PASSENGER CAR OPTIONS	
110	Air Conditioning (Including Heater	$468.10
580	Air Suspension	134.50
412	Brakes, Power	43.05
347	DeLuxe Equipment	16.15
380	Electric Seat Control	102.25
424	Electric Tail Gate Control	32.30
426	Electric Window Control	102.25
410	Engine, Super Turbo-Fire (230 H.P.)	29.10
576	Engine, Turbo-Thrust (250 H.P.)	80.70
576	Engine, Special Turbo Thrust (300 H.P.)	172.20
573	Engine, Super Turbo-Thrust (280 H.P.)	150.65
573	Engine, Special Super Turbo-Thrust (315 H.P.)	195.85
578	Engine, Ramjet Fuel Injection (250 H.P. Std.)	484.20
578	Engine, Special Ramjet Fuel Injection (290 H.P.)	484.20
220	Exhaust, Dual	19.40
398	E Z I	43.05
388	E Z I (Rear Window Only - 17-1837)	21.55
101	Heater, De Luxe	80.25
116	Heater, Recirculating	51.90
237	Oil Filter	9.15
315	Overdrive	107.60
427	Padded Dash	18.30
*675	Positraction	48.45
*313	Powerglide	199.10
324	Power Steering	75.35
335	Seat Cushion - Foam Rubber Front	7.55
302	Turboglide	242.10
	Two-Tone (Biscayne)	21.55
	Two-Tone (Brookwood, Bel Air, Impala)	26.90
	Two-Tone (Parkwood, Kingswood, Nomad)	32.30
117	Wheel Discs	16.05
348	Wheel, Steering	3.80
*465	White Side Wall Tires (7.50x14 - 4 Ply)	31.55
588	White Side Wall Tires (8.00x14 - 4 Ply)	35.85
*333	Windshield Wipers (with Washer)	16.15

Corvette Options

426	Electric Window Control	59.20
469A,B	Engine, 245 H.P. Dual 4 Brl. (Reg. Cam)	150.65
469C	Engine, 270 H.P. Dual 4 Brl. (High Lift Cam)	182.95
579A,C,D	Engine, Fuel Injection, 250 H.P. (Reg. Cam)	484.20
579	Engine, Fuel Injection, 290 H.P. (High-Lift Cam)	484.20
101D	Heater	102.25
108	Light, Courtesy	6.50
107	Parking Brake Alarm	5.40
102	Radio, Signal Seeking	149.80
261	Sunshades; Right & Left	10.80
473	Top, Hydraulic, Folding	139.90
419	Top, Removable, Hard	236.75
685	Transmission, 4 Spd. Close Ratio	188.30
	Two-Tone Paint	16.15
	*Available Same Price on Corvette	

PASSENGER CAR ACCESSORIES

AIR CONDITIONER (Cool Pack) 340.75
ANTENNA, Right Rear 10.85
ANTENNA, Left Rear, Dummy 7.00
AUTRONIC Eye 57.25
BELT, Seat (each) 15.50
BRAKE, Power 43.00
CARRIER, Continental Wheel 216.00
CARRIER, Luggage (Sedans Coupes) 89.50
CARRIER, Luggage (Station Wagons) 103.00
CLOCK, Electric 18.95
CONTAINER, Litter 4.40
COVER, Wheel (Set of four) 24.00
DISPENSER, Tissue 5.90
GLARESHADE, Windshield 17.25
GLARESHADE, Rear Window (Spt. Cpe.) 19.25
GUARD, Rear License Plate Pocket 5.40
GUARD, Door Edge (Two doors) 3.95
GUARD, Door Edge (Four doors) 7.35
GUARD, Front Bumper Grille 31.50
LAMP, Ashtray 2.35
LAMP, Backup 11.95
LAMP, Courtesy (Bel Air & Impala) 4.90
LAMP, Courtesy (Biscayne) 5.80
LAMP, Glove Compartment 2.60
LAMP, Luggage Compartment 3.75
LAMP, Underhood 4.15
LIGHTER, Cigarette 4.50
MAT, Front Contour (pair) 6.95
MAT, Rear Contour (pair) 7.25
MAT, Rear Station Wagon (Gray) 9.85
MAT, Floor (each) 1.85
MIRROR, Rearview, Body Mount 5.95
MIRROR, Nonglare 5.85
MIRROR & Comb Vanity Visor 2.40
MOULDING, Body Sill (pair) 14.50
ORNAMENT, Front Fender (pair) 7.00
PORTS, Exhaust 11.00
RADIO, Manual with front antenna 63.75
RADIO, Push-Button with front antenna 84.00
RADIO, Wonderbar with front antenna 121.50
REST, Arm (pair) (Biscayne Series) 8.50
SAFETY light 34.50
SHIELD, Door Handle (pair) 2.95
SIGNAL, Parking Brake 3.85
SPEAKER, Rear Seat (all except Station Wagon) 15.25
SPEAKER, Rear Seat with Grille (Station Wagon) 18.85
SPEEDMINDER 23.95
SPINNER (Wheel (set of four) 19.25
THROTTLE HOLDER 17.50
TRAY, Vacuum Ash 14.75
VENTSHADES (4 windows) 11.45
VISOR, R.H. Sun (Biscayne Series) 6.85
WASHER, W/S, Push Button 17.35

TRUCK INFORMATION

*1170-(6) $2504.50	3603 . . . . $2159.50	6103 . . . . $3034.75
*1270-(8) 2622.50	3604 . . . . 2286.50	6403 . . . . 3066.75
1180-(6) 2493.50	3609 . . . . 2377.50	6503 . . . . 3129.50
1280-(8) 2611.50	3634 . . . . 2302.50	6703 . . . . 3187.50
3103 . . . . 1957.50	3654-(4 WD) 3404.25	7103 . . . . 4316.40
3104 . . . . 2089.50	3803 . . . . 2318.50	7703 . . . . 4445.40
3105 . . . . 2390.50	3804 . . . . 2452.50	8103 . . . . 3955.00
3106 . . . . 2734.25	3805 . . . . 2802.00	8703 . . . . 4134.40
3116 . . . . 2767.25	3809 . . . . 2587.00	9103 . . . . 5695.40
3134 . . . . 2105.50	4403 . . . . 2608.00	9703 . . . . 5824.40
3154-(4 WD) 3124.00	5103 . . . . 3452.75	10103 . . . . 5265.40
3204 . . . . 2127.50	5403 . . . . 3496.75	10403 . . . . 5319.40
3234 . . . . 2143.50	5703 . . . . 3539.75	10703 . . . . 5406.40

*Add $75.35 For Full Width Seat, Option 482D

OPTIONS - ALL SERIES

210 - R.V. Mirror, RH . . . . $ 4.85	Two-Tone (Exc.Fleetside) 16.15
258 - Foam Rubber Seat 17.25	Two-Tone (Fleetside Only) 37.70
345 - H.D. Battery 7.55	Two-Tone (Panels) 26.90
394 - Pan Window 43.05	W/S Wiper 7.55

OPTIONS - SERIES 30

200-Shock Absrb.(3800) . . . . $ 26.90	316-3 Spd Trans. (3800) 21.55
218-Rear Bump. (Painted) 21.55	318-4 Spd.Trans.
218-Rear Bump. (Chrome) 32.30	(31.34,35,3700) 75.35
227-H.D.Clutch 5.40	318-4 Spd. Trans. (3200) 80.70
237-Oil Filter (1 Qt.) 9.15	318-4 Spd. Trans. (3600) 91.50
592-Oil Filter (2 Qt.) 12.95	341-Tire Carrier (side mt.) 16.15
254-H.D. Rear Springs 6.50	350-Power Steering 123.75
256-H.D. Radiator 16.15	408-V-8 Engine 129.15
263-Auxiliary Seat 40.90	431-Cust. Cab (3105-3805) 69.95
314-Hydramatic 252.90	431-Cust. Cab (31,32,3634) 102.25
316-3 Spd. Trans.(3100) 69.95	431-Custom Cab (3000,
316-3 Spd. Trans.	Exc. Fleetside) 86.10
(32,34,35,3700) 75.35	591-OBAC 4.35
316-3 Spd. Trans. (3600) . . . . $ 86.10	675-Positraction (31,3200) 64.60

OPTIONS-SERIES 40

212-Hydrovac $45.20	321-Hydramatic $252.90
256-H.D.Radiator 16.15	350-Power Steering 145.30
267-Auxiliary Springs 26.90	408-V-8 Engine 129.15
281-Vacuum Tank 23.70	431-Custom Cab 48.45

OPTIONS-SERIES 50-60

201-2 Spd. Rear Axle $150.65	350-Power Steering $145.30
253-H.D. Frt. Springs 5.40	413-Brakes 285.15
254-H.D. Rear Springs 17.25	414-H.D. Brake Booster 26.90
309-Powermatic Trans. 833.90	451-H.D.Whls.(6.75) 22.60
322-5 Spd. Trans. 188.30	584-H.D. Frt. Axle 204.45

TIRE OPTIONS

288-(5) 6.70X15-6 Ply	299-(6) 8X19.5-8 Ply Duals
(31-3200) . . . . $ 44.55	(4000) 87.30
298-(4) 8x17.5-6 Ply	228-(6) 9x22.5-10 Ply Duals
(3600) 32.60	(5-6-7-8000) 216.30
462-(6) 8x19.5-6 Ply Duals	238-(6) 10x22.5-10 Ply Duals
(3800) 190.60	(5-6-7-8000) 389.95
459-(6) 7x22.5-8 Ply Duals . . . . 458-(6)	11x22.5-12 Ply Duals
(4000) 56.70	(9-10000) .429.85

COLORS

700-Jet Black	708-Baltic Blue	718-Golden Yellow
703-Galway Green	710-Tartan Turquoise	719-Yukon Yellow
704-Sherwood Green	712-Frontier Beige	721-Pure White
705-Glade Green	714-Cardinal Red	523-Cadet Gray
707-Dawn Blue	716-Omaha Orange	

ACCESSORIES (Installed) (Except El Camino)

Block, Junction . . . . $ 4.25	Lighter, Cigarette 4.15
Brake, Power .58.00	Mirror, 5 x 7 R.V. 12.50
Bumper, Rear-Step (Fleetside) 44.50	Mirror, 15 x 6b Deluxe (Pair) 39.80
Cover, Wheel (Set of Four) 17.95	Mirror, 1.R.V. (With Bracket) 7.90
Equipment, Legal	Radio & Antenna 83.00
Guard, Bumper (Painted) 13.75	Rest, Arm (Each) 5.50
Guard, Bumper (Chrome) 21.50	Safety Light with Mirror 28.50
Guard, Grille-Com. 40.50	Signal, Dir. (Pickup & Panel) 27.95
Guard, Grille-Truck 46.50	Signal, Dir. (Stake) 38.85
Heater & Defroster-DeLuxe 78.50	Visor, R.H. Sun 5.10
Heater & Defroster-Recir. 57.00	Visor, Outside (Painted) 17.45
Lamp, Backup 17.00	Washer, Windshield 17.75

Back end view of a stylish 1959 convertible.

Virtually the same package that came on the market in 1958 is this 1959 example. The main appearance changes were the removal of the hood louvers and the two stainless bars on the trunk. Approximately 40 units a day left the home base for Corvettes at that time which was St. Louis, Missouri.

As America's only truce sports car, Corvette has superior accelerating, handling, cornering and braking qualities so important in a car of this type. As a pleasure car, it has beauty, comfort and convenience that conform to highest American automotive standards.

Highest quality, Magic-Mirror acrylic lacquer finish, like that on other Chevrolets, is used on Corvette. Finishing process differs only in that plastic Corvette body requires neither rustproofing nor fender undercoating. Lacquer colors for 1959 include seven solid colors and seven optional two-tones in which second color is in sculptured coves of body side panels. Top fabric options and cockpit color options with nearly all exteriors provide extra-large selection of color schemes.

BODY AND OPTIONAL HARDTOP	SCULPTURED COVES IN SIDE PANELS	COCKPIT AND TRUNK INTERIOR	CONVERTIBLE TOP FABRIC	WHEELS
Snowcrest White	Inca Silver*	Black, Blue, Turquoise or Red	Black, White, Turquoise or Blue	Black
Tuxedo Black	Inca Silver*	Black, Blue or Red	Black or White	Black
Inca Silver	Snowcrest White*	Black or Red	Black or White	Black
Roman Red	Snowcrest White*	Black or Red	Black or White	Black
Classic Cream	Snowcrest White*	Black	Black or White	Black
Frost Blue	Snowcrest White*	Blue or Red	Black, White or Blue	Black
Crown Sapphire	Snowcrest White*	Turquoise	Black, White or Turquoise	Black

*Or body color.

CORVETTE CONTROLS

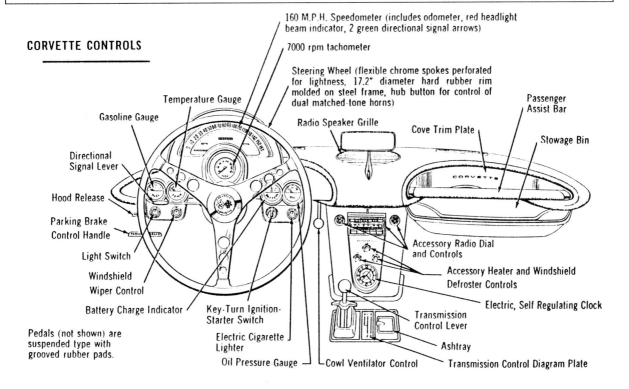

160 M.P.H. Speedometer (includes odometer, red headlight beam indicator, 2 green directional signal arrows)

7000 rpm tachometer

Steering Wheel (flexible chrome spokes perforated for lightness, 17.2" diameter hard rubber rim molded on steel frame, hub button for control of dual matched-tone horns)

Temperature Gauge

Gasoline Gauge

Radio Speaker Grille

Passenger Assist Bar

Cove Trim Plate

Stowage Bin

Directional Signal Lever

Hood Release

Parking Brake Control Handle

Light Switch

Windshield Wiper Control

Battery Charge Indicator

Key-Turn Ignition-Starter Switch

Accessory Radio Dial and Controls

Accessory Heater and Windshield Defroster Controls

Electric, Self Regulating Clock

Pedals (not shown) are suspended type with grooved rubber pads.

Electric Cigarette Lighter

Transmission Control Lever

Oil Pressure Gauge

Cowl Ventilator Control

Ashtray

Transmission Control Diagram Plate

245

CHEVROLET—*What could beat one of these beauties*

(unless it's two of 'em!)

Fresh-minted models for every taste. All with a remarkable new ride, new room, new safety, new handling ease—and Chevy's own special brand of economy and reliability. What more could you want?

1— *BISCAYNE UTILITY SEDAN.* Chevy's low [p]rices start right here—a handy, handsome 2-door with [?]1 cu. ft. of cargo space behind front seat.

2— *BROOKWOOD 2-DOOR,* Chevrolet's lowest [p]riced wagon, is as dutiful as it is beautiful. Seats 6, [h]olds up to 92 cu. ft. of cargo.

3— *IMPALA 4-DOOR,* most elegant family sedan in [th]e line, makes you wonder why anyone would want a [c]ar that costs more.

[4]— *EL CAMINO* combines stunning passenger car [st]yling with the load space of a pickup. Good looks [n]ever carried so much weight!

[5]— *IMPALA CONVERTIBLE.* Chevy's got a [sp]ecial formula for carefree top-down fun.

[6]— *BISCAYNE 2-DOOR.* This beauty's the lowest [pr]iced 6-passenger Chevy you can buy!

7— *NOMAD 4-DOOR,* 6-passenger station wagon—finest of Chevrolet's 5 wonderful wagons.

8— *BEL AIR 4-DOOR.* As luxurious as it looks, yet priced just above Chevy's thriftiest sedans.

9— *BROOKWOOD 4-DOOR.* Chevy's lowest priced 4-door wagon seats 6, holds 92 cu. ft. of cargo with rear seat down.

10— *BEL AIR 2-DOOR,* distinctively styled inside and out, carries a price tag just a notch above Chevy's thriftiest 2-door sedan.

11— *IMPALA SPORT SEDAN.* Here's a 4-door hardtop with the kind of looks and luxury you'd expect only on the most expensive makes.

12— *KINGSWOOD 4-DOOR,* 9-passenger station wagon, offers rear-facing third seat and power-operated rear window at no extra cost.

13— *IMPALA SPORT COUPE.* It's one of Chevy's full series of elegant Impalas for '59. And you won't find a handsomer hardtop anywhere!

14— *PARKWOOD 4-DOOR,* 6-passenger station wagon, distinctively trimmed inside and out, priced a shade above the thrifty Brookwoods.

15— *BEL AIR SPORT SEDAN.* It's Chevy's lowest priced hardtop—and it makes beautiful sense!

16— *CORVETTE.* Take the wheel of America's only authentic sports car and treat yourself to the snappiest, happiest driving you've known.

17— *BISCAYNE 4-DOOR,* thriftiest 4-door sedan in the line, is another big reason Chevy's the car that's wanted for all its worth!

Chevrolet Division of General Motors
Detroit 2, Michigan